New Majority or Old Minority?

NEW MAJORITY
OR
OLD MINORITY?

THE IMPACT OF REPUBLICANS
ON CONGRESS

edited by

NICOL C. RAE and COLTON C. CAMPBELL

ROWMAN & LITTLEFIELD PUBLISHERS, INC.
Lanham • Boulder • New York • Oxford

ROWMAN & LITTLEFIELD PUBLISHERS, INC.

Published in the United States of America
by Rowman & Littlefield Publishers, Inc.
4720 Boston Way, Lanham, Maryland 20706

12 Hid's Copse Road
Cumnor Hill, Oxford OX2 9JJ, England

British Library Cataloguing in Publication Information Available

Library of Congress Cataloging-in-Publication Data
New majority or old minority? : the impact of Republicans on Congress
/ edited by Nicol C. Rae and Colton C. Campbell.
    p.   cm.
    Includes bibliographical references.
    ISBN 0-8476-9168-3 (cloth : alk. paper). — ISBN 0-8476-9169-1
(pbk. : alk. paper)
    1. Republican Party (U.S. : 1854–) 2. United States. Congress.
3. United States—Politics and government—1993– I. Rae, Nicol C.
II. Campbell, Colton C., 1965– .
JK2356.N475 1999
324.2734—dc21   98-54157
                                           CIP

Printed in the United States of America

∞ The paper used in this publication meets the minimum requirements of
American National Standard for Information Sciences—Permanence of Paper
for Printed Library Materials, ANSI Z39.48–1984.

Contents

Tables and Figures

Tables

Figure

Preface

This book springs from discussions we had on the impact of the new Republican majority on Congress during the summer of 1997. The Republican "revolution" on Capitol Hill obviously had considerable ramifications not only in terms of public policy, but also for Congress as a governing institution. We concluded that compiling a volume of essays where leading congressional scholars addressed the impact of the Republicans on Congress (and Congress on the Republicans) would be highly beneficial for students of Congress both in academia and among the public at large. The prominent congressional scholars we approached turned out to be even more enthusiastic than anticipated, and this book is the result.

Time commitments unfortunately precluded Richard Fenno from contributing a chapter, but during our discussions with him, Dick *did* inadvertently suggest our title, "New Majority or Old Minority?" We believe this question captures the essential dilemma of the Republicans since they became the new majority on Capitol Hill: on the one hand, the new majority tried to implement changes in public policy and institutional practice advocated while they were in the minority, but at the same time the Republicans found that electoral survival necessitated some accommodation to the tried-and-trusted ways of doing business in Washington. In short, to establish a long-term congressional majority, Republicans had to, in Fenno's words, "learn to govern."

As the book manuscript was completed and sent to the publishers, the House of Representatives voted to open an inquiry regarding the impeachment of President Bill Clinton for alleged crimes committed in relation to the Monica Lewinsky affair. A few weeks after that momentous decision, the Republicans, although they retained their majority, became the first party not holding the White House to lose seats in a midterm congressional election since 1934, and Speaker Newt Gingrich—the architect of the Republican revolution—was subsequently forced to resign. While most of the essays in this volume do not address these developments, it is legitimate to note that the possible impeachment of the president by the House might have consequences for the balance of power between the legislative and executive branches of the federal government. The impeachment (and near conviction) of President Andrew Johnson ushered in a quarter century during which time the Congress was at its strongest and the Presidency at its weakest in American history. On the other hand, the apparent public perception that Republicans had "misused" the momentous presidential-impeachment process for relatively "trivial" offenses might also provide further evidence that they had not yet accommodated themselves to the proper role of Congress in the modern American political system.

All *that* remains for posterity to work out. What is left for us is to thank all those who contributed to the making of this collection of essays.

We first thank all our contributors for producing such excellent and timely papers and chapters at relatively short notice and for lending us their wisdom and experience in the process of editing and publishing this book. The Jack D. Gordon Institute for Public Policy and Citizenship Studies gave immeasurable assistance in financing and organizing the conference, and we are especially grateful to our strongest supporter, the Director of the Gordon Institute (and chair of the political science department at FIU), John Stack. We should also thank FIU's Vice President for Sponsored Research, Tom Breslin, and Associate Dean of the College of Arts and Sciences, Brian Cutler, for their moral and financial support. At FIU we are also grateful for the help of Carlos Becerra, Diane Dick, Elaine Dillashaw, George Androuin, and Naomi Honig.

All our colleagues in the Political Science department were highly supportive of the project. Particular mention should be made of Becky Salokar, Chris Warren, Kevin Hill, Jenny Chanley, and Barbara Herrera, who provided valuable comments and advice for both editors and contributors. Will Reno, Dario Moreno, Ron Cox, Joel Gottlieb, and Mary Volcansek also deserve special mention for their support, encouragement, and advice to two authors who had never previously organized an edited volume. Graduate students Lourdes Cue, Donald D'Orto, Sean Foreman, and Julio Gonzalez stimulated debate and provided useful insights in Nicol Rae's seminar on Congress. Finally, Danny McGlynn and Aracelys Montoya gave valuable assistance in the production of the manuscript.

At Rowman & Littlefield, Jennifer Knerr has been excited about the project since the time we first approached her with a book proposal, and she has been a consistently patient and supportive editor.

Finally, we once more should thank family and friends, whose unfailing support has helped us through another academic project in more ways than they can imagine. Nicol Rae is once again heavily indebted to his mother, Lily Rae, and also to his good friend Joe Zarranz. Colton Campbell is grateful to his family: parents Budge and Ardis, and sisters Colby and Kenzie.

Without the help of all these fine people this book would not have seen the light of day. Only time will tell whether the observations and conclusions herein were prescient or have been superseded by even more momentous events.

NCR   **CCC**
Miami Beach, Fla.   *Ukiah, Calif.*

CHAPTER ONE

From Revolution to Evolution: Congress under Republican Control

NICOL C. RAE AND COLTON C. CAMPBELL

I find trashing the institution of Congress offensive. We have the greatest deliberative body in the history of mankind, and a model that the rest of the world looks to. What we need to do is shift the popular view of the U.S. Congress from a corrosive cynicism to a healthy skepticism. People should be skeptical of those of us who are representatives, but cynicism is corrosive. I think there was more cynicism two or three years ago, and we have made strides.

Representative David Dreier (Interview, 6 June 1996)

Whether it's term limits or campaign finance reform, or the gift ban, or cutting pensions, it's extremely difficult to cut through the mindset of members who put this institution above the American people. We want an institution that deserves the trust of the American people, but doesn't put itself above the people. It's an institutional corruption, not a legal or ethical corruption, but senior members want to make excuses for a situation that benefits them, and they are unwilling to be objective. If you look at it objectively, you have to say that we have to clean up the campaign system and introduce term limits. This institution needs to be reconnected to the American people.

Representative Zach Wamp (quoted in Rae 1998, 75)

I N NOVEMBER 1994 THE REPUBLICAN PARTY won control of both houses of Congress for the first time in forty years. During the following two Republican congresses, much has been written concerning the ideological "shift" in the direction of public policy engendered by the Republicans toward limited government, deficit reduction, and the decentralization of federal power. But what of the impact of the new Republican majority on Congress itself? As the 106th Congress begins, Washington has experienced the first period of extended Republican con-

1

trol of the legislative branch since the 1920s, and surely it is now time to begin assessing the impact of the Republicans on *the institution* of Congress.

That assessment is the origin and purpose of this volume. In the succeeding pages, ten leading congressional scholars discuss and evaluate the impact of the new Republican majority on the various aspects of Congress: the committee system, party leadership, Speakership, budget process, floor procedures, and the congressional Republican party itself.

As editors, our intent in this introductory chapter is twofold. First, to "set the scene" for what follows by providing a brief chronology of significant events of the 104th and 105th congresses as well as an account of the major legislative and institutional initiatives undertaken by the new Republican majority. Second, we give some indication of the linkages and contrasts among the various essays by reviewing three major themes (or issues) that emerge from the collection: (1) whether the Republicans established themselves as a new congressional majority or, instead, retain the attitudes and behavior of a forty-year congressional minority; (2) the scope of congressional reform under Republican rule; and (3) the extent to which the new majority's approach to conducting the affairs of Congress is due to a distinctive Republican Party culture.

It is also our editorial obligation to establish a consensus from the contributing authors regarding the impact of the Republican majority on Congress and, conversely, the impact of control of Congress on the Republicans. While we have avoided forcing these divergent viewpoints into a single straitjacket, a common theme throughout the essays is the consistent tension between two characteristics of Congress: demands for change from junior members (reflected in the ranks of the new Republican majority) and the institutional mores of the House and Senate. This condition is captured in the contrasting quotes at the beginning of the chapter. The first quote comes from a relatively senior Republican House member serving in a high-ranking position on one of the House's more powerful committees (the Rules Committee), and the second from a militant conservative member of the large Republican freshman class of 1994: the self-proclaimed "guardians" of the "Republican Revolution." How much has the "revolutionary" approach of Representative Zach Wamp and his classmates been tempered by the more "evolutionary" approach of veteran lawmakers like "institutionalist" David Dreier? This is the underlying issue in this introductory chapter and the remainder of this volume.

THE 104TH CONGRESS: REVOLUTION

The results of the 1994 congressional elections represented an earthquake in American politics. In the House of Representatives, the Republicans made a net gain of 52 seats for a 230–204 margin and their first House majority since 1954.

In the Senate contests, the Republicans gained 8 seats for a 52–48 margin (which increased to 53-47 when Democratic Senator Richard Shelby of Alabama switched parties the day after the election).

Congressional observers were confounded not only by the outcome of the election, but also by the nature of the Republican campaign. For at least two decades the prevailing wisdom in congressional elections conformed to former Democratic Speaker (1977–1986) Thomas P. "Tip" O'Neill's dictum that "all politics is local." State and local concerns invariably took precedence over national themes in congressional contests, which, for most voters, boiled down to a referendum on the effectiveness of their individual House member (in terms of accessibility, service provision, and deliverance of federal programs). In 1994 the Republicans engineered a nationalized campaign to win the House based on an explicit party manifesto: the "Contract with America." As Ronald Peters indicates in chapter 3, the nature of this campaign and the exceptionally high profile of the de facto Republican leader, Minority Whip Newt Gingrich (Ga.), in recruiting candidates, devising the Contract, and directing the campaign, marked a decisive break with what had gone before.

In the interim before the 104th Congress met in January 1995, the scope of the Republican revolution continued to puzzle many congressional scholars and observers versed in the truisms of the Democratic era on Capitol Hill. As described in the chapters by Roger H. Davidson, Christopher J. Deering, Peters, and Barbara Sinclair, Speaker-elect Gingrich and the new Republican majority not only submitted their blueprint for change, but also outlined a strategy for fulfilling that plan. The initial order of business was to reshape the procedural environment in which the institution operates, dramatically altering which policy issues were pushed to the top of the legislative agenda and how such policies were processed. Gingrich ignored traditional patterns of collective leadership through standing committee chairs. Instead, Gingrich called upon ad hoc task forces to write legislation, not only to move legislation more rapidly, but as Davidson notes in chapter 4, for other substantive reasons such as circumventing outside committee clienteles. Gingrich also assigned a decisive role to the Speaker's Advisory Group (SAG) that included junior members and excluded most of the Republican committee chairs (Cook 1997; Evans and Oleszek 1997).

House Republican leaders put extraordinary pressure on committees to report legislation quickly. Three months into the 104th Congress, the Republican House majority had systematically passed all but one of their planks of the Contract with America (with the exception of the constitutional amendment prescribing term limits, which passed the House but failed to get the required two-thirds majority). To ensure that the major legislative committees moved with speed, Gingrich used the leverage of his singular support among the rank and file of the House Republican Conference to effectively select the new chairmen of all standing committees, departing in four instances from seniority and choosing more activist and committed conservatives.

Even more uncharacteristic than the uncommon haste in passing the Contract was the extraordinary influence conferred by Gingrich on the large (73-member) Republican freshman class (Rae 1998). Aside from receiving an unprecedented number of positions on key committees, the freshmen assumed a vocal role as "guardians" of the Republican revolution in terms of both change in public policy and in institutional reform within the House (Rae 1998). Moreover, junior members (the freshmen and sophomores), who together constituted over 50 percent of the House Republican Conference, became a prime source of power for the leadership.

In short, the initial impact of the GOP, especially in the House, appeared equivalent in effort and scope to previous instances of dramatic institutional and organizational change in this century, most notably the 1910 revolt against Speaker Joseph Cannon that ushered in the committee-seniority system, and the 1974 "Watergate" election that inaugurated the period of "subcommittee government" (Rhode 1974; Patterson 1978; Davidson 1981; Deering 1982; Deering and Smith 1997).

The dizzying speed of the 104th Congress came to an abrupt halt once the Contract with America reached the more restrained and deliberative Senate. With only 54 Senate seats the Republicans were still well short of the 60 votes ordinarily required to overcome dilatory practices—particularly the filibuster—and secure floor passage of legislation.[1] The first indication that the Republican agenda would stall came when the balanced-budget amendment to the Constitution—an integral part of the Contract—failed by one vote to secure the necessary two-thirds majority (67 votes) for passage. As the rest of the Contract faced inevitable obstruction in the Senate, the Republican House leadership and Senate Majority Leader Robert Dole were compelled to resort to the same tactics of "unorthodox" lawmaking as their Democratic counterparts in the 103rd Congress (Sinclair 1997). That is, they had to package the most contentious items of the Contract together in a fashion calculated to circumvent the possible Senate roadblocks and requirements for "supermajorities."

Because the Senate precludes filibustering on budget-related bills—so-called "must-pass" legislation—the easiest way to ensure approval was by consolidating as much of the Republican legislative agenda into a massive budget and reconciliation bill. The failure of the balanced-budget amendment in the Senate provided Republicans with the ideal pretext for doing this. In the spring of 1996, House and Senate Republicans began constructing an omnibus budget resolution for FY 1996, committing Congress and the president to a series of spending reductions toward a 2002 balanced budget. Simultaneously, Republicans promised a "tax cut for working families," described by House Republican leaders as the "crown jewel" of the Contract, thus enhancing the scale of the spending reductions necessary for reaching stipulated budget targets (Rae 1998). In sum, via the FY 1996 budget process the Republicans hoped to effect important change in the direction of American public policy toward lower taxes, significantly reduce the size of the federal government, reform the welfare system, roll back environmental legislation (by cutting appropriations for the relevant enforcement agencies), and redirect federal government activity to the state and local levels.

While packaging the Contract into the budget process circumvented Senate hurdles, Republicans still faced the risk that Democratic President Clinton would veto their Reconciliation Bill (making the budget resolution legally binding) and several of the thirteen annual Appropriations Bills needed to keep the federal government going into the next fiscal year. Still, they intended to win politically, whatever Clinton did. The president appeared weakened by the 1994 election outcome, and they calculated that public opinion would blame the White House not Capitol Hill, if Clinton's possible vetoes of their budget legislation precipitated a federal government shutdown.

The actual outcome of the 1995–1996 budget battle frustrated the Republicans' hopes, however. Democrats lost no opportunity to inform both the press and the public that the amount of reductions sought by Republicans in the politically popular Medicare program ($270 billion) was uncannily near the level proposed ($245 billion) for what the Democrats depicted as a "tax cut for the wealthy" (Maraniss and Weisskopf 1996, 140). Overheated Republican rhetoric—particularly talk of "revolution"—from the House Republican freshmen was ill-received by the public, nor did the harsh public image of Gingrich help the Republicans.

As a result, when the vetoes of the Republican budget legislation came and the federal government temporarily closed in November and, again, over Christmas and New Year's 1995, it was the Republican Congress that was blamed rather than the president. Realizing the risk this situation posed to their narrow congressional majorities, Gingrich and Majority Leader Dole persuaded their reluctant troops to reopen the government and accept a "stop-gap" budget until the struggle could be resumed after the 1996 elections. Following the easing in the budget battle, the Republican revolution in the House appeared to be utterly deflated. Without a balanced budget—the centerpiece of the Republican legislative agenda—and despite significant institutional reform in the areas of congressional lobbying and gifts and the passage of significant farm and telecommunications legislation, House Republicans were left without a clear strategy for their reelection efforts. Conversely, Democrats were invigorated by the outcome of the budget battle and encouraged by organized labor's television advertising campaign against vulnerable Republican freshmen. They were hopeful of recapturing the House, thereby rendering the 104th Congress an aberration to the same extent as the Republican 80th (1947–1948) and 83rd (1953–1954) Congresses: temporary interruptions in a long-term pattern of Democratic rule on Capitol Hill.

That this did not happen was, in fact, largely due to the Republican senators and their new leader, Trent Lott (Miss.). Lott took over in May 1995, when it became apparent that the presumptive presidential nomination of Majority Leader Dole had effectively brought the Senate to a halt. Not wishing to give Dole the credit for passage of any major legislation, Senate Democrats employed numerous dilatory tactics, and with allegations of a "do-nothing" Congress in the air, the GOP was desperate to pass some substantive measures before the November elections. Dole's resignation to concentrate on his presidential campaign and the incapacitation of the shell-shocked House Republican leadership provided Lott the opportunity to set the agenda and break the Senate logjam. Lott did this by striking compromises with Senate Democrats and the Clinton White House on popular legislation such as raising the minimum wage, welfare reform, immigration reform, and health insurance "portability." While these measures helped to bolster the reelection campaign of President Clinton, Lott calculated, correctly, that some of the credit would rub off on Republican candidates for both the House and Senate in the fall.

Indeed, the 1996 congressional elections for the Republicans turned out to be an exercise in "dissociation" and "localization": practices congressional Democrats had successfully employed in years of Republican presidential victories since the 1950s. Dissociation was evident in the reluctance of many Republicans to link their campaigns to the faltering presidential effort of Bob Dole: the clearest example being national GOP television advertisements late in the campaign, urging voters not to give Clinton a "blank check" by electing a Democratic Congress (Drew 1997). Localization was the deliberate effort by Republican incumbents, including the firebrands of the 1994 freshman class, to use the resources of incumbency—programs, constituent service, fundraising, and media visibility—as ruthlessly as their Democratic counterparts had done over the past forty years (Mayhew 1974; Fiorina 1977). Many freshman incumbents, for instance, intentionally voted against their party in meaningless procedural votes in the House, simply to inflate their overall scores on "opposition" to the unpopular Speaker Gingrich (Rae 1998, 207).

The strategy worked. After the electoral dust had finally settled, the first Republican House majority since 1928 was reelected. Republicans still outnumbered Democrats 227–207 (with one independent), but after a net loss of nine seats, they held the smallest overall margin of control since 1952. In the Senate elections, the Republicans picked up two seats, increasing their margin to 55–45. The context of the 1996 Republican congressional election victory, however, was utterly different from that of 1994, as became evident when the 105th Congress convened.

THE 105TH CONGRESS: EVOLUTION

With the previous Congress's budget deadlock with President Clinton, internal party disagreements about how to handle pressing agenda items, the collapse of Speaker Gingrich's own public support, and the public's discontent with partisan bickering fresh in mind, the Republicans gathered to organize the 105th Congress. They did so with far less consensus on their agenda, more open divisions in their ranks, a tarnished and less united House leadership, committee chairs who felt free to stray from the wishes of the party bosses (Deering and Smith 1997), and significant differences in the tactics and temperaments of the members (Davidson and Campbell forthcoming).

In the 105th Congress, there seemed to be a return to a more traditional model of government in Washington, with most legislation being crafted in committees, and Republican leaders being forced to bargain with the Clinton administration (Davidson and Campbell forthcoming). Career-oriented Republican House members were also beginning to find that traditional congressional career-building—paying their dues by working through the committee system, earning their stripes by rising through the ranks of the formal party structure, and developing expertise with the support of a caucus of members with shared interests—was indeed useful in achieving some of their personal political goals.

The narrow majority, which invited internecine fighting among numerous factions who sought to display their own presumed strength in the party, rendered House Republican leaders in the 105th Congress unable to legislate effectively. Adding to this constraint was the continuing cloud of controversy surrounding Speaker Gingrich. Aside from his national unpopularity, the beleaguered Speaker was tormented for much of 1996 by an Ethics Committee investigation of his activities as head of GOPAC (an organization that he had used while the Republicans were in the minority to recruit and fund candidates and generally spread the House Republican message). Although the charges were still unresolved, Gingrich was narrowly reelected Speaker with nine Republican members voting against him. Later he had to endure a House reprimand for ethics violations and a $300,000 fine.

Rumblings against Gingrich continued in the summer of 1997 as a rebel faction of two dozen conservative sophomores criticized and publicly challenged the Speaker's leadership. Voicing concern that their leader had become too willing to capitulate to President Clinton and the Democrats in budget negotiations, the dissidents even met with Gingrich's four chief deputies in an aborted "coup" (Eilperin and Vande Hei 1997; Rees 1997b).

There was little that the House Republicans could achieve on their own in terms of policy. A public-relations disaster occurred in the early summer when the House Republican leadership tied legislation for disaster relief for the flood-wracked Midwestern states to a commitment by the Clinton administration not to use statistical "sampling" techniques in enumerating the population for the 2000 census (and thereby, it was thought, gaining more congressional seats for Democrats).

On the Senate side, after his agile start at the end of the 104th Congress, Majority Leader Trent Lott was unable to surmount the inevitable resort to dilatory tactics on the part of the Democratic minority on any contentious piece of legislation. Much of the Senate's time in 1997 was taken up with hearings conducted by Senator Fred Thompson (Tenn.) into the financing of President Clinton's reelection campaign, which culminated in a partisan impasse. Republicans in both chambers were thus immobilized by the lack of a clear consensus or agenda and their relatively narrow majorities.

A singular achievement of the first session of the 105th Congress, nevertheless, was the apparent resolution of the budget crisis that had dominated the 104th Congress. This was made possible by a booming economy, which generated revenues to such a degree that the amount of "pain" required to eradicate the deficit reduced dramatically. In such an atmosphere, reaching an accommodation with the Clinton administration became much easier than it had been in the previous Congress. And as a result the White House and Congress concluded a budget deal in the summer of 1996 that temporarily took the deficit issue off the political agenda. Interestingly, in contrast with the 104th Congress where the leadership had directed congressional strategy on budget issues, House committee chairs such as Ron Archer (Tex.) of the Ways and Means committee played a much more prominent role in the negotiations on the 1997 budget "deal."

Despite all these changes, Gingrich clung to power. He did so, as Peters points out in chapter 3, by a masterful accommodation to the changed circumstances of the 105th Congress, which demanded a strategy of consolidation in the hope of expanding the Republican majorities in 1998, rather than the programmatic policy "revolution" of 1995. The "new" Speaker Gingrich now cultivated relations with Republican moderates, avoided unnecessary confrontation with the Clinton administration, and worked closely with the committee chairs.

Prior to the political explosion created by the submission of the Starr Report and the beginnings of impeachment proceedings against the president in its final weeks, the 105th Congress was a stable, "consolidation" Congress in contrast with the 104th. With a precarious margin in the House, the Republican majority proceeded cautiously, generally acting only when reasonably assured of gaining presidential approval (or embarrassing the president) or blocking unpopular

Clinton initiatives. Continued economic prosperity at home and peace abroad were reflected on Capitol Hill in a general reluctance to propose any radical new initiatives that might endanger the status quo.

The outcome of the 1998 elections and the downfall of Speaker Gingrich and his replacement by the more pragmatic "institutionalist" Dennis "Denny" Hastert for the 106th Congress made any further such initiatives even less likely. Five more seats were shaved off a Republican House majority that now was reduced to 223–211, and expected gains in the Senate failed to materialize as the GOP's 55–45 margin was maintained. Gingrich was held responsible for an "issueless" Republican campaign that yielded the worst outcome for a party not holding the White House in a midterm House election since 1934. Republicans were all the more embittered, since they expected that the Lewinsky scandal would substantially increase their precarious House majority. The loudest voices calling for Gingrich's head came from the right of the party. Yet ironically, both Gingrich's original successor, Appropriations Chair Bob Livingston (who had secured the "bipartisan" 1998 budget deal with the Clinton White House that was widely reviled by conservatives), and his eventual successor, Deputy Whip Dennis Hastert, had established reputations as pragmatic dealmakers.

Thus as the 106th Congress opened, the "revolutionary" spirit of the 104th Congress certainly appeared to have been arrested, but it remained unclear whether, with such a narrow majority, Speaker-elect Hastert would be able to fully consolidate the "evolution" toward a new Republican congressional regime.

A NEW CONGRESSIONAL REGIME?

While in the minority the Republicans became used to attacking Congress as an institution. It was clear by 1994 that they had succeeded in persuading public opinion that congressional norms were antiquated and ossified, acting as impediments to the popular will that a representative assembly is supposed to reflect. It later became apparent, however, that if the Republicans were to consolidate their 1994 victory into a solid new congressional majority, some accommodation with those preexisting norms—Sinclair's "institutional constraints" (chapter 2)—would be required. How, and to what extent, was the "new majority" able to cast off the anti-institutional disposition of the "old minority" and make the legislative branch of government serve their purposes?

Certainly in the 104th Congress the inclinations of the old minority appeared to persist, especially in the House. Sinclair informs us that House Republicans were driven by "partisan imperatives" at the outset of the 104th Congress, but by the second session these had been superseded by individual member goals—particularly the primary member goal of reelection (chapter 2). Moreover, she remains unconvinced that the new majority effected such a substantial change in the House's organization and norms as those of the anti-Cannon revolt of 1910–1911 and the revolt against autocratic committee barons of 1974. The elements of the new more partisan regime in the House, Sinclair argues, were already substantially in place prior to the 1994 elections. Using a different theoretical framework, in the last chapter William Connelly and John Pitney arrive at essentially the same conclusion: the Republicans discovered the continuing significance of the Madisonian checks and balances in the American political system after abortive attempts at "Wilsonian" party government in the early days of the 104th Congress (chapter 9).

In chapter 3, Peters agrees that the Republican majority was compelled by changed political circumstances to moderate its strategy and rhetorical tone in the 105th Congress. Yet he differs with Sinclair in his conclusion that the Republican regime—notably the leadership of Speaker Newt Gingrich—was fundamentally different from that which preceded it: a distinctiveness that Peters views as rooted in the differing "cultures" of the Democratic and Republican parties.

Davidson also discusses the new majority from a "regime-building" perspective. He agrees with Sinclair that in their efforts to construct a substantially different House regime in the 104th Congress, the new Republican majority built upon some tendencies toward a more centralized party leadership and enhanced partisanship in the final years of the Democratic era. Like Peters, however, Davidson views the Republican attempt to move the locus of decision making from the committees to the House floor as part of a broader effort to undermine the constituency-based, service-oriented, Democratic regime with a Republican congressional regime based more on national issues.

While there is some disagreement over the impact of the Republicans on the House as an institution, there is broad consensus as far as the Senate is concerned. In that chamber, despite the new Republican majority, "institutional constraints"—in Sinclair's terms—continued to "trump partisan imperatives." Just as the Republican minority in the Senate effectively blocked much of the Democratic agenda during the 103rd Congress, so the Democratic minority in the Senate used all the dilatory devices that the chamber allows to derail most of the Contract with America. Only by accommodating the minority to some extent was the new Republican Majority Leader Trent Lott able to get some parts of the Contract enacted into legislation before the 1996 elections. It was also Senate obstructionism that led Republicans to legislate the way the preceding Democratic majority had done it, via budget-related legislation, which is not subject to Senate filibusters and nongermane amendments. There was some long-term potential for regime change in the Senate, however, contained in the package of changes to Republican Senate Conference rules passed in the wake of Appropriations Chair Mark Hatfield's vote against the balanced-budget amendment. These provided for a party agenda, term limits on committee chairs, and possible votes to confirm or remove committee chairs on the part of the conference as a whole: all momentous changes for the Senate if carried into effect.

In short, at the end of the 105th Congress it remained unclear whether the new Republican congressional majority had succeeded in entrenching itself. While aspects of old House minority behavior—strident partisanship, the public denigration of Congress as an institution, strong centralized party leadership—initially carried over into the majority, there was little indication that the Republicans had yet constructed a new House regime that would keep them in power over an extended period of time. In fact, many of the pathologies of the Democratic *ancient regime*—emphasis on assiduous district service, powerful committee chairs, distributive programs (such as the 1998 Highway bill)—appear to have recurred under Republican rule. Moreover, the "accommodationist" style of the new Republican Speaker, Dennis Hastert, seemed closer to that of Democratic predecessors such as "Tip" O'Neill and Tom Foley than the "revolutionary" approach of the deposed Newt Gingrich. There are still significant differences in style and emphasis between the parties in their conduct of the House however, and should the Republicans considerably expand their majorities in the 106th or 107th Congresses, the likelihood of a return to the aggressive leadership and programmatic orientation of the 104th Congress seems strong. But in the Senate, absent a Republican "supermajority" in excess of 60 votes or (highly unlikely) changes in its rules, such centralized, disciplined House majorities are likely to continue to be frustrated.

THE REPUBLICANS AND INSTITUTIONAL REFORM

According to the Republicans' blistering institutional critique of the House under Democratic rule, the House was run for the benefit of a self-serving, autocratic, and unrepresentative Democratic majority, which did its utmost to stifle the minority viewpoint through the manipulation of rules and procedure. As Connelly and Pitney observe in chapter 9, such feelings of oppression are characteristic of any minority in a chamber that is institutionally structured to favor majority rule. Increasing partisanship in the House and the stronger role played by the party leadership in the 1980s only increased this frustration.

In chapter 3, Peters describes how Gingrich's ascent to power was largely attributable to his confrontational strategy vis-à-vis the Democratic majority. Initially derided inside the beltway, his approach began to bear fruit when he succeeded in forcing the resignation of Democratic Speaker James Wright on ethics grounds in 1989. Over the next two congresses Gingrich's critique of the Democratic House found increasing resonance outside Washington in a series of scandals. Even the more tranquil Senate was not immune, as the Senate Judiciary

Committee was embarrassed by the sexual-harassment allegations it had to investigate in the 1991 Supreme Court confirmation hearings of Justice Clarence Thomas. Greater abashment followed when Senator Robert Packwood of Oregon, the ranking Republican (and chair for the first few months of the 104th Congress) on the powerful Finance Committee, was accused of long-term sexual harassment of several female staff assistants.

The Hill scandals of the early 1990s—most notably the House Bank scandal—involved Republican members to the same extent as Democrats, but their overall effect helped the Republican minority, because they focused media attention on the Democratically controlled Congress and created a public impression of a body that appeared "unresponsive," "privileged," and "corrupt." As Congress's public approval ratings fell, the message driven home by Republicans in the 1994 campaign was that only a change in partisan control could reform and reinvigorate the legislative branch. Putting institutional reform at the forefront of the Contract with America, Republicans pledged, on the opening day of a Republican-controlled House, that they would pass a "Congressional Accountability Act" making Congress subject to the same laws as the rest of the country. They also promised a package of institutional reforms that would streamline the committee system and allow more open procedures for floor debate.

To what extent have these pledges of reform come to fruition? Have they indeed made the operations of Congress more effective and/or efficient? The answers of our authors vary. In chapters 4 and 5, Davidson and Deering demonstrate that the new majority undertook a substantial reform of the committee system in the 104th Congress, abolishing three major committees, placing freshman members on "exclusive" committees, firing over a third of total committee staff, ending proxy voting, streamlining the committee jurisdictions, and reducing multiple referrals of legislation. Though perhaps the larger change, as Peters indicates, was the unprecedented power asserted by Gingrich in naming committee chairs or devising alternative methods to write legislation via such tools as task forces. There is general agreement among our scholars, however, that the Republicans' changes in the committee system were not as dramatic as anticipated and that much of the pattern of decentralization and battles over legislative turf, so characteristic of Democratic rule, had reemerged by the end of the 105th Congress.

In chapter 6, regarding floor procedure, C. Lawrence Evans and Walter J. Oleszek point out that Republican changes toward rules based on overall time restrictions and limiting the types of amendments submitted, made floor debate marginally more "open" compared to the final years of Democratic control. They also conclude that the House leadership still uses procedural rules to advance its own position, but is more likely to succeed in this pursuit the closer the leadership's position is to the median member of the chamber, not the median member of the majority party. Sinclair remains skeptical, however, that there has been any greater degree of openness in House floor debate under Republican rule (chapter 2).

Connelly and Pitney note that majority and minority status in the House have crucial importance in encouraging certain types of behavior among members. Majority status confers tremendous advantages for members to the extent that it serves as a "goal in itself," which can supersede constituent interests and reelection. They maintain that the frustrations of minority status encourage behavior by the new Democratic minority in terms of dilatory tactics, obstructionism, and media publicity stunts, in exactly similar fashion to that of the Republicans under Democratic rule (chapter 9).

As for the Senate, the Republicans did not have the votes (rules changes require a two-thirds majority) or the inclination to effect substantial rules changes in that body. The large Senate freshman class (disproportionately composed of veterans from the House Minority under Gingrich) did nevertheless use Mark Hatfield's vote against the balanced-budget amendment to push for greater change and accountability in the Senate committee system. Rules changes subsequently adopted by the Senate GOP Conference, setting term limits on committee chairs, and "binding" the chairs to support an agenda endorsed by three-fourths of the conference, might have some effect in circumscribing the authority of Senate chairs. The strong pull of institutional loyalty and tradition in the Senate, however, still provides substantial grounds for skepticism.

The verdict on the new majority, as far as reform is concerned, remains mixed. On the constructive side, the Republicans passed substantial reform in the areas of lobbying, gifts, and making Congress subject to federal civil rights and workplace practices laws. In the committee rooms there has been important change and some streamlining, but the real changes here have been in terms of habit and behavior rather than structure, and in the 105th Congress the signs of the reassertion of committee authority indicate that even this change may be short-term rather than permanent. The prospect of term limitations on committee chairs due to come into effect for the 107th Congress (2000–2001) will have significant institutional effects on the committee system. Whether the Republicans actually follow through with this rule change (which also imposed an eight-year term limitation on the Speaker) will be a key indicator of their continuing commitment to congressional reform or accommodation to institutional constraints. On the House floor the Republicans' procedural changes have created some new opportunities in terms of offering legislative alternatives, but time restrictions still constrain the minority's impact on floor debate. While procedural changes in the Senate are minimal, there is some potential for the reforms by the Republican Conference to have a long-term impact. Ultimately, to undertake substantial and durable changes in organization and procedure, the

Republicans will need greater majorities than the relatively slender margins afforded them in the 104th and 105th Congresses.

ARE REPUBLICANS DIFFERENT?

The third and final major theme emerging from our collection is the extent to which the congressional Republican party itself has been affected by the experience of congressional control. Connelly and Pitney conclude that since 1994 the Republicans have been essentially—in Richard F. Fenno's phrase—"learning to govern" (Fenno 1997). They suggest that the House Republican leadership initially had a flawed conception of the governing "mandate" of their new House majority—based on an amalgam of the limited government, states' rights, legislative dominance, ideas of the antifederalists, and Wilsonian notions of "responsible party government"—that ignored the checks and balances intrinsic to America's Madisonian system of government. They also argue, however, that the Republicans were able to achieve significant change in the direction of public policy, and within Congress.

In chapter 3, in his analysis of the Gingrich Speakership, Peters agrees with Connelly and Pitney in this aspect, but unlike them, he goes further. In a challenge to the "contexualist" view of party leadership in Congress, Peters posits the concept of a party culture that differentiates Republicans from Democrats and explains much of the "unconventional" behavior of the new Republican majority. Moreover, he argues that even after the government shutdown and the reprimand at the beginning of the 105th Congress, Gingrich's behavior could still better be explained in terms of Republican party culture rather than just a process of "learning to govern."

Additional evidence for Peters' thesis about the importance of party culture is provided in Robin Kolodny's chapter (chapter 8) on Republican moderates. Like Connelly and Pitney, and in contrast to Peters, Kolodny illustrates that in contrast to the "homogeneity" often ascribed to them, congressional Republicans have always been a very diverse and fractious group—both in the minority and in the majority. In her examination of activities by moderates in the so-called Tuesday Lunch Bunch Kolodny also discovers behavior that distinguishes the GOP centrists in Congress from their Democratic counterparts. Moderate Republicans found themselves in a pivotal position on several crucial issues in the 104th and 105th Congresses. Yet in intraparty debates they succeeded in deflecting action on contentious social issues that divide Republicans—such as abortion and Church/state relations—and helped the leadership by promoting agreement on issues (such as the balanced budget) upon which Republicans were more generally agreed. Kolodny further suggests that despite reports of their extinction, moderate or centrist Republicans continued to play a very important balance of power role on several crucial issues during the 105th Congress.

By contrast with the emphasis on Republican distinctiveness in the Kolodny, Peters, and, to some extent, the Connelly and Pitney chapters, Davidson, Sinclair, and Deering adhere—albeit to varying degrees—to a more contexualist or "learning to govern" approach. For these authors the institutional norms and political context of Washington D.C. have had an impact on the congressional Republicans rather than vice versa. After their initial burst of revolutionary and reforming zeal, the Republicans worked out how Congress really functions and how its seemingly arcane practices, such as the committee system and the seniority rule, actually do serve members' goals regardless of party.

All of our authors primarily agree that the institutional traditions of the Senate generally muted any long-term effects from the change of partisan control in 1994. Davidson, Sinclair, and Deering all discuss the changes in Senate party rules introduced by the Mack committee. Sinclair judges that changes making chairs more accountable to the party conference ultimately will flounder due to the nonmajoritarian nature of the Senate. Deering broadly agrees, although he does note that the changes "move the Senate closer to the house in terms of the relations between committee leaders, party leaders, and the party groups." The thesis of Peters and Kolodny regarding party "culture" should also apply, however, to the Senate, and perhaps the more incremental pace of institutional change in that chamber is masking a long-term drift toward greater partisanship with the Republicans, due to their greater focus on party unity, in the vanguard. Ironically, however, Senate norms and rules entail that unlike the House, a more partisan Senate is likely to be a more "gridlocked" Senate.

LESSONS LEARNED OR CONTINUED SHIFTS?

The three areas of consensus among the congressional scholars writing in this volume are: (1) the 1994 election and the change in partisan control led to change in the internal structures and proceedings of the House of Representatives during the 104th Congress; (2) this change was largely arrested in the 105th Congress; and (3) Republican control has had relatively little impact on the norms and proceedings of the Senate. Beyond this our contributors disagree on the extent and the durability of institutional change in Congress effected by the Republicans. Peters, and to a lesser extent, James Thurber and Evans and Oleszek, see the changes in the House as significant (in Peters' case amounting to a change of congressional regime based on the culture and ideology of the GOP), while Davidson, Deering, and Sinclair are less impressed by the extent of the Republican reforms and emphasize the degree to which the new majority has accommodated itself to the longer-term traditions and practices of the House in order to stay in power; they echo Fenno's (1997) view that the Republicans have been "learning to govern." Kolodny, along with Connelly and Pitney take a middle-ground position on this issue, but do note that the congressional Republican party remains diverse and distinctive in its new majority position in the House.

There are certainly strong grounds for the view that after the electoral "earthquake" of 1994 and the "aftershocks" experienced during the early days of the 104th Congress under the new Republican majority, Congress has returned to a "normal" pattern of institutional behavior characterized by incremental structural and procedural change. Moreover, the further reduction in the Republican House majority after the 1998 midterm elections seems likely to reinforce this tendency. But we caution the reader that Capitol Hill might be sitting on an active fault, and that the congressional landscape might continue to feel aftershocks, not just in institutional behavior, but in its role within the American constitutional system as well.

Perpetuation of the post-1995 congressional status quo is premised on continuing narrow Republican majorities in both chambers. There can be little doubt, however, that further expansion and consolidation of the new Republican majority over the next few election cycles would surely lead to further changes in the way lawmakers do business on Capitol Hill. A Republican gain in excess of the illusive 60 Senate seats required to invoke cloture could place further strain on the institutional constraints of the chamber, as well as encourage procedural change, perhaps as dramatic as the impact of the new Republican majority in the House in 1995. Similarly, an expansion of the Republican House majority might provide additional opportunities to consolidate a new House regime based around the culture and ideology of the GOP.

On the other hand, the impact of a large Republican majority after the millennium might actually have the opposite effect of returning the House to a pattern of decentralized leadership based around largely autonomous committee and subcommittee chairs that prevailed under Democratic rule, simply because the GOP House (or Senate) majority would be too large for the leadership to control and satisfy. That is, much of the partisanship and centralized leadership that distinguishes the new House majority might well be encouraged by the fact that, in historical terms, its margin of control has been very narrow. Naturally, a return to power by the Democrats, in the short term, might see the elimination of changes initiated by the Republicans, their institutional consolidation, or a completely new thrust in the conduct of business on Capitol Hill.

If they maintain or enhance their majorities on Capitol Hill, the major institutional "ticking time-bomb" for the Republicans is the impact of the term limitations on committee chairs introduced during the 104th Congress in *both* the

House and Senate. An interesting test of their continued commitment to institutional change in Congress will be whether or not the Republicans actually make these alterations in the face of some likely resistance from incumbent chairs. If the changeover does occur, the impact would surely be dramatic, particularly as it would also effectively end the seniority system, the primary organizing tool for congressional committees for almost a century. There would probably be profound effects on membership turnover in the House, as most legislators would be unlikely ever to have the prospect of chairing a committee. The institutionalization of term limits on committee chairs should logically strengthen the power of the party leaders and consolidate the emergence of a more powerful Speakership. The fact that the Speaker's own term is limited to eight years is another imponderable factor in this area however. In the Senate, which is even more bound to traditions of seniority than the House, the effects of term limitations on the chairs would surely be even more deep-seated. Again, would a future Democratic majority feel bound to adhere to such changes?

The debate over the impact of the new majority in Congress is not over, for it is still unclear what the long-term institutional impact will be. Our authors offer a lively discussion on the impact of the Republicans in the first two Republican Congresses in forty years, with contrasting interpretations that will provoke further study and dispute among congressional scholars. What is not yet known is whether the process of institutional change in Congress initiated by the new Republican majority is over or is merely the harbinger of more drastic institutional change by either Republican or Democratic congressional majorities.

NOTE

1. The party switch of Colorado Democrat Senator Ben Nighthorse Campbell further augmented Republican numbers in the spring of 1995. The Republican tally went down to fifty-three again at the end of 1995 when Democrat Ron Wyden won the special election in Oregon after the resignation of Republican Robert Packwood.

PART ONE

New Styles of Party Leadership

CHAPTER TWO

Partisan Imperatives and Institutional Constraints: Republican Party Leadership in the House and Senate

BARBARA SINCLAIR

INTRODUCTION

What have we learned about Congress as an institution from the Republican experience in controlling Congress since 1995? What impact has the Republican majority had on Congress as an institution, and vice versa? Specifically what does the experience of the Republican-Party leadership teach us about the extent to which members can reshape the institution to serve their ends and about the extent to which the institution shapes its members' behavior?

We know that institutional arrangements in the House and Senate have changed over time and that alterations have, at least in part, been the result of members' efforts to reshape institutional arrangements so as to make them better suited to furthering their goals. Major changes have come about when a sufficiently large group of members found current arrangements, formal and informal, to be seriously hindering their efforts (Sinclair 1989, 1995; Binder 1997). The aim of many of the changes was an alteration in the internal distribution of influence.

Changes of a magnitude to be labeled "regime" changes can be characterized as alterations in the distribution of influence among committees, the party leadership, and the rank-and-file. For example, we can without too much oversimplification characterize the House in this century as having experienced at least three relatively distinct regimes. The first regime can be characterized as a *strong Speakership,* in which power was centralized in a Speaker who was powerful both as presiding officer and as party leader (one who could and did appoint his chief lieutenants as chairs of the most important committees, thus effectively melding party and committee system). This regime gave way, following a revolt against Speaker Joseph G. Cannon, to a *committee government regime* characterized by autonomous committees and powerful and independent committee chairs. The reforms of the 1970s dismantled this regime, moving influence from the committee chairmen up to the party leadership and the majority caucus, and down to the subcommittee chairs and the rank-and-file members. By the 1980s this *postreform regime* had come to be characterized by an activist majority party leadership that took an increasingly central role in the legislative process. In the Senate, a committee government regime gave way in the 1960s and 1970s to a regime characterized by extreme individualism, one in which senators fully exploit the prerogatives given to individual members by Senate rules.

Did the shift in party control with the 104th Congress bring about changes of that magnitude in either chamber? Whether or not Republican control brought with it regime change, what has been the impact of the Republican majority on Congress as an institution? Did the Republicans believe major changes in institutional arrangements were needed for them to achieve their goals? Did they succeed in making such changes? What are their effects on the way Congress functions? And, whether or not the Republicans changed Congress, did Congress change the Republicans? These are the questions this chapter seeks to answer.

A Majority under Contract: House Republicans, 1995

Although Republicans won control of both the House of Representatives and the Senate in the 1994 elections, the House takeover was the big story. After forty continuous years in the minority, Republicans confounded most political prognosticators and made a net gain of 52 seats, thereby securing a House majority of 230–204, with one independent. This new Republican majority was unusually homogeneous in ideology, and believed itself to be mandated to make far-reaching policy changes. Most of its members, both continuing and new, had signed the "Contract with America," thus pledging themselves to bringing an ambitious policy agenda to the floor for votes. The huge freshman class—seventy-three strong—consisted largely of true believers, deeply committed to cutting the size and scope of government and to balancing the budget; with the sophomores, who were very similar in outlook, they made up over half of the Republican House membership. Many more senior Republican conservatives had been waiting for such an opportunity for years. Even moderate Republicans strongly agreed that, since Republicans had run on the Contract, for the party to maintain its majority, Republicans had to deliver on their promises (Healey 1994, 3210–15).

During their years in the minority, the Republicans who filled the leadership ranks of the new majority had developed an elaborate critique of the institution, damning it as corrupt, unresponsive to the public will, and internally undemocratic. "Mandate for Change in the People's House: Republican House Rules Substitute, 103rd Congress" charged that:

"Democrats" control . . . has produced a bloated, muscle-bound bureaucracy characterized by a multiplicity of semiautonomous subcommittees, multitudes of staff, a muddle of tangled jurisdictional lines, and a multiplicity of mud-fights over turf. Democratic leadership efforts to produce legislative results . . . by relying on ad hoc task forces and restrictive amendment procedures have not only resulted in ill-conceived and unrepresentative legislation but have further undermined deliberative democracy. Key decisions have been moved from the sun-filled committee rooms and Chamber of the People's House to the smoke-filled back-rooms of partisan power brokers. . . . [T]he House Republican Conference again commits itself to nothing less than a comprehensive overhaul of the Congress. (Republican Policy Committee 1992, 1)

Among an extensive list of proposed reforms, the most ambitious included realignment of committee jurisdictions, limitations on restrictive special rules and other restrictive floor procedures, a major staff cut and a three-term limit on committee chairmen and ranking minority members (Republican Policy Committee 1992, 3–4).

The 104th thus saw the coincidence of a new majority committed to non-incremental policy change with a leadership that had advocated major alterations in internal institutional arrangements. Did the new majority make changes in institutional arrangements sufficient to establish a new House regime? And how were changes in formal and informal internal arrangements related to legislative outputs?

Clearly, delivering on the House Republicans' promise of ambitious policy change required active and assertive internal leadership. Lawmaking is a complex and time-consuming enterprise and one that, if successful, produces a collective good; consequently it presents the legislature's members with collective-action problems (Olson 1965). Overcoming these collective-action problems requires the delegation by members of powers and resources to agents—to leaders (Cox and McCubbins 1993). The benefits of such delegation can be great. A party leadership well endowed with powers and resources can significantly facilitate the passage of legislation that furthers its membership's policy, reelection, and power goals. It can do so by providing basic coordination services, such as legislative scheduling; by facilitating (for example, through "side payments" or the coordination of both tacit and explicit "logrolling") the passage of legislation various subgroups of its membership want; and by policy leadership, that is, using leadership powers and resources aggressively to influence the congressional agenda and the substance of legislative outputs in order to translate broadly shared legislative preferences into law. Such delegation is, however, risky for members; agents may use the powers granted them to pursue interests that are not those of their principal. Thus the character of the delegation and the extent to which members are willing to allow their leaders to use their delegated power and resources aggressively depend on the costs and benefits to members of strong leadership, which in turn depend on the political and institutional environment. Most relevant here, when members are ideologically homogeneous and committed to enacting an ambitious legislative program they are most likely to expect their leadership to use its powers and resources expansively and more likely to augment the powers and resources delegated.

Such optimal conditions for strong leadership pertained in the House in 1995. Most House Republicans considered their leader, Newt Gingrich (Ga.), to be largely responsible for their much-desired majority status. Gingrich had worked for years to build a majority; he had recruited many of the challengers who won and had helped them with fundraising and campaign advice; the Contract with America was Gingrich's idea and he had orchestrated its realization (Koopman 1996; Stid 1996; Sinclair 1998). Not only were members grateful to him, they regarded him as a world-class political genius.

Changing the Rules

The House Republican leaders, who promised a revolution in institutional arrangements, delivered significant but far from revolutionary change. What changed was the way the House actually functioned, but this occurred as a result of less formal processes rather than any changes in rules.

Republicans had advocated thoroughgoing reform of committee jurisdictions. They abolished three committees, all of which had primarily Democratic constituencies, and made some other marginal adjustments in jurisdiction. Gingrich backed away from more ambitious plans when it became clear that pursuing them would precipitate a major intraparty battle.

Republicans put into House rules few limits on the use of restrictive procedures, though they continued to promise to be much more open than their Democratic predecessors had been. They fulfilled their promise to cut committee staffs by one-third, a task greatly eased by the fact that all the cuts would come at the expense of Democrats.

The Republican takeover led to a centralization of authority within committees. Because the Republican Conference had never adopted the "subcommittee bill of rights," the new Republican committee chairs exercised control over the entire majority staff of their committees and more control over the choice of subcommittee chairs and over the assignment of members to subcommittees. However, other new rules tended to weaken committee chairs especially vis-à-vis the party leadership. Committee chairs were subjected to a limit of three terms; proxy votes, which absent members would most often give to the chair, were banned; and sunshine rules (committee markups that are conducted in public) were modestly strengthened, making it harder to close a committee meeting. These were all reforms Republicans had committed themselves to when they were in the minority; new committee chairs were thus in no position to fight them.

House and Conference rules changes augmenting the Speaker's powers were quite limited and, at the insistence of the freshmen, the Speaker was subject to an eight-year term limit. A revision of the multiple referral rule did give the Speaker greater discretion in the referral of bills to committee. A Conference rules change gave the Republican leader more clout on the Committee on Committees (assigning GOP members to committees). In previous years, Republicans had gradually increased their leader's powers, imitating the majority Democrats by allowing him to choose Republican members of the Rules Committee and by augmenting his influence in the committee assignment process. A Conference rule on leadership issues, although not new, also took on added importance with the gaining of majority control; it read, "the Speaker may designate certain issues as 'Leadership Issues.' Those issues will require early and ongoing cooperation between the relevant committees and the Leadership as the issue evolves" (House Republican Conference 1987).

Given the relatively modest rules changes the Republicans instituted, the significant alteration in how the House operated is best explained by the extraordinary political circumstances. Relying on his immense prestige with House Republicans, Gingrich in the days after the 1994 elections exercised power well beyond that specified in Republican Conference rules. He designated Republicans to serve as committee chairs, bypassing seniority in several instances. According to the rules, the Party Committee on Committees (GOP party committee that assigns GOP members to committees) nominates chairs and the Conference approves them; Gingrich preempted that process, assuming correctly that his stature would prevent anyone from challenging his choices. He used the party leadership's increased influence on the Committee on Committees to reward junior Republicans, who were his strongest supporters, with choice assignments. Of eleven vacant Republican slots on Appropriations, seven went to freshmen, as did three of ten on Ways and Means and nine of ten on Commerce. Gingrich appointed four sophomores and one freshman to Rules.

The Democratic leadership had in the postreform years gained considerable influence over the appointment of members to committees, and the Democratic Caucus had occasionally unseated sitting committee chairs or passed over the most senior member when a vacancy occurred. Although the leadership had used the requirement that the Caucus (the organization of all Democrats in either chamber) approve all committee chairmen in a secret-ballot vote to pressure chairs to be responsive to Caucus sentiment, it had never initiated or even supported any of the efforts to bypass seniority in choosing chairs. It was not new rules but an ideologically homogeneous membership determined to enact major policy change that allowed Gingrich to act so much more aggressively than had his Democratic predecessors. No Democratic leader during the postreform era enjoyed the sort of political context that allowed Gingrich's actions. The powers Gingrich exercised in choosing committee chairs have not, however, been institutionalized and are thus dependent on member acquiescence.

Leaders and Committees

The relationship between party and committee leaders was different in the 104th Congress than it had been between Democratic leaders and chairs of the postreform era. The Democratic party leadership in the 1980s and early 1990s had been actively involved in all stages of the legislative process. Assuring that when legislation reached the floor it was in a form that could pass the House and was satisfactory to most Democrats sometimes required leaders to intervene in committee, broker compromises after a bill was reported, or even bypass committee altogether. Committees and their leaders accepted, if not always happily, such leadership intervention because the party leaders were acting as agents of the membership.

In the 104th Congress, however, committee leaders were clearly subordinate to party leaders on Contract bills and on much of the major legislation that went into the Republicans' attempt to balance the budget (Aldrich and Rohde 1997; Sinclair 1997). The party set the agenda; party leaders held the committees to a tight schedule and exerted a strong influence on the substance of legislation (Owens 1998).

When a committee was incapable of mustering a majority for legislation that the party leadership and the membership wanted, the leadership stepped in and bypassed the committee; for example, when the Agriculture Committee refused to report the "Freedom to Farm" bill, which made cuts in farm programs as required by the budget resolution, the leadership inserted the language directly into the reconciliation bill. When the legislation a committee reported was unacceptable to a majority of the Republican membership, as on the term-limits constitutional amendment, the leadership altered the language substantially after it had been reported and before it want to the floor. On Medicare, one of the most politically sensitive issues the Republicans took on, Gingrich himself headed the "design group" that made the major substantive decisions; the group did include the Republican leaders of the committees and subcommittees with jurisdiction (Sinclair 1997).

Like their Democratic predecessors, the Republican leadership tried to get the belligerents in intraparty disputes to work out their differences among themselves. However, especially in 1995, Gingrich's stature was such that he could bring more pressure to bear than his predecessors. Thus, when the Republican governors objected to provisions of the job-training bill, Gingrich instructed the members of the committee to work out a deal with the governors. During one of many intraparty fights about abortion language on an appropriations bill, Gingrich threatened the combatants with a rule that would in effect gut the bill altogether if they did not resolve their differences (Maraniss and Weisskopf 1996, 93–94). When anti-environmentalism began to damage the party's image, Gingrich refused to schedule a bill weakening the Endangered Species Act and insisted that Commerce Committee Republicans work out a bipartisan deal on the Safe Drinking Water Bill.

The Republican leadership could act in such an assertive manner because much of the membership was ideologically committed to passing the legislation at issue and almost all were convinced that the party's fate depended on delivering on their promises. Because most senior Republicans had signed the Contract, party leaders had a strong tool for persuading committee leaders to report legislation without making major changes and to do so quickly; the new Republican chairs did not all agree with all elements of the Contract and most would have liked more time to work on their bills. The Republican party leadership could and did remind them that "we promised to do it in one-hundred days, we must deliver." Then, and later when balancing the budget was at issue, the chairs knew that the leadership was backed by the freshmen's strong support.

Although Republicans when in the minority had bitterly criticized the Democratic leadership's use of ad hoc task forces, Gingrich made extensive use of the device and for many of the same reasons that his predecessors had found it useful (see Sinclair 1995). Leadership-appointed task forces worked on legislative issues ranging from agriculture policy to gun control to immigration reform. These task forces provided Republicans not on the committee an opportunity to work on and influence legislation on issues they cared about. Junior members were especially heavily represented on the task forces and were thereby provided with a channel for meaningful participation in the legislative process. By and large, committees were not bypassed on those issues, but the task forces did have the purpose and the effect of keeping the pressure on committees to report legislation satisfactory to the party majority and in a timely fashion.

Members' desire to quickly accomplish a mass of pent-up policy objectives led to the leadership's decision to use the appropriations process, thus bypassing the slower and more cumbersome authorizing process, the products of which the president could more easily veto. Decisions about what "riders"—policy provisions in appropriations bills—to allow were made in Majority Leader Richard Armey's (Tex.) office and he insisted that the bypassed authorizing committee leadership support the rider. Because controversial riders make appropriations bills harder to pass, many senior Republicans on the Appropriations Committee were unhappy with the strategy, but they acquiesced. Early in the year Gingrich had extracted from each of the thirteen subcommittee chairs a written pledge of cooperation and commitment to the agenda. Even more important, they knew the Republican membership, especially the freshmen, strongly supported the strategy.

When the leaders were acting as agents of an intense and determined membership, the committees had little choice but to accede. But the leaders could not ignore such membership sentiment either; they occasionally found themselves forced by their members into courses of action they would have preferred to avoid. The Republican leadership brought to the floor the gift ban, lobbying reform, and campaign finance legislation only because of pressure from a determined group of mostly junior members.

In sum, party leaders played an unusually influential role in shaping legislation during the 104th Congress; they did so as agents of a cohesive majority party that believed itself mandated to bring about major policy change. Changes in House and party rules played little role in this change in how the House functioned. Before the budget debacle, House Republicans were convinced that Gingrich was a master strategist and they knew he shared their goals of enacting comprehensive policy change and retaining their majority—goals they believed to be linked, not conflicting. Thus they were more than willing to let him exercise great power in order to assure that legislation was passed and in a form that would accomplish their objectives.

Structuring Choices

Contemporary House leaders have available much more powerful tools for structuring choices through procedure than did their pre-reform predecessors. Gingrich made extensive and aggressive but not particularly innovative use of these tools.

The Budget Act of 1974 provides central leaders with a powerful tool. Reconciliation instructions that require committees to make changes in legislation under their jurisdiction, which are then packaged into a single bill, give the budget act the potential of serving as a vehicle for making comprehensive policy change. Since its use for that purpose by President Reagan in 1981, the budget process has become the tool of choice for those attempting to bring about comprehensive policy change.

In 1995, the Republicans' program entailed major policy change. Balancing the budget in seven years while also cutting taxes required draconian spending cuts and the fundamental revamping of a number of popular programs, including Medicare. As the Democrats had with Clinton's economic program in 1993, Republicans simply assumed they would use the budget process; it offered the only realistic hope for success. By wrapping the provisions into one omnibus bill, the number of battles that need to be won can be kept to a minimum. Leaders can ask members to cast a handful of tough votes, not dozens. And the stakes become so high, it is actually harder for members to vote against their party leaders. Republican leaders packaged a mass of major policy changes into one huge reconciliation bill and passed it on a largely party-line vote.

Packaging can also be used to structure the president's choices in a way more favorable to the congressional majority. Given the frequency of divided control during the past several decades, congressional majorities often had strong incentives for trying to force the president to accept legislative provisions that, were they sent to him in free-standing form, he would veto. As a new majority bent on forcing "revolutionary" policy change on a resistant president, the House Republicans made extensive use of this strategy. The Republican leadership believed that packaging the mass of major policy changes in one huge reconciliation bill made it harder for the president to veto. For good measure they included in the reconciliation bill a must-pass provision to raise the debt limit. In a separate ploy, they loaded down must-pass legislation such as appropriations bills and legislation to raise the debt limit with provisions the president strongly opposed.

In the 1980s, Democratic House leaders had developed the rules that govern floor consideration into flexible and powerful tools for shaping choices. When in the minority Republicans had labeled restrictive rules "dictatorial" and "illegitimate" and had promised not to use them if they took control. The enormous usefulness of restrictive rules for promoting the party's legislative objectives largely overcame any Republican objections based on principal or the fear of seeming hypocritical. To be sure, the type of restrictions were sometimes of a different character: Republicans often limited amending activity by specifying a maximum number of hours rather than specifying the amendments that could be offered. Nevertheless, 77 percent of rules for the consideration of major measures were restrictive in the 104th—compared to 82 percent in the 103rd and 72 percent in both the 100th and 101st Congresses.[1] On this major legislation, the restrictions by and large were more substantial than just time limits on the amending process or the requirement that amendments be "preprinted" in the Congressional record; according to the Republican Rules Committee's own classification, 63 percent of the rules were either modified closed (which permits some amendments to some parts of a bill) or closed (which prohibits the offering of amendments except those from the committee reporting the bill).

The new majority used rules to structure choices, as had their Democratic predecessors. In 1995, Republicans used a cleverly constructed restrictive rule to protect their rescission bill (a bill cutting already appropriated spending). It specified that anyone wishing to restore spending cuts in the bill had to offset the cost by cutting something else in the same section of the bill; thus, no money could be transferred to social programs from defense spending or from disaster relief for California, in effect, protecting them from cuts (Sinclair 1997, 20–26). The rule for the budget resolution in 1995 required that all substitutes made in order had to balance the budget by 2002. More frequently than his Democratic predecessors, Gingrich simply barred amendments that a significant number of his members wanted to vote on but that went against the party's promises. Thus, over one hundred Republicans signed a letter to their leadership requesting a vote on an amendment to the tax bill lowering the income ceiling for eligibility for the $500-per-child tax credit. Since Democrats favored lowering the limit, the amendment would have passed handily if offered. The Republican leadership refused to allow the vote, making those of its members who favored the amendment choose between that preference and sinking the tax bill, the "crown jewel" of the Contract (Sinclair 1997, 175–216). Those Republicans and others who were put in the same position on other Contract or budget-related legislation knew that the press would have a field day if any of those items failed and that, were they responsible, their colleagues would not soon forget.

House Republicans brought all of the Contract items to a floor vote in the first one hundred days of the 104th Congress as they had promised. They passed all but one; the term-limits constitutional amendment, which required a two-thirds vote, failed on the House floor. Even more impressive, Republicans passed a reconciliation bill balancing the budget in seven years and overhauling a number of major federal programs, including Medicare, Medicaid, and farm price support programs. Republican success depended on the remarkable unity they maintained during 1995. Only 4.7 Republicans on average defected from the party position on final passage votes on Contract items. During all of 1995, 73 percent of roll-call votes pitted a majority of Republicans against a majority of Democrats and, on those, Republicans on average supported their party's position 91 percent of the time (*Congressional Quarterly Weekly Report*, 27 January 1996, 199–201).

In sum, although Republicans when in the minority had argued that the House required a major overhaul of its institutional arrangements, once in the majority they, in fact, made relatively modest changes in House rules and structures. And clearly a major overhaul was not a prerequisite to legislative productivity.

How the legislative process in the House functioned did change, but not as a result of formal rules changes. The party leadership played an extremely active policy leadership role and closely supervised committees that were perforce highly responsive to the party leadership and the party membership. Yet this did not represent an abrupt discontinuity with the past. As a consequence of the reforms of the 1970s and the political climate of the 1980s, the internal distribution of influence in the House had changed significantly well before the Republicans took control. The majority-party leadership had become more active and more central to the legislative process; committees had become less autonomous and more responsive (Sinclair 1995). The effective subordination of committees to the party leaders acting as agents for their members in the 104th Congress represented a difference in degree, not in direction, and was made possible by the extraordinary political circumstances, not by major rules changes.

In fact, by the end of the nineteenth century, the House of Representatives had evolved a set of rules that made it a majority-rule chamber (Binder 1997). The reforms of the 1970s swept away the barriers to a reasonably cohesive majority working its will that had grown up during the committee-government era. The new Republican majority did not need to make fundamental changes in House institutional arrangements in order to pass their ambitious program in the House; a cohesive majority working within current arrangements was sufficient. The House does not place institutional constraints on a determined majority working its will and doing so quickly.

BETWEEN PARTISAN IMPERATIVES AND INSTITUTIONAL CONSTRAINTS: THE REPUBLICAN SENATE

Republicans took control of the Senate in the 1994 elections as well, making a net gain of eight seats. Although more politically experienced than the House Republican freshmen, the eleven new Republican senators were similar in ideology; with one exception (Olympia Snowe of Maine), they were staunch conservatives. Senate Republicans had not endorsed the Contract with America, but the House's actions put great pressure on the Senate to follow suit; clearly the media would judge Republicans by their success in getting the Contract and then the balanced-budget legislation through both houses. Furthermore the Senate majority leader was running for president and touting his ability to get things done. Consequently Senate Republicans and Bob Dole had a stake in passing the legislation as well.

Unlike their House counterparts, Senate Republicans had not advocated significant changes in Senate rules. To the contrary, when in the minority Senate Republicans had used the Senate's permissive rules to stymie many of the legislative initiatives of President Clinton and congressional Democrats. Majority Democrats had complained bitterly about Republican filibusters and other delaying tactics and had proposed rules changes (Evans and Oleszek 1997). At the beginning of the 104th, a few Democrats continued to advocate change in the cloture rule, but found no support on the Republican side of the aisle.

By the end of the first one hundred days, only five of twenty-one Contract items had reached the Senate floor; only four of those had passed and three of those were relatively noncontroversial items. Senate committees had not even begun markup of many of the key pieces of the Contract (*Congressional Quarterly Weekly Report* 8 May 1995, 996–97). By the end of 1995, a mere five of twenty-one Contract items, most of them noncontroversial, had become law. Of the others, some—the national security initiative, much of the anticrime legislation—had gone nowhere in the Senate. Others—the regulatory moratorium, welfare reform—had been severely watered down in order to make Senate passage possible. No compromise that allowed passage had been found on some measures, the regulatory overhaul bills, for example. And the balanced-budget constitutional amendment had been defeated on the Senate floor. The Senate had, however, passed a massive reconciliation bill that, like the House bill, included major alterations in entitlement programs (*Congressional Quarterly Weekly Report* 6 January 1996, 22–23, 52–53).

Why were legislative outcomes so different in the two chambers in 1995? Certainly Senate Majority Leader Robert Dole did not have the prestige Speaker Gingrich had, nor was his membership as mandate-driven. More importantly, however, Gingrich did not require Democratic support to pass legislation in the House; with the important exception of budget legislation, Dole could not win by simply holding together his majority; he required Democratic acquiescence, if not support.

Leadership and Legislating in a Nonmajoritarian Chamber

Senate rules that empower individual senators severely limit the control of the majority leader and the power of the majority party. In most cases, any senator can offer an unlimited number of amendments to a piece of legislation on the Senate floor and those amendments need not even be germane. A senator can hold the Senate floor indefinitely unless cloture is invoked, which requires an extraordinary majority of sixty votes. When the majority leader refuses to schedule nongermane amendments, senators may offer such amendments on the floor, which undermines the majority leadership's control of the schedule and of the agenda more broadly. The ability of forty-one senators to prevent a measure from coming to a vote means that a united minority party can almost always extract concessions, at least, from the majority, and sometimes block action altogether.

The Senate's permissive amending rules and the right of extended debate provide the individual senator with powerful and flexible weapons that few senators now refrain from using. Both the number of floor amendments offered and the number of filibusters has skyrocketed since the 1950s and 1960s (Sinclair 1989; Binder and Smith 1997). Recent congresses have averaged almost thirty filibusters each (where filibusters are defined as those instances where an attempt to invoke cloture was made) (see Beth 1995; Democratic Study Group 1994). In the late 1980s and early 1990s, just under 30 percent of major legislation encountered some extended-debate-related problem identifiable from the public record (Sinclair 1997, 48–49).

With the increase in party voting and the heightening of partisan intensity in both houses of Congress, the filibuster has increasingly become a partisan weapon. In the 103rd Congress, it was used as a partisan tool to an extent unprecedented in this century. In the first congress of the Clinton presidency, almost half of major legislation encountered an extended-debate-related problem. A Republican filibuster killed Clinton's stimulus package; Republicans used the filibuster or the threat thereof to extract concessions on a number of bills— voter-registration legislation ("motor voter") and the national service program, for example. At the end of the 103rd Congress, Republican filibusters killed campaign finance and lobbying reform bills. Although unsuccessful in the end, Republicans filibustered and tried to prevent passage of a massive crime bill, the California Desert Protection Act and a comprehensive education bill. In some cases, filibusters were waged to prevent legislation from being sent to conference and, more frequently, on approving the conference report. Republican threats of obstructionist floor tactics were major contributors to the death of important bills revamping the superfund program, revising clean drinking-water regulations, overhauling outdated telecommunications law, and applying federal labor laws to Congress. In the first year of the 104th, Democrats, now in the minority, returned the favor. In 1995, 44 percent of major legislation encountered extended-debate-related problems. It is no fluke that the massive reconciliation bill incorporating nonincremental policy change passed the Senate, while much less radical legislation failed; budget legislation receives special protection from filibusters, while most other legislation does not.

Senate majority leaders have always had to be negotiators, brokers, and persuaders. They have had to work closely not only with the members of their own party but with the minority leader and often other individual minority-party senators as well. The greater individualism and greater partisanship that characterize the contemporary Senate make that both more necessary and more difficult. The problems faced by a Senate majority leader are well illustrated by the path of welfare reform in the Senate. Although the House passed its bill with relative ease in late March 1995, the Senate Finance Committee did not report a bill until 26 May and problems within the majority party immediately became apparent; Republicans from the South and Southwest who represent fast-growing states with relative low welfare benefits objected to the funding formulas that based federal funds on past welfare expenditures; some very conservative senators decried the dropping of House provisions that were aimed at reducing out-of-wedlock births such as one barring unwed teenage mothers from receiving welfare, and Republican moderates believed the legislation did not provide enough money for child care and would allow states to cut their own welfare spending too much. Because of the saliency and the popular appeal of the issue, no one, including most Democrats, really wanted to vote against a welfare-reform bill, and had the Republican leadership been able to force an up or down vote, the committee bill might well have passed. But because he had no way of protecting the legislation from a barrage of amendments on the floor or from a filibuster, Senate Majority Leader Dole (Kan.) had to deal. He, along with Finance Committee Chairman Robert Packwood (Ore.), took on the task of rewriting the bill. In early August, after several months of negotiations, Dole unveiled a revised bill aimed at satisfying the various factions; in addition to a modified version of the Finance Committee bill, it incorporated in revised form three other pieces of legislation—food stamps overhaul from the Agriculture Committee, and child-care and job-training bills approved by the Labor and Human Resources Committee. Adding these provisions provided a greater scope for compromise.

Floor debate began 7 August and it soon became evident that problems still existed and the bill would not pass before the scheduled recess. Republicans blamed the Democrats, charging that they intended to offer fifty amendments, but in fact the GOP was still split. On 6 September, after the recess, Dole brought the bill back to the floor, but he still lacked a secure winning coalition and continued to make changes to placate various groups of Republicans. He began talking with Democrats as well as with moderate Republicans and on 15 September, a major compromise was reached; among other provisions, it added substantial funds for child care. Four days later, Dole offered for himself and the minority leader the Dole-Daschle amendment, which incorporated the compromise, and it passed on an 87–12 vote, with mostly hard-line conservative Republicans voting in opposition. Acceptance of the amendment significantly moderated the Senate welfare-overhaul bill, which was already more moderate than the House's bill. The Senate passed the bill as amended 87–12, with only one Republican voting in opposition.

After the House-passed legislation overhauling federal regulatory procedures Majority Leader Robert Dole attempted to steer the legislation through the Senate. Dole's efforts in the Senate were similar to those in the House, but less successful. Over the course of months, he bargained and compromised with a large number of senators, Democrats as well as Republicans. Although he mustered a majority on several cloture votes, Dole fell short of the sixty needed to cut off debate and bring the bill to a vote. Thus he was forced to abandon a bill that was important to the Republican Party's core business constituency and most of his members.

The Senate is not a majority-rule chamber. Senate rules make it hard for the majority-party leadership to meet the expectations of members dedicated to major policy change unless the party majority is very large and the public mood emphatically in favor of such change. Although moderates made up more of the Republican membership in the Senate than in the House, most Senate Republicans were strong conservatives who did want to pass much of the Contract.

Junior Senate Republicans, a number of whom had previously served in the House, were particularly frustrated with the barriers to policy change in their chamber. It was the defection of a moderate Republican on a key vote that brought their frustration to a head. After the House had approved it, the constitutional amendment requiring a balanced budget failed in the Senate by one vote, with Mark Hatfield (Ore.), the chairman of the Appropriations Committee, casting the only Republican vote against it. The amendment was a part of the Senate Republicans' agenda, and the ideologically-driven junior Republicans, many of whom were Gingrich admirers and allies, believed that on such a crucial vote a senior committee chair should not be allowed with impunity to vote against the party to which he owed his chairmanship. They proposed stripping Hatfield of his chairmanship, but were placated with a reform task force to which three freshmen were appointed.

The provisions proposed by the task force, which the Senate Republican Conference adopted, included limiting chairs and party leaders (except the top leader) to three terms; requiring a secret-ballot vote on committee chairs, both in committee and in the Conference; and providing for the adoption of a Senate GOP agenda in the Conference by a three-quarters vote. The new rules went into effect at the beginning of 1997 and were intended by the junior conservatives to make their more senior (and often more moderate) party colleagues responsive to the predominantly conservative party membership as a whole.

In the Senate, however, attempts at party government come up against the Senate's nonmajoritarian rules (see Jones 1998). On controversial legislation, a majority is not enough and Republicans fell far short of the 60-member majority needed to enact legislation without regard for the minority party. Increasingly the Senate's usual problems were exacerbated by Robert Dole's presidential candidacy. With Dole intent on running as the man who can get things done, the incentives for Senate Democrats to stall were magnified. By the time Dole decided to resign from the Senate in summer of 1996, the Senate had ground to a halt.

A New Leader for a More Partisan, but Still Individualist Senate

Senate Republicans elected Trent Lott (Miss.) as their new majority leader in June 1996. Younger and considered more ideologically conservative than Dole, a former House member and a friend of Gingrich's, Lott had served as whip in both chambers and was known as a savvy politician. Under Lott, who had been elected Senate Republican whip in late 1994, the Republican whip system had become larger, more structured, and more active (Jacoby 1995). When he succeeded Dole as majority leader, Lott instituted a similar form of leadership at the top level, relying more heavily on and sharing more duties with other elected leaders, attempting to provide more structure but also more openness to leadership endeavors, and striving to include as many senators as possible in party-based activities. Lott sees congressional party leadership as a team enterprise.

Partisan polarization has made participation through their parties more attractive to senators than it was when the parties were more heterogeneous and the ideological distance between them was less great. It has transformed the preferred leadership style. Previous leaders such as Robert Byrd (D-W.Va.) and Dole were, in effect, solo operators; they (along with their top staff) largely carried out the leadership's tasks themselves; they did not rely on other leaders. In an atomistic chamber, this modus operandi provided maximum flexibility. George Mitchell (D-Maine) started delegating and decentralizing the organization, though he himself was inclined to a solo leadership style. Lott and his minority counterpart Tom Daschle (D-S.D.) have much more inclusive leadership styles, both in terms of organization and in term of actual operations; they are heads of party teams. Still, individual senators exercise a great deal more discretion about when and under what conditions to participate on the party team than do House members; they have available attractive alternative channels for participation and they pay little price when they go off on their own.

Soon after he took over, Lott broke the legislative logjam. Urged on by Republican members from both chambers increasingly concerned about the media's branding the 104th "a do-nothing Congress," Lott compromised with Democrats who now had less reason to hang tough. He quickly cut a deal that allowed the minimum-wage legislation, which Democrats were advocating, to come to a vote and pass. Decoupling Medicaid changes from welfare reform and backing off Dole's strong support for the inclusion of medical savings accounts in the Kennedy-Kassebaum health-insurance reform bill allowed welfare reform and modest healthcare reform to become law.

Lott began the 105th Congress in a strong position. The final months of the 104th had enhanced his reputation as a leader who could get things done. The 1996 elections increased his membership by two, and the nine new Republicans were from the same increasingly dominant activist-conservative wing of the party as was Lott. The new rules that strengthen party influence went into effect. Lott had the legitimacy and credibility of having won his position recently and overwhelmingly and he was untainted by scandal.

Yet those who expected Lott to parlay these resources into a record of party-based legislative achievement were quickly disappointed. Even with a bigger and more conservative majority, Lott was no more successful than Dole had been in engineering passage of the balanced-budget constitutional amendment, and it again failed by one vote. Most Senate Republicans, including Lott, favored limiting the hearings into campaign finance abuses to the Clinton–Gore reelection campaign. Yet Democrats' threat to block funding for the investigation and the public defection of the senator Lott had chose to chair those hearings forced Lott to expand the committee's charge. In return for their support for the resolution financing the investigative committee, Democrats also extracted a provision terminating the committee at the end of 1997. In late September 1997, Lott was forced to bring campaign-finance legislation—sponsored by Senators John McCain (R-Ariz.) and Russell Feingold (D-Wis.)—that he and most Republicans opposed to the Senate floor. Democrats and the few Republican proponents of the legislation had threatened to attach the McCain-Feingold bill as a nongermane amendment to whatever legislation was brought to the floor, and very little business had gotten done. Media coverage was becoming more and more harshly anti-Republican.

Lott gave in but used his powers as majority leader to give the proponents little prior warning and thus little time for final preparations. Furthermore, he then "filled the amendment tree"; that is, he used the majority leader's power of first recognition to offer an amendment that Democrats saw as anti-labor and strongly opposed and then offered the full complement of amendments allowable under Senate rules, thus assuring that his amendment could not be further amended. Lott's purpose was to force a Democratic filibuster of his amendment and thus both stymie action and shift the blame to Democrats. The maneuver did produce stalemate; the legislation was on the floor for several days, but when neither side had the votes to impose cloture, Lott pulled the bill.

Proponents were furious. Democrats began blocking everything except the appropriations bills by again threatening to offer McCain-Feingold as a nongermane amendment, and the Senate again ground to a halt. Lott's maneuver had not succeeded in shifting the onus onto the Democrats; it only intensified media criticism of Senate Republicans. Finally, in late October, Lott gave in and made a deal; he promised that there would be a full debate on campaign-finance reform in 1998 with an up-or-down vote on McCain-Feingold (Doherty and Koszczuk 1997).

In 1998 when it was considered again, the bill failed to muster the 60 votes necessary to break a filibuster, but the debate brought with it another round of bad publicity for Senate Republicans. By midsummer of 1998, Lott found himself in a situation reminiscent of that Dole had confronted two years earlier. In the run-up to the elections, he was forced to pull bill after bill off the floor to prevent Democrats from attaching their own agenda—especially managed-care reform—to legislation Republicans wanted.

A minority party that numbered over forty and that was frequently cohesive enough to make effective use of Senate rules made Lott's job as majority-party leader very different from the House leadership's job. Furthermore, the individualism that Senate institutional arrangements breed greatly exacerbated Lott's problems. When Senator Fred Thompson (R-Tenn.), Lott's choice to head the campaign-finance investigations, refused to support the party's position on the scope of the investigation, or when respected conservative Senator John McCain (R-Ariz.) became a leading advocate of campaign-finance reform and cosponsored the bill Democrats were supporting, Republicans could not paint the Democrats' position as simply crass partisanship. These actions by individual Republicans made it much more difficult for Lott to present the Republicans' stance in a favorable light and severely handicapped the Republicans in the battle for favorable media coverage.

A Senate majority may be able to prevent or halt minority obstructionism by winning the public-relations battle and thereby making the perceived electoral costs of continued obstruction too high for minority-party members. Near the end of the 103rd Congress, for example, the Republican filibuster of the so-called Brady Bill (imposing a seven-day waiting period for buying a gun) collapsed when a number of Republican senators began to fear the political price of their participation. President Clinton and allied interest groups had effectively kept the spotlight on the issue. The tendency of senators to freelance even against the great majority of their own party makes it less likely that the majority leader can successfully orchestrate such a public-relations battle.

For those Republicans most committed to nonincremental policy change, the compromises necessary to pass legislation in the Senate are a bitter pill. "We always compromise too early," complained Senator Robert C. Smith (R-N.H.). "It's like we're punting on second down" (Doherty 1997, 2743).

In the Senate, institutional constraints trump partisan imperatives. The Senate is not a majority-rule chamber. The Senate majority leader prefers to lead through accommodation. Oversized coalitions are required to pass most legislation, and that usually means bipartisan coalitions—and to put them together usually requires extensive compromise.

THE REPUBLICAN HOUSE AFTER THE BUDGET DEBACLE

The constraints of the American governmental system led to the demise of House Republicans as a "revolutionary force." The Senate and, even more, the presidential veto proved to be insurmountable barriers to much of the radical policy change the new majority had hoped to bring about. Then, when President Clinton won the public-relations war over the Republicans' budget bill and the American public increasingly came to regard the Republican Congress as both "extreme" and "do nothing," another form of constitutionally derived constraint came into play. When, as in the wake of the 1994 elections, a congressional majority perceives itself to be mandated to enact major policy change, policy, power, and reelection goals for members of the majority all dictate the same course of action—delivering on the mandate. In 1995 it was this alignment of goals that made possible the unusually strong policy leadership and the swift passage of a mass of nonincremental legislation in the House. Losing the budget battle undermined members' confidence that their goals were, in fact, congruent, and forced members into a more normal and complex calculus. Each Republican now had to ask himself if the pursuit of good public policy as he saw it would help or hinder his reelection chances and if the course of action most likely to lead to retention of the Republican majority would entail severe reelection or policy costs. Given differences in their constituencies, members answered these questions quite differently and the extraordinary unity House Republicans had displayed in 1995 began to break down.

In 1996, Republican defections for constituency reasons became more common and the majority lost some major votes. Threats of a revolt by Northeastern moderates forced the leadership to allow a floor vote on a minimum-wage increase, which they and a majority of their members strongly opposed. To counter the "do-nothing" label that was hurting them with the public, House Republican leaders switched strategy and began to compromise enough to enact some legislation into law. They began to help vulnerable Republicans secure district projects and to suggest they run locally oriented campaigns (Taylor 1996). With these changes in strategy and enormous amounts of money, Republicans managed to hang on to a House majority in the 1996 elections; but their margin narrowed and their sense of mandate was gone. There was no consensus within the party on strategy for the new Congress. No longer did members believe their own goals were necessarily congruent, much less that their goals and those of their fellow party members were congruent.

The party leaders responded by exercising less aggressive leadership. They proposed no ambitious agenda. The leadership did not have the same credibility with its membership as it had had in the 104th, and thus had less leeway to be innovative in strategy and aggressive in using its resources. With less trust in their leaders' judgment, members were more likely to second-guess its strategic decisions, to bicker among themselves about strategy and policy, and to go their own way when they disagreed with leadership decisions. Because the Republican Party leadership in the 105th was not in as strong a position vis-à-vis its members as it had been in the 104th, it was not in as strong a position vis-à-vis the committees and their chairs as it had been. Committees were subject to less direction from the leadership and were freer to pursue their own agendas.

Intraparty divisions and the collective malaise led to more defections and more Republican defeats. The attempt to topple Gingrich as Speaker, in which some of the other party leaders were involved, was another consequence. They did not, however, lead to a peripheral, inactive party leadership.

Although the House Republican-Party leadership was less aggressive, less dominant, and less successful in the 105th than it was in the 104th, it nevertheless remained an activist-engaged leadership. Members complained bitterly about the lack of an agenda, even though a consensus on its contents was lacking. Because what the committees do affects the party as a whole, leadership intervention on behalf of its members was often required. Members still need an activist leadership to advance their goals. Republicans now faced an adverse climate for advancing their true policy preferences without endangering their electoral goals. They confronted an opposition-party president who had proven himself tougher and more skillful in the public-relations wars than they ever expected, and an electoral imperative to avoid gridlock and produce legislative accomplishments. In this context, activist leadership might not enable members to accomplish their goals, but members knew they could succeed as individuals.

The budget situation illustrates the problems members faced and their need for activist leadership. Republicans badly needed a budget agreement in 1997. The media were already pounding them as a "do-nothing" Congress. Yet Republicans wanted to avoid having to propose and pass their own budget. Many members were unwilling to take the lead on making the unpopular decisions on programs like Medicare; the only way of making those choices less draconian was to scale back substantially the tax cuts, a course of action anathema to many Republicans. Since Republicans could count on no Democratic votes for a partisan budget resolution, and thus had to hold all but a handful of their own members, they probably could not pass a budget resolution on their own.

Given these circumstances, a budget agreement with the president was essential and, as past experience has demonstrated, only the party leadership could negotiate a deal. Achieving a budget deal required extensive bipartisan compromise, including spending increases for Clinton's domestic priorities. (It also required a major assist from a swiftly growing economy.) Conservatives outside the Congress were scathing in their attacks on the "timid, minimalist" deal the leaders made. Yet, while there was a good deal of private grumbling, all but the most purist of the Republican revolutionaries in the House kept quiet; all but one voted for the tax component and all but thirty-two voted for the spending component of the deal.

The 1997 deal that balanced the budget will probably be seen as the 105th Congress's signal accomplishment. Inter- and intraparty differences stymied the enactment of most significant legislation in 1998. The major exception was a huge highway bill that contained something for every state and almost every district in the country. A number of the most conservative junior Republicans did vote against it, but most Republicans managed to surmount their aversion to pork and adherence to spending discipline and voted for a bill that provided rich district benefits.

The House Republicans' public posture on the budget deal—their willingness to follow their leaders and "declare victory and go home"—illustrates that the Congress had indeed changed the Republicans. In the space of two years, the firebrand revolutionaries of the 104th who would not allow their revered leader to compromise would acquiesce to leaders with much less stature making a deal that represented much greater compromise. They have learned that, given the barriers to major policy change erected by the American governmental system, incremental change is often the best one can accomplish. As the highway bill shows, junior Republicans have also learned that to make good public policy, you have to be reelected and, in the American electoral system, purely national party appeals are seldom sufficient; reelection requires some deference to local constituency opinion and concerns and thus members' reelection calculus often puts a break on partisan imperatives.

NOTES

In addition to the sources cited, this essay is based on interviews conducted by the author. All unattributed quotes are from those interviews.

1. *Congressional Quarterly*'s list of major legislation, augmented by those measures on which key votes occurred (again according to *Congressional Quarterly*) are used. See Sinclair 1997 for more detail.

CHAPTER THREE

Institutional Context and Leadership Style: The Case of Newt Gingrich

RONALD M. PETERS, JR.

INTRODUCTION

On 26 January 1993, House Speaker Tom Foley of Washington testified before the Joint Committee on the Organization of the 103rd Congress (1993–1995) to express his views on congressional reform. On that day Speaker Foley, a Democrat, said: ". . . I do not believe that the Speaker, in this time and circumstance, ought to appoint committee chairmen beyond those committee chairmen that he presently appoints or have the total responsibility of directing the House affairs that still exists in some legislatures. But marginally, I wouldn't object to that direction" (Foley 1993).[1]

Two years later, in January of 1995, the House elected Republican Newt Gingrich of Georgia as Speaker of the 104th Congress (1995–1997). Gingrich imposed a highly centralized regime. He established leadership control over the committee system for the first time since the turn of the century. Revamping the Republican Committee on Committees to give control of committee appointments to the leadership for the first time since 1919, he bypassed three senior members in appointing committee chairs. He demanded leadership approval of committee staff directors. In pushing the "Contract with America" legislation through the House, he often bypassed the committees altogether in favor of appointed task forces. When the committees did produce bills, the Speaker was not reluctant to alter them in the Rules Committee. The leadership attached substantive riders to appropriations bills. Under the Gingrich regime, policy was made by the Speaker's Advisory Group (SAG), a small band of elected and appointed party leaders. Gingrich himself chaired task forces on budget and

43

Medicare reform. Not only did the Republicans pass most of the Contract legislation in the House, they also passed other substantial legislation, such as a major agriculture-reform bill and a major telecommunications bill.

On the opening day of the 105th Congress (1997–1999) with the Republicans still in the majority, the Democrats sought to defer the election of the Speaker until ethics charges against Gingrich could be fully resolved. The Republicans defeated the Democratic ploy, but four Republicans voted with the Democrats. The House moved to ballot for the election of the Speaker, and nine Republicans refused to vote for Gingrich, who was elected by a bare plurality of members voting for a candidate by name. In his acceptance speech Gingrich humbled himself and offered his apologies to the House for having brought dishonor upon it. His power at a low ebb, Gingrich followed seniority uniformly in appointing committee chairs and indicated that he intended for the committee system to resume its traditional role. Seven months later a group of Republican renegades launched an abortive attempt to oust him from the Speakership.

As we compare the 103rd, 104th, and 105th Congresses, we witness three distinct variations of the Speakership. In the 103rd Congress, the House was led by a characteristically Democratic Speaker who was reluctant to embrace reform, who was reluctant to assume additional powers, and who moved reluctantly to reform the administration of the House. Due in part to the autonomy of strong committee chairs, Speaker Foley was unable to lead the House to enactment of reform, and the Democrats' failure to act on their reform agenda contributed to their defeat in the 1994 elections. In the 104th Congress, Speaker Gingrich, fresh from the electoral triumph of 1994, was able to establish a strong central-party leadership regime. As the Republican leader and historical nemesis of the Democrats, he became the object of intense partisan attack that eventually drove down his public approval ratings and eroded his position in the House. In the 105th Congress, Gingrich survived two challenges to his leadership and was able to lead the Republicans in reaching a historic agreement with President Clinton and the Senate to balance the federal budget. However, the Republicans were not able to develop a substantial legislative agenda, and amidst the controversy surrounding the impeachment proceedings, the Republicans lost five seats in the November elections. Faced with a challenge to his leadership by Appropriations Committee Chair Bob Livingston, Speaker Gingrich resigned from the House. After his initial election by the Republican Conference as its nominee for Speaker, Livingston withdrew and Representative Dennis Hastert of Illinois was elected Speaker of the 106th Congress.

Congressional leadership theory has held since 1981 that leadership style is defined by institutional context. In "Institutional Context and Leadership Style: The House from Cannon to Rayburn," Joseph Cooper and David Brady (1981) launched a generation of congressional-leadership research that has embraced the main contention of their article, that congressional party leaders are constrained by the institutional context in which they function. For Cooper and Brady, the main determinant of institutional context is party cohesion: cohesive parties produce strong leadership; divided parties produce weak leadership. Building upon the contextual premise, scholars such as David Rohde (1991) and Barbara Sinclair (1995) have held that party leadership opportunities are shaped by member expectations, which are in turn related to the nature of their constituencies. Yet the 1990s have witnessed different renditions of the Speakership within roughly the same institutional context. In this chapter, I argue that Newt Gingrich's Speakership suggested limitations on the contextual theory of legislative party leadership. I begin by reviewing that theory.

THE CONTEXTUAL THESIS

In "Institutional Context and Leadership Style," Cooper and Brady distinguish between two eras in the history of the House and two corresponding styles of leadership. The first era ran from 1881 to 1921. During this period the Republicans were in the majority most of the time, and when they were, they imposed a strong leadership regime. The second era began with the emergence of the conservative coalition after 1937, and lasted at least through the Speakership of Sam Rayburn, which ended with his death in 1961. The Democrats were in the majority during most of this period, and when they were, they imposed a weak leadership regime. The respective styles of the Republican Speakers of what I have elsewhere termed the "partisan era" and Speaker Rayburn, the Democratic Speaker of what I have called the "feudal era" (Peters 1997), were contextually determined. During the partisan era the two major political parties were more homogeneous, reflecting their respective constituencies; during the feudal era the two parties (and especially the Democratic party) were more heterogeneous in their constituency base. The former circumstance led to a stronger Speakership under House and party rules, and the style of the Republican Speakers of that era reflected their formal power; the latter circumstance led to a weaker Speakership under House and party rules, and Speaker Rayburn's style reflected that circumstance. Hence, institutional context drives leadership style.

Cooper and Brady code each Congress during these two periods and find that all but two Congresses in the partisan era were marked by strong party leadership under the rules of the House and majority-party caucus, and all of the Congresses during the feudal era were marked by weak central-party leadership. During the former, the parties were relatively homogenous due to the fact that the congressional districts were polarized. During the latter, the parties were more heterogenous, because the districts were not as polarized. This was largely due to the hold of the Democratic Party on the South, which led to the rise of the conservative coalition. The conservative coalition (or the underlying political divisions that it manifested) explains both the low party-unity scores in the feudal era as well as the decentralized leadership that the Democrats adopted. This tendency—for strength of party leadership to be dependent upon levels of party cohesion, which is in turn tied to the polarization of districts—was more clearly indicated during the partisan era because, unlike the feudal era, control of the House switched back and forth, and there was more variation in the pattern of party leadership. For example, during the 50th (1887–1889), 51st (1889–1891), and 52nd (1891–1893) Congresses, control of the House switched from the Democrats to the Republicans and back to the Democrats. The districts were less polarized during the 50th, more polarized during the 51st, and less polarized during the 52nd. Party leadership was weak in the 50th and 52nd Congresses under Democrats John Carlisle and Charles Crisp, and strong during the 51st Congress under Republican Thomas Brackett Reed (Maine). The inference is that Reed was strong because he was the beneficiary of a polarized political system that produced a homogenous Republican party in the House, whereas Carlisle and Crisp were weak because the political system produced more heterogeneous Democratic majorities.

During the feudal era, when the House was controlled by the Democrats for all but the 80th (1947–1949) and 83rd (1953–1955) Congresses, the districts were not highly polarized by party, party cohesion was thus low, and party leadership was weak. Even though the Democrats controlled the 79th (1945–1947), 81st (1949–1951), 82nd (1951–1953), and 84th (1955–1957) Congresses, while the Republicans controlled the 80th and 83rd, party polarization remained low and party leadership remained weak. The change in control of the House was not marked by the same sort of purification of the districts as had been the case in the 51st Congress, and party cohesion remained relatively constant. Speakers Rayburn and Martin operated under essentially the same rules, and adopted similar leadership styles.

Thus, Cooper and Brady (1981) conclude: ". . . institutional context rather than personal skill is the primary determinant of leadership power in the House" (p. 423). Again, ". . . institutional context rather than personal traits primarily determines leadership style in the House" (p. 423). Therefore, ". . . there is no direct relationship between leadership style and effectiveness in the House" (p. 424). Finally, the impact of institutional context on leadership power and style is determined primarily by party strength" (p. 424). On this interpretation, leadership style and skill are dependent upon institutional context. A party leader will be effective if his style is congruent with the context in which he functions. He will be powerful if the rules permit it, and the rules will permit it if the members want it so. Leaders cannot change the parameters within which they are called upon to lead; they can only react to them.

This is a powerful argument, buttressed by substantial evidence. Yet it seems inadequate to explain all observed facts. In particular, it gives insufficient consideration to the role of leadership and party culture in shaping the conditions of legislative party leadership. In all but two Congresses during the partisan era that demonstrated very low percentages of party voting and noncentralized leadership (the 47th [1881–1883] and 66th [1919–1921]) the Democrats were in the majority, while during all Congresses with a high percentage of party voting the Republicans were in control. In the 47th and 66th Congresses, the Speakers were Warren Keifer and Frederick Gillette, lesser lights in the Republican pantheon. Were Keifer and Gillette weak Republican Speakers or were they simply contextually constrained in a way that Reed and Cannon were not?[2] Keifer served before the adoption of the Reed rules, whereas Gillette was the first Republican Speaker (other than Cannon himself) to serve after the revolt against Cannon in 1910. Thus, their Speakerships are coded as noncentralized by Cooper and Brady because they could not control the floor, in Keifer's case, or the committees, in Gillette's case.[3] Yet it is undeniably the case that during the partisan era the Democrat Crisp offered a weak Speakership (he refused to count a quorum), while Gillette's successor, Longworth, offered a stronger Speakership than either Gillette before him or Democrat John Nance Garner after him. One might, in fact, argue that every Republican administration of the House since the Civil War has offered stronger party leadership than its historically adjacent Democratic counterparts (James G. Blaine/Samuel Randall; John Carlisle/Thomas Reed; Charles Crisp/David Henderson; Joseph Cannon/ Champ Clark; Nicholas Longworth/John Nance Garner; Sam Rayburn/Joe Martin; Tom Foley/Newt Gingrich).[4]

It would seem that party control makes a difference and that it is related to party culture. If one simply correlated party control and the dependent variable in Cooper's and Brady's table (Table 1, p. 414), one would reach nearly the same results without the intervening variables of party unity or district homogeneity. However, we should ponder further the relationship between district homogeneity and party unity. When control of the House passes from one party to the other, control of some number of districts must do likewise. Considering the 50th, 51st, and 52nd Congresses, for example, the shift in control of the "swing" districts might have "polarized" the parties during the 51st Congress in comparison to the one before and the one after. Yet normally, swing districts are more marginal for both parties, since by definition they can go either way. We would expect members elected from swing districts in either party to be further from the party median than members from safe districts whose constituencies reflect the party core. If, for example, the Republicans gained their narrow majority in the 51st Congress by capturing marginal, nonagricultural districts, there is little reason to expect that the members elected from those districts would toe the party line as much as their safe-seat counterparts. They might lose the next election by doing so, and in fact all of them did.[5]

If we compare the switch from a Democratic majority in the 103rd Congress to a Republican majority in the 104th Congress, we observe that the Republican gains were in open-seat and swing districts in the South and West. Districts held by moderate Democrats, or open seats previously held by moderate Democrats, were the killing ground of the Democratic majority. Yet it was precisely those seats that the Democrats targeted in their effort to recapture the House in the 1996 election. One would have expected the newly elected Republican members to have temporized their voting patterns as their Democratic predecessors had done in order to pacify their districts. Instead, the Republican class of 1994 demonstrated high party unity and if anything sought to push the party further to the right. This suggests that factors other than district homogeneity were affecting member behavior. Thus, there are grounds to suppose that party control is in and of itself an important variable; if so we can ask, how do Democrats and Republicans differ in ways that often produce higher party voting when the Republicans are in charge and lower party voting when the Democrats are in charge?[6]

Cooper and Brady run "leadership style" into "organization." The style of a Speaker is conditioned by the form of organization. Centralized regimes will give rise to different styles than noncentralized regimes. Within the context of a particular organizational form, centralized or decentralized, there can be variation in the personality and style among Speakers, but these differences are cosmetic and do not reach fundamentals. Reed and Cannon are simply two versions of the strong-Speaker style (urban Northeast and rural Midwest), whereas Rayburn and McCormack are two different versions of the weak-Speaker style (rural Southwest and urban Northeast). In any case, the style of the Speaker is conditional upon the institutional context. A Speaker can adapt to the context, but he cannot change it.

Yet in the election of 1888, Reed staked his Speakership explicitly on rules reform. The Republicans made reform a part of their campaign, and in the period leading up to the adoption of the Reed rules the party conference openly discussed the issue and planned strategies. Again, in the 61st Congress (1909–1911) the Republican insurgents, led by George Norris of Nebraska, had openly broken with Cannon. In the campaign of 1908 the Democrats sought to make Cannonism an issue in both the presidential and congressional elections. After the election, Democratic leader Champ Clark sought to forge a coalition with the insurgent Republicans to break Cannon's power. Without Norris's "profile in courage," the revolt against Cannon might not have occurred. Since the adoption of the Reed rules, on the one hand, and the revolt against Cannon, on the other hand, are the means by which Cooper and Brady operationalize their dependent variable, it seems worth noting that the major changes in the rules that created the conditions of strong party leadership and then later undermined it, both were marked by strong individual leadership.

This analysis of the contextualist thesis as developed by Cooper and Brady has been intended to nibble around its edges rather than to challenge its core. We may accept their contention that forces in the political system shape institutional context, which in turn sets the conditions of party leadership. In doing so, however, we want to avoid allowing this generally correct notion to lead us into the thicket of determinism, where Cooper and Brady may wander near when they say:

> . . . institutional context rather than personal traits primarily determines leadership style in the House. To be sure, style is affected by personal traits. Nonetheless, style is and must be responsive to and congruent with both the inducements available to leaders and member expectations regarding proper behavior. Indeed, the personal traits of leaders are themselves shaped by the character of the House as a political institution at particular points in time through the impact of socialization and selection processes that enforce prevailing norms. (1981, 423)

SPEAKER NEWT GINGRICH

I now address several aspects of Newt Gingrich's Speakership that may qualify the contextual thesis. These are: (1) the role of party leaders in winning and maintaining majority control of the chamber; (2) the impact of party leaders in shaping the expectations of members; (3) the role of party culture; (4) leadership conception; and (5) the symbolic role that party leaders play.

Winning Control

With respect to a party leader's role in winning and maintaining majorities, contextual theory assumes that larger social and political forces shape congressional majorities and influence the institutional arrangements they put in place. Of course no individual leader can by himself direct the voting patterns of voters in all 435 congressional districts. A leader can affect the underlying political dynamic, but he cannot control it. Still, it is evident that some leaders go to greater efforts to try to influence elections than do others, and among those who try, some are more effective than others. Uncle Joe Cannon canvassed extensively for Republican candidates as Speaker, and in fact may have campaigned more extensively than did Sam Rayburn a half-century later, notwithstanding the greater ease of travel available to Rayburn. In recent times, Speakers such as Tip O'Neill, Jim Wright, and Tom Foley have been active in congressional campaigns both by appearing on behalf of members and by contributing to their campaign coffers via leadership PACs. Yet none of the three Democratic Speakers was in charge of the party's congressional campaign apparatus and all took direction from the Democratic congressional campaign committee and its professional staff. No Democratic Speaker served as the principal organizer, recruiter, and fundraiser of the party's campaign.

Newt Gingrich played these roles across four election cycles from 1990 to 1998. There is no close historical comparison to Newt Gingrich's role in leading the House Republicans to their majority. He was actively involved in recruiting candidates for office, he provided training for them through GOPAC workshops, he articulated their campaign themes on audiotapes that most of them drew upon, he planned campaign strategy for the party, he raised vast sums of money for candidates, he organized the incumbent GOP members to contribute to the campaigns of nonincumbent GOP candidates, he planned the 1994 "Contract with America" strategy—in short there was no aspect of the Republican effort to elect a House majority that he was not responsible for initiating and leading. In interviews with me, Gingrich, his staff, and Republican members said that Gingrich differed from all previous Speakers because he had created his own majority. Political scientists can identify the many factors that came into play in enabling the Republicans to capture the House in 1994; but from the perspective of the House Republicans, their majority was due to Gingrich's leadership.

Contextual theory would, in the first instance, point to the general social and political conditions that enabled Gingrich to succeed in building his congressional majority. He did not shape those conditions; he simply analyzed and acted upon them. But the fact that he did act made a difference, and there are few Republicans who believe that they would have won the 1994 election had Edward Madigan defeated Newt Gingrich to become their whip in 1989. Contextual theory takes elections as independent variables, swinging districts and reshaping congressional majorities. But insofar as party leaders can influence election results they have a hand in shaping their own majorities, and that is what Newt Gingrich plainly did. Gingrich entered the Speakership with the majority of his conference directly indebted to him for their own elections and all of the GOP members indebted to him for the Republican majority. In the 104th Congress, this was a dominant contextual fact. In the 105th Congress, it helps explain why Gingrich was able to survive ethics charges to retain the Speakership.

It also suggests why Gingrich had to resign after the 1998 elections. Previous Speakers, no matter how extensively involved in individual members' campaigns, had not assumed the responsibility for managing their party's campaigns nationally. Gingrich did. He was the chief strategist for the Republicans. When they lost seats to the Democrats in 1996 and 1998, Gingrich carried the blame. And, he deserved it. For the disappointing Republican showing in 1998 could be traced directly to a number of decisions that the Speaker had made. It was he who had decided that the normal rhythms of the sixth-year election (of a president's term) would produce "natural" gains for the congressional opposition party. It was he who had decided to avoid pushing controversial legislative proposals. It was he who had decided to make an issue of the scandals surrounding the president. It was he who had decided to cave in to the administration on the massive omnibus appropriation bill. These decisions produced a result that failed to meet the expectations that Gingrich had himself set. Had his strategy been successful, he would without doubt have been able to retain his Speakership, newly empowered. When his strategy failed, he failed with it. Had he not chosen to play such a central role in the campaign process, he would not have been held accountable either way.

Shaping Expectations

Gingrich's role in bringing the Republicans to power was also related to another main plank of contextual theory. According to the theory, leadership style is shaped by member expectations. Party leaders are just as strong as members allow them to be, and no stronger. Member expectations are shaped by the reelection goal, or institutional goals such as building a career in the House or beyond it, or shaping public policy. Can congressional leaders affect member expectations? An answer built upon the evidence of Democratic Speakerships would be yes and no. Under Rayburn, Democratic members were taught "to get along, go along." New members were to be seen and not heard. In socializing Democratic (and hence Republican) members (in conformity to the prevailing power structure in both parties) by this mantra, Rayburn shaped member expectations. Yet there is little evidence that recent Democratic Speakers sought to shape the way that members thought about their roles. Speaker Wright often called party leadership a "license to persuade," acknowledging the limits on his power and his ability to alter member expectations. Rayburn's ability to socialize members to norms conducive to his leadership style and Wright's inability to alter member expectations by the strong leadership he sought to provide show the limits of leadership in the Democratic caucus. Democratic Speakers could reinforce but not change institutional norms.

Speaker Gingrich was not given a blank slate in the 104th Congress, but he plainly had more room to operate than his Democratic predecessors and a greater disposition to take advantage of the opportunity. Gingrich's understanding of his role as Speaker was in fact a direct counterpoint to the Democratic Speakers. From the outset Gingrich sought to mold the Republican Conference, to impose a new kind of regime on the House. The initial phase of socialization occurred during the recruitment and training of GOP candidates. The GOPAC workshops and the Gingrich audiotapes were designed to both win elections and socialize members. The next phase occurred between November of 1994 and

January of 1995 as the Republicans organized their new regime. The various reforms that they implemented were designed to undercut Democratic power and to alter the culture of the House as it had evolved under Democratic control. This was necessary in order to prevent Republican members from adopting Democratic attitudes, as they had under the Democratic regime. The third phase was the Contract period, from January to April 1995. Speaker Gingrich had two goals for the Contract, to pass it in the House and to build around it a new Republican regime grounded in Republican values and centered in the party leadership. He saw the processes developed during the Contract period, such as the use of task forces to design law and the use of the Rules Committee to alter it, as models for a new kind of legislative management. In order for this to succeed, it was necessary to foster a sense of teamwork within the Republican Conference. Borrowing from contemporary management and military command theories, Gingrich sought to develop a doctrine for House Republicans that would unify them under his direction. In all of this, Gingrich clearly believed that it was possible to shape member expectations. His premise was not that member expectations were a given (an independent variable); to the contrary, he believed that member expectations were bound to be shaped by someone or something, and he was determined to make sure that the members took their cues from the leadership rather than from anyone else.

Did he succeed? Obviously, the erosion of his public support and standing in the House in the 105th Congress undermined his ability to shape member expectations. Still, there is evidence to suggest that he affected member attitudes. Reports about Republican Conference meetings suggest that Gingrich was able to keep the focus on party interests as well as on member needs. A main role of an organizational leader is to influence the terms of discussion and debate. Gingrich has sought to shape dialogue within the Republican Conference around the lodestar of party purpose. Political parties are, he believed, cultures, and culture can be shaped by leaders.

Gingrich's experiment in offering transformational leadership to the Republican conference made progress only so long as he had the political clout to command attention, mostly during 1995. At the end of that year the Congress became embroiled in the government shutdown, and Speaker Gingrich never recovered his commanding political position. During 1996 he was slowly bled by the ethics investigation, and he limped into the 105th Congress hobbled by a censure and fine, a narrow reelection as Speaker, and a diminished majority. Caught between his own political instincts, which told him that he needed to moderate his image and move the party towards the center, and the attitudes of the hard-shell conservatives in the GOP conference (whom he had recruited and socialized), he seemed to wander without a sense of direction. This lack of strategic direction undermined any attempt to raise the level of discourse in the Conference, and instead the Republicans were riven by ideological, regional, and personal factions. As the Conference disintegrated, its cultural foundations hove more clearly into view.

Party Culture

Jo Freeman argued in 1986 that political scientists ought to pay more attention to party culture, since the cultures of the two major parties differ in ways that make a difference (Freeman 1986). She was right. In the case of Newt Gingrich and the House Republicans, we may ask whether aspects of institutional context as well as leadership style are affected by the party's culture. Empirical measures of party culture are hard to come by, but one need go no further than the national party conventions to be made aware of the cultural differences between Democrats and Republicans. In the House, the Republicans have always been less diverse than the Democrats by any measure, and Republican homogeneity is related to the character of the districts they represent and the social class they draw upon. Republicans are the party of the business class and they reflect its culture and values. They tend to be more accepting of hierarchy, more ideological, less tied to politics as a vocation, and they take a different attitude toward organizations than do Democrats. Whereas Democratic members see organizations serving the needs of entrepreneurial members (Loomis 1988), Republicans see organizations serving group goals. The Democrats set up an elaborate (and arcane) administrative and legislative apparatus because efficiency and effectiveness were at the bottom of their list of priorities; Republicans sought to establish different organizational arrangements because their party culture values organizational efficiency (even when they fail to achieve it).

Richard Fenno (1997) has recently written that Republicans had to learn how to govern because they brought little prior legislative experience to their majority It is apparent that many House Republicans elected in 1994 seem not to have the basic grasp of constitutional structure that compromise presupposes. They carried nonpolitical instincts into a political arena. In searching for the source of this aspect of GOP behavior, one is eventually led to the party's grass roots, which is the seedbed of its culture. At a local meeting of Democrats one is likely to encounter people who value government, including many seasoned politicos who have long experienced government as a source of programs and benefits that they wish to sustain. At a local meeting of Republicans one may expect to find members of the business community or the professional class whose experience with government is as a source of regulation and control, and who are skeptical of it. The former know how to govern, the latter, according to Fenno, need to learn.

But what does it mean to govern? This question is itself culturally conditioned. Fenno takes governing to mean accepting the responsibility of enacting legislation via the range of behavior that political science associates with legislative institutions—bargaining, compromise, logrolling, pork-barreling, coalition-building, and so forth. Many in the Republican class of 1994 had little experience in these tasks, little appetite for them, and some degree of ideological disdain for them. Hence, they needed to learn how to govern. A House Republican might respond by saying that "learning to govern" means "learning to behave like Democrats," which they had vowed not to do. Early in his Speakership some Republicans held that as soon as they heard people say that Gingrich was "growing" in office (precisely in Fenno's sense of learning to govern), they would know that he had gone native. There are two distinct questions: (1) what does governing entail?; and (2) how do Republicans come to think this way? It is on the latter question that I now focus. Republicans think this way because of deep-rooted cultural differences between them and the Democrats. There are no universals here: some Republicans are pragmatic politicians and some Democrats are ideologically driven; but each party's culture is a reflection of its social foundations, and fosters a preponderant tendency.

Political novices are more likely to be naive about power than are experienced politicians. The current crop of Republicans is more naive than most because fewer of them are politically experienced. When experiencing frustration at their inability to impose their agenda on the government, some Republicans blamed Speaker Gingrich. But in fact Gingrich understood that the Republican's main problem was that they did not have enough power to impose their will on the constitutional system of separated powers. The consistent tendency of Republicans to charge into blazing guns, as they did in the case of the government shutdown in the 104th Congress and in the case of the disaster relief provided in an emergency spending bill in the 105th Congress, is grounded in the culture of the party.

A strong party culture offers both opportunities and constraints to party leaders. Gingrich believed that he could shape the culture of the GOP Conference by taking advantage of the natural cultural tendencies of the Republican Party. Republicans are more homogeneous than Democrats and more inclined to party unity.[7] The trick was to impose a regime grounded in these values before other forces interceded. According to the "electoral connection" thesis advanced by David Mayhew (1974), members of Congress will ultimately be driven by reelection goals. Fenno (1973) specifies career development and policy impact as other goals that members will naturally seek. Obviously, all of these goals are relevant for any elected legislator. Understanding this, Speaker Gingrich wanted to reinforce naturally occurring cultural tendencies within the

GOP Conference in order to inoculate the Conference against the centrifugal force that these other incentives provided. The Republican leadership stressed the team concept, put in place a coordinated staffing system, and stressed the development of a party "doctrine" that would, as in military-command doctrine, bind the conference together. During the Contract period, indeed during most of 1995, the emphasis within the Republican Conference was on teamwork, participation, and the inculcation of shared institutional values.

This effort to impose a Republican institutional culture eventually ran up against internal divisions within the Conference in a manner that context theory predicts. Conflict between the party's left and right wings, a new assertiveness by some committee chairmen, and general frustration in dealing with the White House led to intraparty conflict. In seeking to resolve conflict, Gingrich engaged in a variety of therapeutic activities that included extended rounds of meetings and role-reversal games within the Republican conference. These strategies are characteristic of the modern Speakership (Peters 1997). They were not always successful, yet in considering Speaker Gingrich's most troubled moments—the shutdowns, the crisis of his reelection, the disaster-relief fiasco, and the coup—we see that in each case the party held together when under tremendous strain.[8] Given the narrowness of the Republican majority, the cohesiveness of the party was crucial in enabling it to maintain control of the legislative agenda.

In the 105th Congress Gingrich was undeniably weakened by the ethics charges and the circumstances of his reelection, and operated with an even narrower majority. The coup attempt against him in July of 1997 was a reflection of disaffection on the Republican right. Later, some moderate Republicans signed a discharge petition for a campaign-finance reform bill, challenging the most basic of majority-party prerogatives, control of the floor. While Gingrich was in a less commanding position, he did not abandon his commitment to a leadership that would reflect a Republican culture of the House. He was committed to the concept of teamwork, open dialogue, and tolerance within the Republican Conference. Instead of trying to impose a cultural regime from the top, as had seemed possible in the 104th Congress, Gingrich now sought to build a cultural regime from the bottom. This was a longer road to travel, along which he encountered many obstacles. Gingrich wanted to bond the Conference through persuasion rather than force, and he was reluctant to punish recalcitrant members on the left or the right. This led some party stalwarts to complain that he was too accommodating. In their description, Gingrich was made to appear more similar to Tom Foley than Joe Cannon. Yet Gingrich was different from Foley and the other Democratic Speakers, because he never abandoned the goal of imposing a Republican culture on the House. Context theory holds that party leaders adapt to context; Gingrich sought to shape it.

Speaker Gingrich's resignation from the House in the wake of the 1998 elections revealed consistent tendency of Republican party culture. The fact that Republicans are generally more homogenous than Democrats and demonstrate higher party unity, has never prevented them from squabbling. To the contrary, the Republicans' general ideological cohesion has permitted them greater latitude to fight with each other for different reasons. They have a long and consistent record of leadership struggles. Incumbent leaders are often challenged and unseated. Conservative ideologues have divided the Conference over tactical issues as well as over legislative priorities. When the party does not fare well in elections, upheaval follows. The challenge to Speaker Gingrich by Congressman Livingston and the contested elections for majority leader and Conference chair are norma for Republicans. When the Democrats lost their majority in 1994, not a single incumbent leader was challenged. When the Republicans retained their majority in 1998, all hell broke loose. Speaker Gingrich's resignation was no doubt grounded in a realistic perception of his prospects of defeating Livingston, but it was also consistent with his conception of the Party and his leadership role in it. Gingrich believed that the Speaker should stand for the corporate interest of the Party, and should be willing to step down when the Party's interest demanded it. Thus, his last act of leadership was his decision to relinquish it, reflecting his conception of it.

Leadership

A staple of context theory is that member expectations shape leadership response. When member's expectations are in accord, they will expect leaders to lead, that is, to assert central control. When member expectations are divided, leaders are constrained, and must cope with conflict. Under the Democratic regime, leaders sought to broker compromise: during the feudal era, Rayburn did so by working with the committee barons; in the postreform period (which I have labeled the Speakership's "democratic era"), O'Neill, Wright, and Foley did so by fostering member participation and by agenda control. It is clear that the conception of leadership to which this theory gives rise was accepted by recent Democratic Speakers. Did Speaker Gingrich offer a new conception of party leadership?

Undeniably, in 1995 Gingrich offered a new form of leadership for the House. He assumed more influence over the leadership structure, the committee system, and individual members, than did any modern Speaker. He revamped the administration of the House. He became a visible national leader for the party, giving an unprecedented national television address at the end of the Contract period. He put in place a more extensive and well-coordinated communications strategy than any Speaker before him. He continued to spend much of his time away from the House, promoting the party agenda and rais-ing money for campaigns. Through the use of legislative task forces, the Rules Committee, and leadership staff, he exercised more direct control over the sub-stance of legislation than any Speaker since Cannon. Contextual theory sug-gests that Gingrich assumed this remarkable role because it comported with member expectations; however, the Speaker and his leadership group saw it dif-ferently. Gingrich assumed this role in order to shape member expectations around it.

After the government shutdowns and the accumulating weight of ethics charges dragged down his approval ratings, Speaker Gingrich stepped back from the role that he played in 1995. Cracks appeared in the unity of the GOP Conference, committees and their chairs resumed more normal operations, and at times the Republican Conference seemed to drift while Gingrich licked his wounds. That Gingrich's power eroded in 1996 and 1997 is as undeniable as the power he held in 1995. Again, contextual theory predicts this result. The role that Gingrich had tried to assume was inconsistent with member preferences under normal legislative circumstances, and he had to back away. Yet this inter-pretation overlooks an important fact. Republicans, including those who plot-ted the coup against him, never complained that Gingrich was too strong; to the contrary, they complained that he was too weak. It was his failure to stand firmly for a conservative agenda (in the eyes of the right wing of the Conference) or his unwillingness to discipline maverick members on the left and right (in the eyes of party regulars) that brought about the most criticism. Pilloried in the press and by Democrats when he was outspoken, Gingrich earned criticism among some Republicans when he failed to speak out.[9]

Gingrich was caught in a thicket, and his path through it took many turns. He started out in the 104th Congress with tight leadership control over the agenda through SAG. At the outset of the 105th Congress he disbanded SAG in favor of a larger and more inclusive leadership group, and re-empowered the committees and their chairs. Then, a few months into the first session, he decided to revive SAG and recentralize decision-making. Then came the coup attempt. Gingrich revised SAG's membership, moving away from inclusion and essentially circled the wagons by surrounding himself with loyalists. As he moved back and forth between centralization and delegation, inclusiveness and exclusiveness, his own role kept changing. During 1995 he was often directly involved in legislative negotiations, within the GOP conference, with external interest groups, and with the White House. In 1996, in the wake of the budget debacle, he withdrew from sight and devoted his attention to fundraising and strategy for the 1996 election. In 1997, he decided to spend more time in the House, and he led the House to a budget deal with the administration. After the coup attempt he devoted considerable attention to reinforcing his position within the Conference, and by the fall of 1997 he began to reemerge as a spokesman for the party. In 1998 he reprised his role as chief election strategist and fundraiser.

Was this a Speaker chasing member expectations, or trying to figure out how to shape them? Was this a politician scurrying to survive by nurturing a minimum winning coalition within his party Conference, or is it an organizational leader seeking to recast his leadership role in light of changing circumstances? Gingrich understood the limitations placed on this leadership by the fact that his members were autonomous. He grasped that events had provided him with a very unusual opportunity to shape his party's culture and hence socialize members and shape their expectations. He had seen how very constrained the Democratic Speakers were, and was determined that under the Republican regime the party leadership would not be hamstrung by the committee system or intraparty factionalism. As his position eroded, he sought to adapt to the circumstances, at first as a matter of strategy, later as a matter of survival. Thus far, he reacted. At no point along the way, however, did he waver from a belief that the House Republican regime should be fundamentally different than its Democratic predecessors and an intention to build his Speakership on a different principle. He would see his adjustments as tactical rather than strategic. Even in his darkest hour, Speaker Gingrich articulated a different principle of party governance than any Democratic Speaker had been able or willing to embrace.[10]

That principle was essentially parliamentary. Gingrich saw politics as a struggle between opposing forces, armies in military parlance, teams in sports vernacular. He believed that the Democrats had maintained power over sixty years by obfuscating differences between themselves and Republicans. The Democrats wanted to disaggregate politics, to make all politics local, to denationalize elections, and to bury public policy in committee rooms that they could control. The Republicans had locked themselves into the minority by acquiescing. Gingrich believed that if the Republican Party could assert itself in opposition to the Democrats; if elections could be nationalized and fought on principles; and if his party was better manned, equipped, and organized than the opposition, then it could win. Having won, he then sought to use control of the House to reshape it along lines conducive to Republican interests and values. There was no role in this scheme for Democrats. Therefore, all of Gingrich's strategies focused on building consensus within the Republican ranks rather than by forging coalitions with the Democrats. This made his leadership task very difficult, because it made Republican moderates vulnerable and Republican radicals frustrated. To bring the GOP Conference together, Gingrich appealed specifically to the principle of party governance. Being Republican was the linchpin of his appeal to Republicans. And it resonated among them.

In articulating the principle of party governance, however, Gingrich established himself as the most visible Republican. As such, he came to assume a symbolic role that can be identified with no other Speaker since Joe Cannon.

The Speaker as Symbol

Speaker Gingrich cast himself in a more publicly visible role than had any of his Democratic predecessors. By taking center stage, he made himself a symbol of the Republican program and a natural object of Democratic attack. This some Democrats were happy to do in retribution for Gingrich's role in deposing Speaker Wright. But revenge aside, it made political sense for the Democrats to attack the symbol of the Republican revolution. Republicans had attacked Speakers O'Neill, Wright, and Foley, but they did not get much purchase out of the effort. Even the resignation of Speaker Wright in 1989 did not translate into voter disaffection with the Democrats, who had a larger majority in 1993 than they did in 1989. But the Republican attacks on the Democratic Speakers were blunted by the nature of the Democratic regime; no one believed that a Democratic Speaker had much power or that life would be different if one Democratic Speaker was replaced with another. The Republicans had to convince voters that a Republican Speaker would be different than a Democratic Speaker, that a Republican majority would offer cleaner, more efficient, and more effective government. Gingrich symbolized his party's program as had no Speaker since Cannon, and now he was under the glow of the television lights.

Institutional context theory makes no reference to the Speaker's symbolic role except perhaps to suggest that in a centralized party system it is more likely that a Speaker will become a political symbol than in a decentralized party system; thus, Joe Cannon was a symbol and Sam Rayburn was not. Certainly, Cannon became a symbol and an object of attack in the elections of 1908 and 1910. The role of a Speaker as a symbolic leader is more complex than this, however. In Cannon's case he became a symbol not perhaps primarily because of the manner in which he ran the House, but rather because he stood in the path of progressive policies promoted by a very popular president of his own party. One searches Sam Rayburn's career in vain for any example of him running his own reputation up against that of an incumbent president; to the contrary, Rayburn always held that it was a duty of the Speaker to support the president, be he Franklin Roosevelt, Harry Truman, Dwight Eisenhower, or John Kennedy. Rayburn would never have attacked the Rules Committee Chairman, "Judge" Howard W. Smith (D-Va.) if Kennedy had not pushed him to it. A better parallel is to the role that Speaker O'Neill played in the first Reagan administration. Between 1981 and 1986, O'Neill was the leading national Democrat, and he staked out real and symbolic opposition to the Reagan program. This invited and received Republican attacks, which were unavailing.

Speaker Gingrich made himself a symbol of the Republican revolution and bore the brunt of the Democratic attacks. He was also the chief strategist for the Republican congressional campaigns, and a natural political target. He was also the chief fundraiser for the GOP, providing further grounds for partisan attack. This dimension of his leadership was external to the House of Representatives. If Gingrich leaves an enduring legacy for the House, it will be revealed if future Speakers play a more substantial external role than did any previous Speaker. In 1961, Richard Bolling tried to become the Democratic majority leader by appealing for external support; he played the outside game and lost to Carl Albert, a quintessential insider (Polsby 1976 [1963]). Newt Gingrich established the Speaker's external role. Future Speakers may not chose to adapt to this role in the same way that Gingrich carved it. In fact, his demise may suggest to future Speakers that it is unwise for a Speaker to stake his prospects on his party's electoral outcomes. Still, Gingrich has established that in a competitive two-party environment, no Speaker can be indifferent to his party's electoral prospects. The best evidence of this is the role that Minority Leader Richard Gephardt of Missouri has played over the last two election cycles in managing his party's national campaign. The difference between Gingrich and Gephardt is that Gingrich sought to be the national spokesman for the party as well as the national strategist. Gephardt was heavily involved in shaping his party's strategy, in recruiting candidates, and in raising money; but he eschewed the role of national party leader. Speaker Hastert says that he will be a "manager" of the House and not a national party leader; but he will not escape his obligation to manage his party's electoral strategy as well.

Conclusion

What, in the end, do we mean by "institutional context" and "leadership style"? As to context, it would appear that in its broadest signification, context refers to the entire environment of leadership conduct: constitutional structure, political system, social milieu, institutional rules and norms, and partisan alignment. Cooper and Brady operationalize institutional context primarily according to partisan alignment, and then suggest that this variable is in turn related to the others. If we accept the trend toward greater party unity in the 1980s and 1990s in the House as marking an equivalent tendency to the data that they report for the 1880–1910 period, we should infer that the greater distance between the two parties should produce a tendency toward stronger party leadership. Yet in fact the political system and the rules and norms of the House are very different now than they were a century ago. Then, the two parties were undergirded by strong party loyalty. According to Brinkley (1997, 537):

The most striking feature of the late-nineteenth century party system was its remarkable stability. From the end of Reconstruction until the late 1890s, the electorate was divided almost precisely evenly between the Republicans and the Democrats. Loyalties fluctuated almost not at all. . . . As striking as the balance between the parties was the intensity of public loyalty to them. In most of the country, Americans viewed their party affiliations with a passion and enthusiasm that is difficult for later generations to understand. Voter turnout in presidential elections between 1860 and 1900 averaged over 78 percent of all eligible voters. . . . Even in nonpresidential years, from 60 to 80 percent of the voters turned out to cast ballots for congressional candidates. . . . The remarkable turnout represented a genuinely mass-based politics.

How to explain this phenomenon? Brinkley attributes it to cultural rather than policy positions or economic factors: "[P]arty identification, then, was usually more a reflection of cultural inclinations than a calculation of economic interests" (p. 537). But if so, then can we say that the institutional context that drove the centralized leadership regimes of the late-nineteenth century is in any way related to the institutional context that shapes the House in the late-twentieth century? And if not, then upon what ground does the institutional context of the House now rest?

One might contend that since the parties, once strong, centralized, and culturally grounded, are now weak, decentralized, and ideologically ingrained, the basis of party legislative regimes must be very different than a century ago. Then, the parties could control their own nominations and hence their own destinies. Now they cannot.

Today's partisanship comes at a time when the two parties' leaders do not have the power they once had. And, ironically, says David Mayhew, increased party unity might come because of the decline of the party system, not in spite of it. "With an open primary system," Mayhew says, "the power of party bosses to put forward moderate candidates is greatly diminished, since it is often hard-line conservatives and liberals who vote in primaries" (quoted in Carney [1996, 201]).

To contend that the high levels of party voting as measured by the party-unity scores relied upon by recent congressional scholarship are comparable to the 90/90 standard employed by Cooper and Brady is to miss the underlying foundations of party support.[11] We now have institutionally weaker parties with more ideologically homogenous members. How does this context affect leadership style?

This depends upon what we mean by leadership "style." Cooper and Brady translate it into centralized and decentralized leadership regimes under the rules of the House and the party caucuses. Yet it is clear that Cannon and Reed were stronger Speakers than Henderson, and their styles were not in all respects alike. If we reduce the concept of leadership style to something on the order of "strategies and tactics available to leaders under the rules," then we would still face the task of differentiating strong and weak regimes. For example, Cannon lost formal control over the Rules Committee in the 61st Congress, and so Cooper and Brady code it centralized/decentralized. Yet Cannon retained operational control over the committee for the balance of that Congress. Similarly, when the leadership finally wrested control over Rules in the early 1970s under the Democrats (by giving the Steering and Policy Committee of the House Democratic Caucus control over its membership), they were situated similarly to Cannon after the revolt. Should O'Neill, Wright, and Foley then be called strong Speakers under centralized regimes? In comparison to Rayburn, the answer is yes; in comparison to Cannon, the answer is no. Mayhew is quoted above to the effect that party leaders are weak, just at the peak of Gingrich's power. Gingrich had no more formal power than Clark or Longworth under the rules of the House or GOP Conference; he still had to operate through party and House committees. Yet he was able to dictate to those committees, at least for a time.

One might argue that Gingrich was the weakest Speaker since Cannon. His control over committee appointments was mediated by a party committee that he could influence but to which he could not dictate, and the Republicans imposed upon the office a four-term limit as Speaker, unprecedented in the history of the House. If one were coding the Speakerships of the late-nineteenth century under term limits, would they then be coded weak or strong? In fact, the features of Gingrich's Speakership that call upon us to label him very strong in the 104th Congress, less strong in the 105th Congress, but still stronger than Foley altogether, have less to do with his power under the rules than with the use that he made of the power at his disposal. It was not simply member expectations that enabled him to govern; it was that combined with or shaped by the culture of the Republican Conference and his own attitude and approach to leadership. It was also, of course, affected by externalities, primarily the public's reaction to him and to the Republican program. No one can doubt that his low standing in the polls eroded the foundations of his power and undercut his support in the Republican Conference. In this sense, no one can doubt that context matters.

The coup attempt can be taken to suggest that Gingrich, as all other Speakers, is very much at the whim of members. I draw the opposite inference from the fact that he survived it. It is not likely, in my view, that any Democratic Speaker could have sustained the protracted barrage of attacks, the low public-approval ratings, the media attacks, the ethics charges, and the coup attempt, and survived as Speaker; certainly, Jim Wright did not. That Gingrich did survive tells us something about him, his Republican colleagues, and the Republican Party itself. So does his resignation. Context theory suggests that Gingrich's leadership style was at odds with the institutional context in which he led, and declares his downfall inevitable because he failed to satisfy member expectations. There is no doubt that member disaffection was the proximate cause of his resignation. But that this explanation is not adequate is revealed in two ways: First, if the Republicans had done well in the 1998 elections, Gingrich would have emerged stronger and not weaker; second, Democratic leaders have paid no such price when their party has lost seats in the House. Therefore, operating within essentially the same institutional context, Republicans have differed from Democrats, and their leader, Newt Gingrich, differed from his Democratic counterparts. Speaker Hastert will offer a different rendition of the Speakership under Republican control. He will not seek to be a premier. But neither will he seek to be a Democrat.

Our analysis suggests some qualifications of any contextual view of the Speakership. In part, these qualifications speak to the definition of context, which needs to be broadened to include cultural variables that Cooper and Brady and their progeny generally have not addressed. In part, they go to influence of leaders in shaping context, a generally unresearched subject in congressional studies. As it ends, political science may conclude of Newt Gingrich's Speakership that it conformed in many ways to familiar patterns of House leadership; but its most interesting lessons will lie in those areas where it did not.

NOTES

This chapter was originally presented at a conference on "The Impact of the New Majority: Republican Control of Congress," sponsored by Florida International University at Miami. The author thanks Nicol Rae and Colton Campbell, the conference organizers and editors of this book, for their comments. The author would like to thank Gary Copeland and Keith Gaddie for their comments, and Hans Seidenstucker for his research assistance.

1. The historical events described in this chapter are more fully described in Peters 1997 [1990].

2. This is not to forget Speaker David Henderson, who presided over strong Republican leaderships in the 56th and 57th Congresses, without, it must be said, earning a statue on the Mall.

3. Gillette, the oldest Republican member, was elected Speaker by the Longworth faction, who opposed James R. Mann. Mann, a Cannon protégé, had served as Republican leader during Clark's Speakership. Mann retained his influence, however, by winning creation of a new Committee on Committees on which he had disproportionate influence. See Peters 1997, 98–103.

4. Henderson was not an assertive Speaker, but he had more power under the rules than Crisp because Crisp would not count a quorum until Reed forced him into it. The most controversial contention might be that Martin was more powerful than Rayburn. The pattern of Republican policy making under Martin is remarkably similar to that

under Gingrich and also to that of the 97th Congress (1981–1983) when the Republican/conservative-Democrat coalition controlled policy. Policy was made either by the White House or by a party policy committee, and the committees were expected to produce party bills. The Republicans sought across-the-board tax cuts and reductions in expenditures. When, in 1953, Ways and Means Committee Chairman Dan Reed refused to report President Eisenhower's tax bill, Speaker Martin called a meeting of Ways and Means Republicans and insisted that the bill be reported. Rayburn would never have done that. See Peters 1997, 129.

5. The propensity of some Republicans to cast votes contrary to the perceived preferences and/or interests of their constituencies is widely recognized among members of the Republican conference, and may help explain their long period in the minority. It clearly creates a problem for the party leadership that Democratic regimes rarely encounter. The Democrats have been a diverse party and get locked up when members vote their constituencies. The Republicans have been a more ideological and homogeneous party, and run into trouble when members vote their beliefs rather than their districts. The McKinley Tariff may be a case in point. In the 51st Congress, in which it was enacted, there was a Republican majority of 173; in the 52nd Congress, they held a minority of 88 seats.

6. One might argue that the Democratic party has more diverse constituencies, whereas the Republican party has more homogeneous constituencies. Thus, when the Democrats are in power there will be lower party voting and while the Republicans are in power there will be higher party voting. This hypothesis would appear to demand some intervening assumptions. For example, it might be argued that a diverse party, when in the majority, will structure rules, procedures, and votes to accommodate its factions, leading to lower cohesion; a homogeneous party, when in the majority, will structure rules, procedures, and votes to reflect its more unified majority, leading to higher cohesion. Thus, with Democrats in charge, policy will reflect the split in the party's caucus, while when Republicans are in charge, policy will reflect their greater unanimity. What, then, would happen if both parties were more homogeneous? We would expect to see higher cohesion no matter who is in control. This is, I believe, David Rohde's (1991) thesis. However, neither the difference in the homogeneity of districts between the 103rd and 104th Congresses nor the marginal increase in party unity scores seems adequate to explain the stronger GOP regime in the 104th and 105th Congresses. The main differences between the 103rd Congress, on the one hand, and the 104th and 105th Congresses, on the other hand, were, first, that in the latter the Republicans were in charge, and they do business differently than do the Democrats, and second, that the GOP produced Gingrich and the Democrats produced Foley, and Gingrich was a stronger leader than Foley was.

7. Some might argue that the Republicans value member autonomy more than Democrats value it. This is certainly the view of those Republicans who switched from the Democratic Party in recent years. But member autonomy is not inconsistent with a culture that values party unity. I can be an autonomous member and still feel a sense of obligation to my party. Indeed, my sense of obligation may be all the stronger if I do not feel coerced and if I feel that I have had a fair hearing for my views among members who

will listen to them seriously. In fact, if I am an autonomous member it may be more effective to influence my behavior by socialization to a strong party culture than to offer me contingent rewards.

8. In her analysis of Republican and Democratic moderate factions in chapter 8, Robin Kolodny observes substantial differences in the attitudes, strategies, and tactics of moderates. Republican moderates tend to be more team-oriented and more supportive of the party than do Democratic moderates. Democratic moderates are typically the strongest critics of the Democratic leadership, while Republican moderates were among Gingrich's strongest supporters. An explanation of these differences would have to look beyond constituency preference to the culture of the two parties.

9. In the midst of the government shutdown crisis in 1995 and 1996, many Republicans told the Speaker to "shut up" (Maraniss and Weisskopf 1996). Gingrich's penchant for bombast often got him into trouble. It was not long, however, before Republicans were demanding more assertive leadership from him. It appears that House Republicans wanted Speaker Gingrich to speak out, but wanted him to look good doing it. Yet when in 1997 Gingrich sought to cast a softer image (Gingrich 1998), he was criticized by some on the Republican hard right for going soft on the Democrats. This illustrates what I mean when I say that the Speaker has been in a thicket, albeit one considerably of his own making.

10. When I interviewed Speaker Gingrich in July of 1996 he was reeling in the polls. He stressed the limitations on his power, the difficulty in corralling autonomous members, and the many circumstances beyond his control. He thus confirmed contextual assumptions. He also, however, emphasized the differences between Republicans and Democrats, the importance of shaping party culture, and his commitment to be the leader of a Republican team that would think like a team. He thus challenged the contextual perspective.

11. If one applies the Cooper/Brady 90–90 rule to the 103rd, 104th, and 105th (first session) Congresses, one finds party voting at 17.42, 21.24, and 18.17 percent, respectively. By this measure, none of these Congresses would predict centralized party leadership as was predicted for the 1890–1910 period. Of course, the formal powers held by Speaker Gingrich in the 104th Congress would not perhaps have qualified for centralized leadership on the Reed–Cannon model either. All of which would seem to reinforce doubt about the ability of the dependent and independent variables that Cooper and Brady employed to explain nuances in leadership behavior.

PART TWO

Change and Continuity in Congressional Committees

CHAPTER FOUR

Building the Republican Regime: Leaders and Committees

ROGER H. DAVIDSON

INTRODUCTION

Congressional government may or may not be committee government, as Woodrow Wilson contended. But much of Congress's deliberation takes place in its committee and subcommittee rooms, especially on the House side of Capitol Hill. These work groups are critical to deliberation; they are gatherers of information, sifters of alternatives, drafters and refiners of legislation.

Of the two chambers, the House especially has come to follow specialized arrangements for formal, detailed policy-making. Through a complex division of labor in its committee system, House members cultivate expertise in policy issues that normally exceeds that of their counterparts in the Senate. For individual House members who want to have an impact upon policy-making, this decision to specialize is virtually imperative. For the chamber, this habit of specialization has proved to be a source of influence in negotiations with the Senate and the White House.

The quality of committee and subcommittee leaders is therefore an essential ingredient in the House's deliberations, not to mention its leverage with competing decision makers. The seniority principle virtually assures that chairs (and ranking minority-party members) will be seasoned lawmakers who are familiar with the legislation within their purview. Equally important is that chairs remain responsive to their committee colleagues and to the chamber at large. The latter goal is facilitated by rules, developed in the "reform era" of the 1960s and 1970s, that encourage consultation on such matters as subcommittee assignments and chairs, scheduling meetings, and to a limited extent the policy agenda itself. This goal remains problematic, inasmuch as senior members may not accurately reflect their party's overall views, much less those of the larger chamber. Following the Republican victories in the 1994 elections, therefore, Speaker Newt Gingrich moved to assure that committee chairs and Appropriations subcommittee chairs would not obstruct action on the "Contract with America" and other core party-programmatic objectives. To achieve this goal, in four instances the most senior committee members were bypassed in the selection of committee chairs.

The Committee Systems

Congressional committees comprise two complex systems. The House in the 105th Congress (1997–1999) boasted no less than 112 formal work groups— 20 full committees and 92 subcommittees. The Senate had 20 committees and 68 subcommittees, for a total of 88 work groups. There were four joint House–Senate panels. In addition, each chamber in 1998 had occasion to create a new special committee.[1] The average senator serves on nearly ten panels: 3.5 full committees and 6.3 subcommittees. Representatives claim nearly five assignments—1.8 committees and 3.1 subcommittees. For the chambers this means that on any given topic, not one but many work groups may have a piece of the action. On an individual level, multiple assignments mean inevitable scheduling conflicts and the practice of "committee hopping" when two or more panels are meeting at the same hour.

Informal caucuses or voting-bloc groups outside the committee system allow members to involve themselves further in policies that interest them or affect their constituents. At least 176 informal groups and congressional member organizations operated during the 105th Congress (1997–1999) (*Congressional Yellow Book 1997,* VI 1–4). A survey the previous year (Richardson 1996) identified 134 informal groups to which House members belonged, 56 of which were registered with the House Oversight Committee as congressional member organizations (CMOs).[2] Many of these reflect members' common interests in regional, industry, or other constituency matters—for example, the Automotive Caucus, the Great Lakes Task Force, or the Older Americans Caucus. Others serve specific issue or ideological goals—for example, the Porkbusters Coalition, the Pro-Life Caucus, or the Progressive Caucus. Others are factional meeting grounds for like-minded partisans—for example, the Coalition ("Blue Dog," or conservative, Democrats), the Conservative Democratic Forum (the "Boll Weevils"), the Tuesday Lunch Bunch (moderate Republicans), the Conservative Action Team (CAT) (conservative Republicans), and various Democratic or Republican "class clubs" (for instance, the Republican Sophomore Class).

Informal task forces come and go with great frequency, as political parties seek to involve interested members and group representatives in shaping legislative provisions and designing legislative strategy. The Republican leaders of the 104th Congress (1995–1997), distrustful of the traditional standing committees and their outside clienteles, often formed task forces to spearhead specific bills. A preliminary inventory of task forces in the 105th Congress (1997–1999) counted fifty-four of these more or less informal groups (Oleszek 1997). Thirty-three of these were formed by House Republicans. "Too many!" exclaimed Majority Leader Richard Armey when I asked him how many such groups had been formed.

"CRUMBLING COMMITTEES"

By the 1990s, it became apparent that congressional committees were ailing—beset by mounting workloads, duplication and jurisdictional battles, and conflicts between program and funding panels. Their effective control over important portions of the legislative workload was threatened, especially when controversial or broad-gauged legislation was at stake. "Today, committees are often irrelevant or, worse yet, obstacles," wrote journalist Richard E. Cohen, who termed the phenomenon "crumbling committees" (Cohen 1990). Because of its heavier reliance upon committees, the House is more at risk than the Senate as a result of this trend.

Increasingly, committees have been obliged to cooperate in processing legislation; sometimes they have been bypassed altogether. As one of its 1970s reforms, the House for the first time formalized procedures for referring proposed measures to more than a single committee. The Senate has always been able to achieve this informally or by motion, though the latter course is rarely invoked. In the 94th Congress (1975–1977), just after the House adopted its multiple referral procedures, only 8.6 percent of major bills and resolutions were referred to two or more committees. By 1995, four out every ten major measures were referred to multiple panels (Sinclair 1997, 84). In that latter year, almost half of all major measures were subject to postcommittee adjustment in the House; in 11 percent of the cases, the committee of jurisdiction was bypassed altogether (Sinclair 1997, 86).

Complaints are frequently heard these days. The 1993 Joint Committee on the Organization of Congress—the most recent large-scale effort at internal reform—uncovered widespread member dissatisfaction, and its own deliberations ended in stalemate. More than nine out of ten House respondents asserted in the Joint Committee's survey that "major procedural or organizational improvements [are] needed in the way Congress conducts its legislative business" (U.S. Congress, Joint Committee on the Organization of Congress 1993, 246). (Eight out of ten senators agreed with the same proposition.) The Republican takeover in 1995 altered the work of the House in many ways, but resulted in relatively few major alterations in workplace structures or procedures. In any event, complaints about workplace hardships—especially involving scheduling and deliberation—have been at least as prevalent under the new regime.

With a multiplicity of committee and subcommittee assignments, lawmakers are hard pressed to control their daily schedules. Committee quorums are sometimes difficult to achieve or maintain, and members' attentions are often focused elsewhere. All too often working sessions are composed of the chairman, perhaps one or two colleagues, and staff aides. Recent House rules tightening committee quorum requirements may have made scheduling problems even worse.

Political scientists sometimes contend that Congress runs in harmony with members' goals and desires, but the members know otherwise. In a 1987 survey of 114 House and Senate members (Center for Responsive Politics 1988), "inefficiency" was the thing that most surprised them about Congress (45 percent gave this response). Members report that their duties permit little time for personal or family matters. Nearly half of the respondents in the 1987 survey agreed that they had "no personal time after work"; a third said they had "no time for family."

Prerevolutionary Skirmishes

In the years before the Republican takeover, criticism of the congressional committee system mounted among members and outside critics. Committee jurisdictions and procedures loomed large in the reform politics of the 1980s and 1990s (Solomon and Wolfensberger 1994). By the 103rd Congress (1993–1995), questions of committee organization were addressed by several House study groups, including partisan study panels and the bipartisan, bicameral Joint Committee on the Organization of Congress.

Member and staff surveys conducted in 1993 revealed widespread support for committee reform. "Committee structure and membership assignments" ranked very high on the reorganization agendas of the 161 responding to the Joint Committee's survey. More than half the respondents claimed they would support "comprehensive" committee realignment; only 14 percent preferred few changes or none at all (U.S. Congress, Joint Committee on the Organization of Congress 1993, vol. 2, 261). During the Joint Committee's 1993 hearings, thirty-four representatives, eight senators, and a number of outside witnesses endorsed the goal of rationalizing committee jurisdictions. A large number of witnesses favored cutting the numbers and sizes of committees and/or subcommittees.

Representatives seem more dissatisfied with their lot than their Senate colleagues. No doubt that is one reason why so many of them consider running for open or vulnerable Senate seats (Maisel, Falkenstein, and Quigley 1997). Even though House members insist upon the coequal status of the two chambers, no less than thirty-four senators who served during the 105th Congress were ex-representatives. In the 1993 survey of members (U.S. Congress, Joint Committee on the Organization of Congress 1993, vol. 2, 246–51), representatives were more convinced than senators of the need for major procedural and organizational improvements (91 percent versus 78 percent). They were also more eager to support specific changes—in ethics processes, floor procedures, and scheduling—and wanted more assistance from staffing and support agencies and from information technology. They also worried more about overall public understanding of Congress.

Despite this favorable atmosphere, the Joint Committee had little or no formal impact on the conduct of House or Senate business, much less their committee systems. When it went out of business after a year of concerted hearings and meetings, its membership from the two chambers could not even agree upon a common report. Nor were the separate compromise reports of the Committee's Senate and House contingents—Representative Gerald Solomon (R-N.Y.) termed the latter "a 'minimalist approach' to tinkering"—ever acted upon.

Reformers struggled to keep the issue alive and to bring public and media pressures to bear on leaders and members. But theirs was a losing struggle. House and Senate leaders had reluctantly acquiesced to the idea of a reform panel in 1992, when public anger at the House bank scandal and other matters was at its height. But public agitation never seemed to translate into demands for broad-scale reform plans; and by 1994 neither the public nor the press seemed interested. Reformers were unsuccessful in identifying, or agreeing upon, proposals that would capture and hold the public's attention.

In the absence of compelling public pressure, Democratic leaders (and many senior Republicans) saw little reason to agree to structural changes. In the Senate, the Rules and Administration Committee killed the key reform proposals—for shrinking the number of committees through attrition, eliminating four joint committees, and banning proxy voting in Senate committees. A watered-down version of the Joint Committee package was approved, but efforts to gain floor approval were futile. In the House, leadership opposition kept the reform plans bottled up in the Rules Committee. Speaker Thomas S. Foley (D-Wash.) opted to stand by the senior committee chairs, who had protected his Speakership in the dark hours of the "bank" affair and who remained fiercely opposed to any curbs upon their power or jurisdictions.

Although the whole effort was judged a failure, the Joint Committee had two important legacies. First, its extensive hearings and staff reports comprise an invaluable historical record of House and Senate operations—the first such compilation in almost two decades. Second, the lengthy list of recommendations contained in the Committee's reports and in its proceedings (many of which were not accepted by the Committee) served as a laundry list of potential changes in House and Senate procedures. Included, most particularly, were many Republican-proposed reforms that could be considered and adopted only after a change in party control.

Despite the Joint Committee's disappointing history, however, the 103rd Congress yielded to reformist impulses in several important respects. The rules adopted in January 1993, although dictated by leaders of the Democratic majority, embraced several changes that had been pushed by Democratic reformers. These changes: (1) reduced the number of subcommittees; (2) limited certain powers of committee chairs; (3) protected authorizing committees from Senate amendments; and (4) permitted "rolling quorums" in committees.

The leaders were, moreover, challenged later that year by two backbench revolts. In the first encounter, the House ended up eliminating four of its five select committees, temporary panels that nonetheless had vocal supporters and clienteles both inside and outside the chamber.[3] An alliance of Republicans and reformers of both parties forced floor votes on reauthorizing the panels; when the first one lost, the others were doomed. Even though floor leaders in both parties were caught off guard, it appeared that rank-and-file members were eager to strike a blow for reform.

A second backbench revolt succeeded when Republican reformers masterminded a drive to open up the committee discharge process. This was conceived as a way of bringing public pressure on committees that had bottled up popular conservative proposals—for example, the balanced-budget amendment, the line-item veto, and term limits. Under the new scheme, the public and press would have access to the names of members who signed petitions to discharge committees from considering these and other issues. Although originally intended to embarrass Democratic leaders, the device can be used to pry popular measures from committee no matter which party is in power. Discharge petition threats that, for example, helped to persuade reluctant GOP leaders in mid-1998 to schedule floor debate on the campaign finance bill coauthored by Christopher Shays (R-Conn.) and Martin T. Meehan (D-Mass.).

Late in the summer of 1994, as the Joint Committee's proposals were breathing their last breath, House Republicans were dredging those proposals (and other documents as well) for a reformist platform that could be sold to a restless electorate. This responsibility fell to three Republicans who had served on the Joint Committee—Co-Chair David Dreier (Calif.), freshman Jennifer Dunn (Wash.), and Gerald Solomon (N.Y.).

This GOP task force had no lack of material with which to work. Many ideas came from a 43-point plan, "Mandate for Change in the People's House," that had been offered in January 1993 by Minority Leader Robert H. Michel (R-Ill.) as an alternative to the Democratic rules package. The GOP plan, although scuttled virtually without debate, was itself the product of years of frustration on the part of minority-party lawmakers. Other reform ideas came from the Joint Committee—its reports and testimony as well as its ill-fated final rec-ommendations. Proposals from all these sources were combined into a wide-ranging list of reforms that were incorporated into the "Contract with America."

The Contract, signed by virtually all GOP candidates in a ceremony at the Capitol's West Front on 27 September 1994, trumpeted congressional reform as one of its planks. "On the first day of the 104th Congress," announced the Contract's mastermind, Newt Gingrich (R-Ga.), "the new Republican majority will immediately pass . . . major reforms aimed at restoring the faith and trust of the American people in their government" (Federal News Service 1994, 11). He promised that his party would: (1) apply workplace laws to Congress; (2) launch an independent House audit; (3) cut House committees and committee staffs by one-third; (4) limit terms of House committee chairs; (5) ban proxy voting in committees; (6) open committee meetings to the public; (7) require three-fifths majorities for tax increases; and (8) implement baseline budgeting.

THE INCOMPLETE REVOLUTION

After the Republicans triumphed in the 1994 elections, they acted swiftly to change the way the majoritarian House of Representatives operated. At the time the reforms were viewed simply as part of the "revolution" perpetrated by Speaker Gingrich and his troops. With the passage of time, however, a somewhat more nuanced assessment of the content and effects of these changes is in order.

Centralized Leadership

Speaker-designate Gingrich was, strictly speaking, straying beyond his authority when in December 1994 he named the House committee chairs, departing from seniority in four instances. But no one objected, and the Conference readily rat-ified his choices and strengthened their leaders' leverage over the party's Committee on Committees. It was a preemptory strike that sent a powerful message to all senior committee leaders. (After all, Democratic reformers in 1974 needed to oust only three committee chairs in order to bring the rest into line.) Chairs were warned that their posts depended upon their pledge to report out (to send legislation from a committee on to the next congressional phase [e.g., to the Rules Committee]) items from the Contract with America, even if they personally disagreed with them. Tenure of chairs was capped at three terms (compared to the Speaker's four-term limit). Leadership staffs were augmented while committee staffs were cut.

These developments were spectacular evidence of centralized leadership, at least at the outset of the Republican regime. In fact, strengthened leadership has been one of the themes of the postreform House of Representatives. Since the mid-1970s, Democrats had tried with some success to rectify the problems brought about by the reform era's extreme fragmentation. Little by little their caucus invested party leaders with added powers. In his brief tenure, Speaker Jim Wright (1987–1989) showed what a purposeful leader could achieve under the existing rules.

The Republicans Write the Rules

The GOP-drafted rules adopted for the 104th Congress bore the imprint of the party's 43-point package of two years earlier, as well as Representative David Dreier's (R-Calif.) unsuccessful attempts to incorporate major changes in the Joint Committee's 1993 report (Davidson 1995). Easy targets for elimination (actually, the work was transferred to other panels) were committees closely linked to Democrats' clienteles—District of Columbia (mostly Democratic voters), Merchant Marine and Fisheries (environmentalists, maritime unions, and seaport cities), and Post Office and Civil Service (postal and public employee unions). A few jurisdictions were rearranged—most notably financial institutions, transportation, and nonmilitary nuclear issues.

The new regime also marginalized informal caucuses with status as legislative service organizations (LSOs), which allowed them to occupy House office space and procure staff and supplies with members' pooled funds. Liberal groups were especially enfeebled. The twenty-eight LSOs included eleven liberal and eleven industry or regional groups, two state delegations, along with two Republican and two Democratic groups. Prominent among the defunded LSOs were the Democratic Study Group, the black, Hispanic, and women's caucuses, and groups supporting the arts, environmental protection, arms control, human rights, and federal employees.

Although three committees were eliminated and a few jurisdictional lines adjusted, however, more comprehensive jurisdictional realignment was scuttled. Of the four plans seriously debated by Republican leaders after the 1994 elections, the leading contender was drawn up by Dreier, Dunn, and Solomon— based largely on Dreier's earlier scheme. In addition to dropping three targeted panels (District of Columbia, Merchant Marine and Fisheries, and Post Office and Civil Service), the 17-committee plan would have rebuilt several others: Empowerment (education, labor, nutrition, housing, welfare), Ways and Means (revenues, minus welfare and health care), Public Infrastructure (public works, railroads, environment), and Ethics and Administration (combining House Administration, Standards of Official Conduct).

Needless to say, the Dreier plan touched off frenzied debate within Republican ranks (Hosansky 1994). Speaker-designate Gingrich, after intense negotiations with his close advisors, decided against extensive committee realignment (Kahn 1995, A44–A45). "We have a committee structure that . . . is a very efficient structure," explained incoming majority leader Dick Armey of

Texas. Although no doubt achievable, major jurisdictional shifts would set off bruising competition among newly named committee leaders and would jeopardize fragile working relationships between senior moderates and junior firebrands. Perhaps most important, it was thought that realignment would divert energies from the substantive goal of implementing the Contract with America. The Small Business and Veterans Affairs committees, often mentioned as candidates for phase-out, both had powerful constituencies and close Republican ties.

Protecting committee turf is a bipartisan trait. Republican would-be chairs, it turned out, were as quick to defend existing jurisdictions as Democrats had been prior to the 1994 elections. Mild-mannered Thomas J. Bliley, Jr. (R-Va.), who replaced blustery John Dingell (D-Mich.) as chair of the Commerce Committee, fought skillfully to preserve his newfound patrimony. The initial realignment plan would have dismantled large chunks of the panel's turf (securities regulation, health care, transportation, energy, and environmental regulation). Bliley's arguments and horse trading left his committee largely intact—ceding only railroads (to Transportation), some securities (to Banking), energy research (to Science), and the Alaska pipeline (to Resources). "My goal was to hold on to as much jurisdiction as I could," he said, "and I think I did a pretty good job of it" (Andrews 1994, D11).

Promised cuts in committee sizes and in members' assignments were modest. Senior committee leaders tended to favor such cuts, in order to facilitate committee management and combat what Senator Robert C. Byrd (D-W.Va.) called the "fractured attention" of members (U.S. Congress, Joint Committee on the Organization of Congress 1993, 4). New Republican chairs like Bill Archer (R-Tex.) of Ways and Means voiced the same concerns in arguing for smaller committees. However, many GOP members, including otherwise reform-minded newcomers, clamored for choice assignments; party leaders found it impossible to resist pressures to expand available seats on committees, especially those with visible constituency benefits (Hook and Cloud 1994).

The Republicans' new rules were designed to encourage members to focus on their committee duties by requiring them to be present for votes (no more proxies or "rolling quorums"), by publishing votes on committee reports, and by further discouraging committee meetings while the House was in session.

The new rules did clarify the procedures for multicommittee consideration of bills. Joint referrals of measures to committees were prohibited, but split or sequential referrals were not. Indeed, the Speaker now announced a new multiple-referral procedure, sending measures to a "lead" committee and thence to other committees (termed "additional initial referrals") with the option of imposing deadlines upon any or all of the involved committees. The new majority also made unprecedented use of entities outside the committee framework—even for the purpose of drafting legislation—with decidedly mixed results.

Institutional Strategies

Today's political elites, argue Benjamin Ginsberg, Walter Mebane, and Martin Shefter, compete not so much by waging electoral warfare as by building governmental institutions that will bind them to significant interests in American society. Their strategy is to "[seek] to colonize existing governmental agencies, establish new ones, and undermine agencies controlled by their opponents" (Ginsberg, Mebane, and Shefter 1998, 368). In pursuing this strategy, all sides have aggressively exploited the huge and growing scandal-mongering machinery, in the process damaging the reputations of individuals and institutions throughout the system.

Regime-building is regarded, historically speaking, as primarily a presidential activity (Skowronek 1993). Thus, leaders of the new Republican majority on Capitol Hill sought to emulate presidential politics in many ways—including the construction of platforms, the initial promise of action within the "first hundred days," and the use of leadership posts as a bully pulpit. But nowhere did GOP leaders seem more presidential than in their tough-minded efforts to build linkages with interest groups and the general public and, wherever possible, to deconstruct their opponents' political bases.

Consider the new Republican majority's daunting strategic challenge: to eliminate or at least pare back the accretions of more than sixty years of liberals' distributive policy-making and institution building. The Democrats' nearly unbroken reign on Capitol Hill allowed them to draw the blueprints, if not all the details, of the modern-day federal establishment. (Not a few Republican lawmakers learned to play the game, and these members have proved to be major stumbling blocks for the militant revolutionaries.) Republican presidents, having promised to slash taxes and maintain law and order and a strong defense, mostly came to terms with the modern liberal state.

Congressional structures were shaped by this interest-group–public-policy connection as much or more than as by the much-cited electoral connection. The decentralized House and Senate structures that emerged in the reform era (late 1960s to early 1970s) were ideally suited to promoting high legislative productivity and facilitating multiple group access to lawmakers, both individually and collectively. Activist Democrats stressed participation and decentralization primarily because they wanted to pass laws conferring distributive benefits. And the committee and subcommittee rooms of Capitol Hill were ideal venues for that purpose—as we have understood ever since Woodrow Wilson's critique of Gilded Age policy-making.

As congressional Republicans (especially in the House) became more cohesively and militantly conservative, they rightly sensed that their enemies were not just the Democrats' policies but also their prevailing policy-making structures. Long before the Contract with America was unveiled, GOP leaders and parliamentary experts had compiled a lengthy laundry list of reform proposals.

To govern, Republican militants felt they had to make good on their pledge to change the character of the federal establishment, reducing or wiping out distributive or regulatory programs. Thus, they faced the politician's most challenging task: redistribution of benefits, in many cases shifting them from previously advantaged groups and conferring them upon a new set of clients. For this endeavor the established committees, subcommittees, and informal caucuses were seen as minefields of entrenched interests. Such massive changes, they perceived, were best made on the chamber floor, with cohesive majorities driven by focused leadership. By and large this has been where the Republican revolution has been fought—and where its victories and defeats have been recorded.

Bypassing the Committee System

The new Republican leadership's initial strategy called for neutralizing or even displacing the standing committees and the Appropriations subcommittees. In the past, committee obduracy had often thwarted effective legislative scheduling; now central scheduling was achieved at the cost of careful deliberation.

During the first hundred days of the 104th Congress, the committees were led on a forced march to complete action on the Contract with America (Gimpel 1996). Often bypassing hearings or extended deliberation, the panels were rushed into action by the leadership in order to bring bills to the floor on time. At the first organization meeting of the Government Reform and Oversight Committee—which had charge of five Contract items—Chairman William F. Clinger (Pa.) moved immediately from adopting committee rules to marking up the unfunded mandates bill, on which no hearings had been held. "It was chaos," Clinger admitted.

Prestige committees were stacked with junior members, most of them Contract loyalists. Six freshmen were placed on Appropriations, six on Budget, three on Ways and Means, and one on Rules. Appropriations subcommittee chairs were asked to sign a statement that they could be removed if they failed to follow the GOP Conference agenda (Bruck 1995, 71–72). These steps brought unaccustomed partisanship to Appropriations subcommittees and expedited large numbers of "riders" (limitation amendments) to implement the party's policy goals.

To write high-priority legislation, GOP leaders often went outside the committee structure entirely, employing leadership committees (such as Budget or Rules) or ad hoc task forces, sometimes with the Speaker or majority leader personally superintending the negotiations. During its first year, the new leaders issued directives to committee chairs on such disparate subjects as agriculture, legal services, defense appropriations, banking reform, tax provisions, telecommunications, and District of Columbia government. "You can't depend on the committee system to make bold changes," explained Rules Chair Solomon. "The leadership needs to pick up the slack." Needless to say, committee leaders and members did not accept their preemption without protest. After the leadership had revised their pork-rich highway bill, Transportation and Infrastructure Committee members complained they had been rendered "meaningless" by the Budget Committee (Kahn 1995).

Finally, task forces were frequently employed to counterbalance the standing committees. They were used to write or rewrite legislation, keep in touch with allied groups, and design themes or messages for public-relations purposes. The most conspicuous example was the eight-member "design team," chaired by the Speaker, that crafted the party's Medicare proposal—over the objections of Ways and Means Chair Archer and Commerce Chair Bliley. Some of the subcommittees of jurisdiction held perfunctory hearings, but without a bill before them. Needless to add, the House Republicans' foray into health care was no more successful than that of the White House.

Such task forces served several functions. First, as under the Democrats, they can be "inclusionary" devices, dispersing specific tasks among a large number of interested members, staff aides, and even outsiders. Second, they are a way of inviting friendly lobbyists to the table and excluding opposing groups. Given an ambitious agenda and a shortage of expertise—hordes of inexperienced members served by staffs that were often equally green—it was perhaps inevitable that Republicans turned to friendly lobbyists to help draft legislation. Task forces are ideal vehicles for such infiltration: they are informal and short on rules, staff, and press coverage.

THE COUNTERREVOLUTION

The initial strategy of a leadership-driven agenda seemed to make sense. After all, the committees and their allied clientele groups were seen as minefields for many of the goals of the Republican "revolution." However, there were problems from the outset. The threat of being marginalized angered many of the committee chairmen and senior committee members. Many senior Republicans, as well as Democrats, had invested years in learning and mastering the issues considered by their committees. Now their accumulated knowledge was being ignored, at the very moment that their expertise was most needed. There were scheduling and coordination problems as well.

As for the minority Democrats, they had been crushed in the early days of the 104th Congress. They walked out of meetings, threw bills on the floor, engaged in shoving matches, even held their own committee meeting in the rain out on the Capitol grounds. Once the easy votes on the Contract items were over, however, they would have to be a part of negotiations on controversial bills—as the GOP leaders learned.

The Return of Committee Power

A core part of the leaders' strategy—using substantive provisions in appropriations bills to achieve goals pushed by conservative militants but not apt to be approved by authorizing committees—proved especially troublesome. The strategy assumed that President Bill Clinton would retreat and sign the funding bills—not an unreasonable assumption. But on selected provisions the White House stood firm and, remembering their militant constituency, the leaders were reluctant to back down. As we know, the Republicans as a party were blamed for the mess, which shut down the federal government on two separate occasions. Not only was the leaderships' management of the agenda thrown awry, but the leaders' public ratings plummeted.

The extreme centralization of the early 104th Congress therefore proved to be an aberration. A more equitable balance of power between Republican leaders and the committees emerged in 1996 and was confirmed in the 105th Congress (1997–1998). Committees and their chairs reclaimed important ground in the tug and pull between party leaders and committees.

The shift was signalled by a simple event that occurred in late December 1996. Bill Archer (R-Tex.), chair of the House Ways and Means Committee, paid a one-on-one visit to the White House that was billed as "courtesy call," not budget talks (Gray 1997). It was a sign that the money committees would be the major players in forthcoming budget negotiations. Indeed, the chairs of the four committees played central parts in the talks that led to the historic "balanced-budget" pact of 1997.

There were several reasons for this reversion to the "regular order" of politics on Capitol Hill. For one thing, Speaker Gingrich was hard pressed to retain his position because of his ethics problems and low popular-standing. In order to preserve his leadership, in November 1996 he made common cause with committee chairs, agreeing to changes that would expand their power. (Ironically, this was the same strategy followed by Speaker Foley in 1992 when his position was placed in jeopardy by the House "bank" scandal.)

Several adjustments were agreed upon. The GOP Leadership Group was expanded to include more committee chairs. The Speaker's Advisory Group— an inner leadership cabinet that recommended policy, strategy, and legislation— was abolished. Committee chairs were assured of their prerogative of developing legislation largely free of leadership interference. "The last Congress is dead," announced Chief Whip Tom DeLay (Tex.). Or as an aide put it, chairs "can run free as long as they're on a leash. Last Congress they had a choke collar on."

A second consideration was the realization that committees and their chairs were, after all, in a better position to shape legislation than leadership or ad hoc groups. Lack of detailed preparation and compromise was blamed for the fact that many bills in the 104th Congress met with opposition from the White House and the general public. With an even narrower margin of control in the House in the 105th Congress, committees were indispensable forums for hammering out bipartisan compromises and minimizing partisan conflict during floor consideration.

Not that this new balance of power has been without its problems. Asserting their committees' prerogatives, chairs have occasionally feuded publicly with party leaders. House Appropriations Chair Bob Livingston (R-La.) clashed with Majority Leader Dick Armey (R-Tex.) over the issue of attaching riders to supplemental appropriations bills (appropriators tend to oppose such amendments).

Transportation Chair Bud Shuster (R-Pa.) has defied leadership efforts to rein in budget-busting highway and mass-transit authorizations favored by his committee. Indeed, Shuster's 1998 transportation bill—entitled the "Transportation Equity Act for the Twenty-First Century"—was later discovered to include a proviso that would preclude any future floor action that might reduce the bill's current or future spending levels (Eilperin 1998). This effort to lock in transportation spending angered the appropriators, who normally cut spending levels contained in the highway authorization bills. "I thought it was an intrusion into the legislative process," Livingston told reporters. Also miffed was the leadership-dominated House Rules Committee, whose duties include writing "special rules" governing floor debate.

Slower Change in the Senate

The Senate, usually slower than the House to change its ways, served as a brake on impetuous legislative action during the 104th Congress (Salant 1995). But the Senate was not unaffected by the wave of reformism sweeping Capitol Hill. Although no major structural changes were instituted, the chamber did eliminate a few subcommittees and cut its operating budgets by 15 percent and its committee staffs by 20 percent.

Serious confrontations broke out over loyalty to the party on core issues between some of the younger senators (several of whom had migrated from the House) and the senior committee leaders. Out of this conflict grew a special Senate committee chaired by Connie Mack (R-Fla.). Some of the recommendations, adopted by the Senate Republican Conference and put into practice in January 1997, may have the effect of tightening party responsibility. Among the new requirements are term limits for committee chairs and establishment of a legislative agenda at the start of each Congress.

In 1997 a Senate inquiry was launched in order to, in Majority Leader Trent Lott's words, "modernize some of the outdated operations of the institution while preserving its wonderful tradition" (Henry 1997, 1). The chair of the ten-person task force, Senator Bob Bennett (R-Utah), declared that the subject of filibuster and cloture would be off limits, but other topics, such as the practice of holds, could be addressed. The group's work was to be completed during the 105th Congress. The inquiry was a low-key affair, consisting mainly of private conversations between Bennett and his colleagues. It seems doubtful that the effort will yield any substantial public record.

THE COMMITTEE SYSTEM'S UNSOLVED ISSUES

The Republican takeover, then, fell short of being revolutionary as far as the committees' relationships with party leaders are concerned. Its effort at extreme centralization was damaging to the committees and eventually to the party leaders themselves. In any event the experiment was short-lived. Nor has the new regime addressed some of the long-standing problems of the committee system—problems that the Democrats had declined to resolve.

Committee Assignments and Sizes

Republican reforms since 1995, while clearly aimed at focusing members' attention on committee deliberation, failed to resolve some of the underlying defects of the current committee system. In the first place, committees in both chambers, and especially in the House, remain excessively large (see Table 4.1). At seventy-three members, the House Transportation and Infrastructure is the largest committee on Capitol Hill; House Appropriations has sixty and works almost exclusively through its thirteen subcommittees. Other major committees are quite large: the House's fourteen primary standing committees average almost fifty members apiece.

The Senate has been more successful than the House in limiting the size of its committees, and especially in keeping down its numbers of subcommittees. Still, Senate Appropriations has 28 members, and four other committees have 20 or more members. And committee sizes grew 6 percent in the 105th Congress.

There is no mystery about the large size of House committees. Like their Democratic predecessors, Republican leaders have faced strong pressure from their rank-and-file members who desire politically attractive assignments. That is the only explanation for the popularity of the Transportation and Infrastructure Committee (and its Surface Transportation Subcommittee), whose jurisdiction embraces the federal highway and mass-transit grants of the aforementioned intermodal surface transportation enactment—one of the most

TABLE 4.1
CONGRESSIONAL COMMITTEE STATISTICS, 1991–1998

	102nd (1991–92)	103rd (1993–94)	104th (1995–96)	105th (1997–98)
House of Representatives				
Number of Committees	27	23	20	20
Number of Subcommittees	149	117	86	92
Ave. Committee Size	37.9	38.6	39.2	40.1
Ave. Number of Assignments	7	5.9	4.8	5
Largest Committee Size	68	62	62	73
Senate				
Number of Committees	20	20	20	20
Number of Subcommittees	87	86	68	68
Ave. Committee Size	17.6	17.7	16.7	17.8
Ave. No. of Assignments	11	11	11	10
Largest Committee Size	29	29	28	28

Source: Author's calculations from *Congressional Quarterly, The 102nd Congress: A Committee Directory* (4 May 1991); *Players, Politics and Turf of the 103rd Congress* (1 May 1993); *Players, Politics and Turf of the 104th Congress* (25 March 1995); *Players, Politics and Turf of the 105th Congress* (22 March 1997).

visible remaining sources of distributive benefits for discrete states and districts. Seats on key money committees are prized also because they assure members of campaign funds from business firms and PACs affected by the committees' work. House Republicans have been especially effective in placing their most vulnerable members on such panels. "We adopted a plan to help out our own through committee assignments, fundraising appearances, leadership political action committee donations, and personal contributions," explained a leadership aide (Vande Hei 1997). Twenty (43 percent) of the 47 most vulnerable House Republicans in the 105th Congress—those elected since 1994 who won reelection with less than 55 percent of the vote—held seats on the "Big Three" money committees (Appropriations, Commerce, Ways and Means).

Such work groups have grown too large for real deliberation on the part of their members; indeed, few available committee rooms can comfortably accommodate them. It is little wonder that the primary burden of legislative deliberation falls on the subcommittees. However, members of subcommittees may also find themselves lost in the crowd: largest is the forty-six-member Subcommittee on Surface Transportation, whose jurisdiction embraces highway and mass-transit projects—among the few remaining trophies that incumbents can gain for their constituencies.

Committee Jurisdictions

Secondly, standing committee jurisdictions are often outdated and inflexible in comparison with today's complex, interlocked policy questions. Definitions of jurisdictional metes and bounds can grow into the equivalents of jealously guarded land rights, in which boundaries are stoutly defended and trespassers fiercely fought off. Yet evolving policy challenges rarely fit neatly into the jurisdictional definitions that were codified years or even decades ago. Crosscutting issues—involving, for example, the environment, trade, health, and welfare— demand more integrated deliberation and oversight.

The House's mature committee system is increasingly challenged by alternative organizational entities—multicommittee arrangements, partisan or bipartisan task forces, leadership-convened panels, outside blue-ribbon commissions, and high-level "summit" conferences between legislative leaders and the executive branch. The challenge for the future will be to combine the traditional virtues of committee expertise with the need for flexible responses to broad-scale policy issues.

In the end, the Republicans have proven themselves little more inclined to address jurisdictional issues than their Democratic predecessors. On election night 1994, Representative David Dreier (R-Calif.) was awakened by a phone call from Speaker-to-be Gingrich. "David, this is Newt. I want you to reform the committees" (Kosova 1995). As vice chair of the 1993 Joint Committee, Dreier was an advocate of committee realignment and had developed a sweeping plan to overhaul committee jurisdictions. The early days of the Republican takeover would have been a propitious moment for committee realignment. Reform was in the air; scores of freshman votes were available to back up a new set of arrangements; and the GOP committee chairs had not yet settled into their new duties. As related earlier, however, the leadership decided to reject Dreier's ambitious plans and settle for a few marginal adjustments.

So that committee realignment would not be totally forgotten, the GOP Conference authorized a task force headed by Dreier to address jurisdictional entanglement and to "further reduce the number of committees . . . and clarify questions of multi-committee jurisdiction." When the task force reported in November 1996, it repeated several bold reorganization schemes, but neither endorsed nor took a position on them. Moreover, the task force acknowledged that significant realignment would "disrupt the institutional culture and environment of the House, and it would take several years to assimilate to the resulting changes" (U.S. House of Representatives 1996, 14).

Even marginal changes were approached cautiously. The Small Business Committee, the task force admitted, "by itself, does not constitute a sufficiently heavy workload to merit standing committee status" (p. 10). On the other hand, "it is crucial for the House to have a focal and access point for America's small business entrepreneurs" (p. 11). Other committees' jurisdictions were discussed similarly.

The task force offered justifications for the Republicans' abandonment of structural reform of the committee system. For one thing, stronger party leadership had limited intercommittee conflict and prevented the return of the kind of power wielded by chairs under the Democrats. As one leadership aide put it, "committees have not been an obstacle to our legislative agenda" (Eilperin 1998). For another, the task force cited favorably GOP leaders' use of extra-committee entities as "flexible and adaptable devices for addressing problems which either do not fall nearly within the committees' jurisdictional boundaries or are simply not reflected in any committee's mandate" (p. 3).

Staff Support and Working Conditions

Beginning with the Legislative Reorganization Act of 1946, Congress moved in the direction of equipping itself with modern, professionalized staff support. The staff component on Capitol Hill has grown in size, reaching a plateau in the mid-1970s that has only recently begun to shrink. In 1997 there were 9,490 persons employed by the House of Representatives; of these, personal office staffs accounted for 71 percent, committee staffs 12 percent, and other staff 17 percent (Dwyer and Pontius 1997, 7). At the same time Senate staffing totalled 6,535, of which approximately 60 percent were employed by individual senators, 12.5 by the committees, and 26 percent by the chamber (U.S. Senate 1997, 23; Hardy-Vincent 1997, 14–15). Additional staff support is provided by the congressional support agencies: most notably, the Congressional Research Service, General Accounting Office, and Congressional Budget Office.

Many journalistic critics, and even some members, have lamented the size of the Capitol Hill establishment. By the 1990s, the consensus view on the Hill seemed to be that staffs, especially committee staffs, had grown too large. Accordingly, when the Republicans took charge of the House in January 1995, they vowed to reduce committee staffs by one-third. Senate Republicans promised reductions of 10 percent, although they did not specify where these savings would occur.

As Table 4.2 reveals, staff reductions under the Republicans actually exceeded their initial promises. House committee staffs dropped by almost one-half, compared with a drop of only 7.5 percent for personal staffs and 15.6 percent overall. In a separate action, Congress eliminated the Office of Technology Assessment—which, although the smallest of the support agencies, had compiled a much-

TABLE 4.2
CONGRESSIONAL STAFFING LEVELS, 1980–1997

Staff Type	1980–1994 Dem. control (8 Congresses)	1995–1997 GOP control (2 Congresses)	Reduction Number	Reduction Percentage
	House of Representatives			
Committee staff	2,113	1,147	966	45.7
Personal staff	7,537	6,975	562	7.5
Other Staff	2,041	1,741	300	14.7
Total Staff	11,691	9,862	1,829	15.6
	Senate			
Total Staff	7,165	6,446	719	10.0
Committee staff	1,214	1,080	134	11.0
	Supporting Agencies			
CBO	218	230	+12	+5.5
CRS	830	740	90	10.8
GAO	5,210	3,564	1,646	31.6
OTA	190	6*	184*	96.8*

*The Office of Technology Assessment (OTA) was phased out in 1995.

Source: Paul Dwyer and John Pontius, *Legislative Branch Employment, 1960–1997*, CRS Report 97-112 GOV (6 June 1997), 6–7; Carol Hardy Vincent, *Senate Committee Staff and Funding*, CRS Report 97-222 GOV (10 February 1997), 14–15.

praised record of preparing technical reports on a wide range of emerging public issues (Bimber 1996).

As the GOP settled in to the business of governing, some of these early staff cuts were restored or at least moderated. In the House, some of the most severely hit committees subsequently bettered their position. Two committees—Judiciary and Government Reform and Oversight—are actually more generously staffed than under the Democrats. Over in the Senate, staff reductions of 1993 and 1995 have to a great extent been neutralized (Ornstein, Mann, and Malbin 1998, 142). Indeed, overall Senate staff levels have recently risen, although they are still below pre-1993 figures.

Staff cuts no doubt impaired the Congress's work at a crucial moment in the institution's history: the advent of a new Republican majority brandishing an extensive legislative agenda but headed by many inexperienced and untested leaders. True, a number of Senate Republicans, including Majority Leader Dole and several committee chairs, had held majority posts as recently as six years earlier, and in any event law-making chores are more equitably shared in that chamber. On the House side, however, not one of their members had ever served in the majority, much less chaired a committee or written a "special rule" for floor debate. It is probable that at least some of the House's substantive and procedural miscalculations during the 104th and 105th Congress can be traced to inadequate preparation or thin staffing. To be sure, GOP floor and committee leaders themselves were unused to their new majority status, and no doubt needed time to gain confidence in performing tasks that were unfamiliar to them. Yet this was exactly the moment when seasoned staffing would be most needed.

How much expertise did the House, and especially its committees, lose in the process? Some committees were especially hard hit. The three committees that were eliminated (Post Office and Civil Service, Merchant Marine and Fisheries, District of Columbia) were stripped of most of their staffs, a few being reassigned to Government Reform and Oversight. Three panels—Banking, Commerce, and Ways and Means—lost more than half of their staffs between 1994 and 1995 (Ornstein, Mann, and Malbin 1998, 140–41). Several other committees lost a third or more of their staff support: Appropriations, Budget, Judiciary, Education and the Workforce, National Security, Science, Small Business, House Oversight, and Veterans' Affairs. Some committees, such as Appropriations, protected their staff expertise by shifting former majority-party staffers to the new majority's payroll. Other committees—for example, Budget and Government Reform and Oversight—called upon staffs from the Congressional Research Service (CRS) and the Congressional Budget Office (CBO) to take up the slack.

Senate committees were dealt with more gently. A few, such as Governmental Affairs, Labor and Human Resources, Budget, and Indian Affairs, lost at least 30 percent of their staff aides. In any event, many Senate committees had substantially recovered their staffing levels four years after the Republican takeover.

Other questions surround staff morale and working conditions. According to a 1993 staff survey (Congressional Management Foundation 1995), three-quarters or more of House staff members "like their jobs" and are "generally satisfied with most aspects of their work." Staffers cited such positive benefits as opportunities to serve people and to learn, the quality of co-workers, and the variety of job activities. At the same time many of the interviewees pointed to dissatisfactions with House jobs: the amount of work-related stress; few opportunities for promotion, job development, or recognition; poor feedback on job performance; low salaries; haphazard office management; poor physical working conditions; and the unpredictability of the work schedule.

As a result of these and other factors, Senate and House employees tend to be young, inexperienced, and poorly paid. According to the most recent survey of individual House members' staffs (Klouda et al. 1996, 2–3), high turnover is found at all levels and has in fact risen over the last four years. Representatives' Washington-based staffers (about 60 percent of the total) were on average paid 33 percent less than the region's federal employees; salaries for most categories of House employees trail those of Senate counterparts in equivalent posts. Little wonder that nearly half of the Washington-based staffers surveyed in 1993 said they wanted to leave their jobs within three years (Congressional Management Foundation 1995, 26).

Many of the most severe workplace issues, which affect members as well as staffs, could be ameliorated if the House and its leaders determined to do so. As the Congressional Management Foundation concluded:

> The workplace issues with which staff are most dissatisfied—workload and work hours, unpredictable work schedules, job-related stress, insufficient training, and ineffective management practices—are all problems that can be successfully addressed directly, promptly, and without significant cost. Reducing these common and increasingly debilitating workplace problems, however, will require both greater institutional discipline and a greater commitment to improving the quality of work life on the Hill. (1995, 49)

CONCLUSIONS

Out of this examination of the politics of change during the Republican regime's turbulent first few years, several lessons may be drawn.

First, the 1990s will surely be remembered as one of the most concentrated periods of change on Capitol Hill. As in other times of institutional upheaval—the 1910 Progressive revolt against Cannonism, the post–World War II modernization embodied in the Reorganization Act of 1946, and the reform era of the 1970s with its paradoxical mixture of centralized power and decentralized influence—the recent past has altered the Congress's structure, personnel, and traditions.

Second, although the partisan turnover in 1995 may have been its defining moment, the boundaries of this recent reform era embrace a much more extended time period. The upheaval was rooted in the scandals of the early 1990s and the citizen anger that greeted them. The last Democratically-controlled Congress—the much-maligned 103rd—in fact adopted several significant changes, despite the opposition of Speaker Foley and other Democratic (and Republican) leaders.

Third, the new Republican regime built upon rather than departed from longer-term trends in congressional organization—most particularly, the tendency toward strengthening central party leadership and increasingly bypassing the standing committees. "As party power grows, committee power wanes," in the words of the Republican reform task force (U.S. House of Representatives 1996, 3).

Fourth, this seesaw between party leadership and committee prerogatives provides a core theme for the evolution of the Republican regime during the 104th and 105th Congresses. The zenith of the leaders' power occurred before, during, and after the Republican Congress convened in January 1995. As their centrally-driven agenda ran into opposition and eventually public disapproval, the committees and their leaders—having been roughed up during the frantic deliberations over the Contract with America—began to reassert their prerogatives. Eventually the leadership was forced to make tangible concessions, and committees' control over their jurisdictional subjects returned to something like the *status quo ante*.

Fifth, the Republican "revolution" thus turned into something less than than a wholesale change, at least in comparison to the lengthy agenda of proposed structural or procedural reforms in the House and Senate. Basic problems remain not only in committee operations but in the workplace conditions of both chambers. Indeed, some of the Republicans' boldest innovations—including drastic cuts in both chambers' committee staffs as well as certain revisions in House floor proceedings—have proved to be unwelcome hindrances, especially to the majority party's performance of its tasks. The Republican majorities, it seems, have not escaped the "law of unintended consequences."

NOTES

1. The Senate's committee was charged with examining plans for coping with the Year-2000 problem ("Y2K") in federal agencies' computer systems. The House panel was to investigate alleged leakages of military secrets in the course of trade with the People's Republic of China.

2. These are House or bicameral groups that meet the House Oversight Committee's definitional and registration requirements. Registration is required for any organization of House members who join together to share official resources (e.g., staff or office facilities) to pursue common legislative or research objectives.

3. These were the select committees on Aging; Hunger; Narcotics Abuse and Control; and Children, Youth, and Families.

CHAPTER FIVE

Learning to Legislate: Committees in the Republican Congress

CHRISTOPHER J. DEERING

INTRODUCTION

By virtually all accounts the 104th Congress (1995–1997) exhibited the most centralized party leadership and the highest levels of partisanship in the twentieth century. Victorious for the first time since the 83rd Congress (1953–1955), House and Senate Republicans set about the task of agenda setting and governing. For the first one hundred days things went pretty well and, although skeptics on the Hill and in the press could be found, the mood among House Republicans was jubilant. At the center, Speaker Newt Gingrich (R-Ga.) had amassed great power and nearly unanimous support among his party colleagues. Shell-shocked Democrats were floundering. By end of the 104th Congress, however, the mood and the sense of success, in effect, had reversed as President Clinton successfully employed a Trumanesque strategy of confrontation with GOP congressional leaders—particularly in the House. What happened?

Richard Fenno (1997) has argued that the House Republicans' long period in the political wilderness of minority status left them ill-prepared to *interpret* the 1994 elections and subsequently to *govern* effectively once they gained the reins of power on 4 January 1995. Worse yet, Fenno adds, House Republicans misinterpreted the mandate of the 1994 elections, which compounded subsequent decisions about how to go about the process of governing. The result, writes Fenno, was that "House Republicans missed their golden governing opportunity and made possible the rehabilitation, resurgence, and reelection of Bill Clinton" (Fenno 1997, 3; see also Jones 1994).

The 104th Congress represented a high-water mark for party leadership strength and centralized agenda management. Put more strongly, the 104th Congress was an aberration largely confined to the House of Representatives. The aberration was born out of an excessively long period of Democratic dominance in the House—a notion quite compatible with Fenno's institutional interpretation of the 104th Congress. Fenno argues that the distinctiveness of the 104th Congress can be traced to the long period of Democratic control, the confrontational style of Speaker Gingrich, the demise of interparty cooperation, reduced public faith in the institution, and increased public support for congressional term limits. Republicans in both chambers faced serious obstacles—some of their own making and some not. But I would contend that the Senate's lack of change is not only an institutional feature in and of itself, but also additional evidence for Fenno's observations about the House. The Senate had experienced two recent majority-party shifts and, although most of the Senate had turned over, many experienced majority- and minority-party members remained. This is not to say that Senate Republicans faced no obstacles. To some degree, they too were dragged along in the confrontational public-relations battle with Democrats and against big government. Moreover, the Senate, and especially its leadership ranks, had become populated by veterans of the House party wars.

My focus is primarily upon committees. But no treatment of Congress today can ignore the larger partisan and chamber contexts within which committee politics take place. After briefly reviewing the House and Senate reforms I will discuss a series of roadblocks faced by committees and committee chairs as they learned to legislate. Not surprisingly, I will show that Senate Republicans had a much easier time of it. They had learned these lessons in the recent past, making the transition from minority to majority and from majority to minority. Finally I will discuss larger themes about committee politics that seem to endure despite occasional "Tsunamis."[1] Indeed, my underlying theme is that the congressional committee system's ingrained conservatism, while not immutable, tends to win out over personalistic leadership in the long run.

REFORM REPUBLICAN STYLE

Throughout the twentieth century, periods of reform have generally been punctuated by de jure or de facto partisan change.[2] The most obvious of these are the institutional changes that accompanied—sometimes preceding and other times succeeding—changing House and/or Senate majorities in 1911, 1913, 1919, 1947, and 1995. The early 1970s did not witness a shift in party control—although some might argue that only Watergate forestalled such a change—but a power shift within the Democratic party did occur as northern liberals became a majority within their own party and pushed conservative southern Democrats to the side. By the 103rd Congress, substantial pressures for reform had built up, but entrenched Democratic leaders had no taste for the sort of changes discussed by the Joint Committee on the Organization of Congress (the Boren-Hamilton Committee).

The missing ingredient, partisan change, was provided in dramatic form by the 1994 midterm elections. As with the 1992 elections, a large class of new senators and representatives was assured due to numerous retirements. More importantly, however, a seemingly distant but plausible chance for a Republican takeover of the Senate and House hung in the air. Journalists, political pundits, and even scholars talked about a Republican victory in fairly serious terms. The Congress elected in 1974 will always be remembered as the Watergate Congress, just as the Class of 1974 will always be known as the "Watergate Babies." In much the same way, the Congress elected in 1994 is likely to be remembered as the Contract Congress because of the "Contract with America"—the ten-point platform masterminded by House Republican Whip (and Speaker-to-be) Newt Gingrich in an attempt to nationalize the notoriously local character of congressional elections. If elected, Gingrich and his fellow partisans promised, the Republican House would vote on each item in the contract in the first one hundred days of the new Congress. Furthermore, Gingrich promised that a sweeping set of changes within the institution, point one of the contract, would be passed on the first day of the new session.[3] Republicans succeeded on both counts.

Revolution and Reform in the House

The most recent round of reforms—both in the 103rd and in the 104th Congresses—are described and discussed at great length elsewhere (see Thurber and Davidson 1995; Evans and Oleszek 1997; Deering and Smith 1997) and need not take much space here. The House of Representatives of the 104th Congress came to order at 10:58 A.M. on 4 January 1995 and did not adjourn until 2:42 A.M. 5 January (details from Palmer 1997). After a good many ceremonial activities, the Republican House adopted the set of landmark rules changes. These changes altered the House committee system, applied term limits to a variety of House leaders, changed floor procedures, and set in motion administrative reforms designed to cut costs and depoliticize House operations. A summary of the major House and Senate reforms appears in Table 5.1.

The package of rules changes had taken shape over an extended period and amounted to a "bill of particulars" authored by House Republicans. Republicans believed that Democrats had grown overly content with their role as the majority party. Indeed, Gingrich and his colleagues frequently used strong language to describe Democratic hegemony in the House. Details of the reform plan were hammered out during the House Republican Conference's organizing sessions in December 1994 for presentation and adoption in the House on opening day.[4]

TABLE 5.1
Major House and Senate Reforms of the 104th Congress
(1995–1996)

House	Senate
Six-year term limits for committee and sub-committee chairs	Six-year term limits for committee chairs
Eight-year term limit for Speaker of the House	Six-year term limits for Republican-Party leaders other than floor leader and president pro tempore
Elimination of three standing committees and some jurisdictional shifts	Senator prohibited from "reclaiming" seniority upon return to a committee on which they previously served
Limitation of five subcommittees for most committees (Appropriations, Government Reform and Oversight, and Transportation excepted)	Secret-ballot elections for committee chairs in committee and party conference; majority leader can nominate chair in case of conference rejection
Joint referrals eliminated; Speaker gains enhanced authority over split and sequential referrals— including authority to designate a "lead" committee with deadline for reporting	GOP Conference to adopt (by a three-fourths vote) a formal legislative agenda prior to beginning each Congress and prior to selection of committee chairs
"Rolling quorums" prohibited	
Proxy voting in committees prohibited	
Majority-party leaders given enhanced authority over committee chair selection	
Members' assignments cut back to two full committees and four subcommittees	
Verbatim transcripts of hearings and meetings required	
Members' committee votes to be published	
Subcommittee staff hired by the full committee chair	
Committee staff reduced by one-third; House Oversight gains authority to establish committee staff sizes	
Motion to recommit with instructions guaranteed	
Motion to rise from Committee of the Whole reserved to the majority leader	
Three-fifths floor vote required for measures that raise income tax rates	

Source: For the changes in the House see David S. Cloud, "GOP, to Its Own Great Delight, Enacts House Rules Changes," *Congressional Quarterly Weekly Report,* 7 January 1995, 13–15; and for the Senate, David S. Cloud, "GOP Senators Limit Chairmen to Six Years Heading Panel," *Congressional Quarterly Weekly Report,* 22 July 1995, 2147.

The most visible changes included the elimination of three committees (District of Columbia, Merchant Marine and Fisheries, and Post Office and Civil Service),[5] 31 subcommittees, and 484 committee and subcommittee seats. These reductions were reinforced, and in some senses facilitated, by new limits on members' committee assignments (two) and subcommittee assignments (four). Somewhat less visible to the public was a series of relatively minor changes in committee jurisdictions on financial institutions, transportation, and nonmilitary nuclear issues. Republicans also cut back substantially on staff by establishing caps one-third below those permitted in the 103rd Congress and forced a long list of so-called legislative service organizations—nonlegislative issue groups supported by members' office allowances and political contributions—out of House office space. Thus, Republicans were able to make good on their promise to reduce Congress's own bureaucracy and realize some budget savings at the same time.

Another series of changes that went largely unmarked by the public increased the power of the Speaker while reducing the power of committee and subcommittee chairs. Full committee and subcommittee chairs are now limited to three two-year terms, permitting them less independence and further weakening the seniority system. The Speaker, who also has a term limit of eight years, gained additional influence in making committee assignments and chair selection. Speaker Gingrich used this power at once to elevate less senior colleagues to chairs over more senior colleagues on three important committees—Appropriations, Commerce, and Judiciary.[6] Committee chairs suffered some additional loss of power with a ban on proxy voting, the elimination of "rolling quorums" (which allowed committees to operate with less than a majority present), and reinforcement of certain open committee rules that prevent work from being done in executive session. Committee chairs were not total losers, however, as they gained the authority to appoint subcommittee staff and, if they were willing to work with party leaders, the authority to work out the details of Contract legislation.

In the short term, at least, there is no mystery about the actual and intended consequences of these reforms. The corporate party leadership, and the Speaker in particular, gained substantial power at the expense of committees and committee chairs. Leadership control of the agenda, fewer staff, diminished procedural powers, more open committee procedures, reduced protection on the floor, and the ultimate threat of simply being dismissed by party leaders transformed the balance of power for Republicans in the House. Where did this leave the new Republican chairs after a wait in the wilderness of minority status? "I'm just the *subchairman*," said Chairman Henry Hyde (R-Ill.) of the Judiciary Committee, acknowledging that the leadership-dominated schedule of the first hundred days had given the new committee leaders very little leeway (Cohen 1995).

Continuity and Change in the Senate

Although Republicans also regained control of the Senate in the 104th, the new majority party (which had been out of power in that chamber for only eight years) simply went about the business of switching offices and hiring new (but somewhat fewer) staff. This was, in part, a matter of experience. But it also stems from basic institutional differences. House rules are adopted anew at the beginning of each Congress along with any changes a majority supports. But the Senate operates as a continuing body, carrying its rules over from Congress to Congress. Thus, there were no dramatic rules changes, no committees were eliminated, and no changes were made in the authority of the party leaders. Pressures for reform certainly existed in the Senate but they tended to break along generational rather than ideological or partisan lines. By and large, younger senators with House experience and ties to Speaker Gingrich favored changes that would strengthen the hand of the majority leader, limit the power of seniority, and permit a more majoritarian (that is, Houselike) process to emerge.

On 2 March 1995, this core group became agitated when Appropriations Committee Chair Mark O. Hatfield (R-Ore.) voted against the balanced-budget amendment to the Constitution. The amendment failed by a single vote.[7] Some of the backbench group advocated stripping Hatfield of his chair for failing to support an otherwise unified Republican party. Majority Leader Robert Dole (R-Kan.) snuffed out the revolt at the price of agreeing to appoint a Republican task force, headed by Senator Connie Mack (R-Fla.), to study possible changes in the Conference's rules. Mack's task force returned to the Conference two months later with eight proposed rule changes designed to reduce the power of the committee chairs, enhance the power of the floor leader, and improve the leverage of rank-and-file members within the party (Dewar 1995; Hosansky 1995).

On 19 July 1995, the Republican Conference adopted most of the proposals. Republican committee leaders, like their House counterparts, are now limited to three two-year terms as chair of a full committee. This limitation also applies to each Republican-Party leadership position except the floor leader and the largely ceremonial president pro tempore. Another proposal that would have given the floor leader the power to nominate committee chairs—a process currently handled within committees and strictly according to seniority—was defeated. The reformers did succeed in adopting a secret-ballot procedure for the election of committee chairs that allows the leader to present a nominee in the event that the committee's choice failed to gain a majority from the Conference. Finally, the Republicans adopted a procedure for establishing a formal GOP legislative agenda *prior* to the election of committee chairs. The new agenda, which requires the support of three-fourths of the Republican Conference, is not binding upon members of the Conference but its adoption permits subsequent votes on chairs to be taken in light of members' positions on agenda items.

These new rules do not dramatically alter the character of the Senate. Seniority was not overthrown. The Republican leader has not gained much power. But they do move the Senate closer to the House in terms of the relations between committee leaders, party leaders, and the party groups. Secret ballots will allow dissatisfied senators to "send a message" to their colleagues, and term limits will force rotation in the system. Or, as the leader of the task force, Connie Mack, put it: "Basically, it's to enhance the leadership's authority and to encourage team play" (Hosansky 1995, 1392). The changes did not appeal to all senators. Orrin G. Hatch (R-Utah) was reported to be nonplussed when he said in response to the new rules: "Whatever they want to do." But others, such as Senator John McCain (R-Ariz.), wanted more: "It didn't go as far as I wanted, but we got the secret ballot" (Cloud 1995).

LEARNING CURVES AND ROADBLOCKS

As the 104th Congress commenced, the new Republican majority faced a series of roadblocks that would retard the learning process for committees. In some cases, as Fenno (1997) argues, these were self-imposed (or self-inflicted). Although much more acute in the House, the Senate experienced problems as well. The most important of the roadblocks include: leadership inexperience, task-force rivalries, an emphasis on partisan rather than policy oversight, staff cuts, and highly centralized agenda management. Leadership inexperience was exacerbated by an emphasis on the Contract that delayed the commencement of "normal" legislating. Staff cuts left Republicans with fewer resources than their Democratic predecessors enjoyed, but staff turnover (some would say purges) was more harmful than actual reductions. Of these, the centralized, leadership-determined agenda was the linchpin, because it prevented senior chairs from inheriting the power they so longed to obtain and ultimately left Gingrich vulnerable to an abortive coup in July 1997. In sum, these roadblocks meant that Republican committees got off to a slow start and many did not begin the learning process in earnest until the outset of the 105th Congress.

Committee Leader Experience

Experience obviously makes a good deal of difference for a new majority party. Indeed, the primary defense of the seniority system is that it ensures experienced leaders in positions that allegedly benefit from institutional memory. Establishing a committee agenda, hiring staff, managing a committee budget, forming coalitions, anticipating floor activity, and interacting with party leaders on scheduling matters can all be observed while one is in the minority. But, particularly in the House, they are *learned* through experience while in the majority. Thus, much has been made of the inexperience among majority Republicans of the 104th Congress: inexperience as a majority party, inexperience in positions of authority, and inexperience chairing a committee or subcommittee. As we will see, House Republicans of the 104th Congress were substantially disadvantaged by comparison to Senate Republicans. But *neither* group was much worse off, if worse of at all, than its predecessors in 1947 and 1981.

First, as we know, no House Republican had previously served in the majority and, therefore, none had ever chaired a House committee or subcommittee. By contrast, seventeen senators in the 104th Congress had experienced the last majority change (1981) and twenty-three 104th Congress senators had experienced majority-party status for part or all of the 1981–1986 period. Moreover, nine Republican committee chairs had experience chairing a Senate panel. This is not to say that House Republican chairs were totally inexperienced. The least senior of the new chairs were John Kasich (R-Ohio, six terms) on Budget and Larry Combest (R-Texas, five terms) on Intelligence—both panels with rotating memberships. The most senior, Jan Meyers (R-Kan.) of Small Business, Floyd Spence (R-S.C.) of National Security, and Bill Archer (R-Tex.) of Ways and Means, had served fourteen, twelve, and twelve terms, respectively. The entire group of chairs averaged more than nine terms in the House. But again, none had ever served in the majority party. And by contrast, the outgoing group of Democratic chairs had among them an even six hundred years of combined service in the House or, on average, 13.5 terms of service when they began the 103rd Congress.[8] How does this compare to previous Republican takeovers?

In 1947, Republicans regained a House majority for the first time in sixteen years and a Senate majority for the first time in fourteen years—to that point the longest periods of uninterrupted one-party rule in this century. In terms of experience, new Republican chairs of the 80th Congress, who would inhabit a new committee system created by the Legislative Reorganization Act of 1946, had served an average of 9.7 years in the House (see Table 5.2).[9] A modest proportion of House Republicans had previously served in the majority, but none of the new chairs had previous experience as chair. The longest-serving of the group was Ways and Means' Harold Knutson (R-Minn.), who had served sixteen years in the House but only eight on the committee. Circumstances in the Senate were little different. Average service for the new Republican chairs was 10.2 years. And only three of those—Albert Capper (R-Kan.) of Agriculture, Wallace H. White, Jr. (R-Maine) of Commerce, and Arthur H. Vandenberg (R-Mich.) of Foreign Relations—had experienced majority-party status.[10]

As the 104th Congress began, eighty-six Republicans became subcommittee chairs for the first time. Of those, thirty-nine gained subcommittee chairs on committees on which they had not previously held a ranking-member slot. Under the old Republican rules, committees were categorized in a fashion that paralleled the Democratic practice of exclusive, major, and nonmajor commit-

TABLE 5.2
NEW REPUBLICAN MAJORITIES AND THE EXPERIENCE OF
NEW CHAIRS: 80TH, 97TH, AND 104TH CONGRESSES
(AVERAGE NUMBER OF YEARS SERVED PRIOR TO PARTY CHANGE)

	Congress		
Chamber	*80th (1947–49)*	*97th (1981–83)*	*104th (1995–97)*
House	9.7	—	18.5
Senate	10.2	12.5	19.4

Source: 80th and 97th Congress calculated from Garrison Nelson, *Committees in the U.S. Congress 1947–1992 (Vol. 1: Committee Jurisdictions and their Rosters)*. Washington, D.C.: Congressional Quarterly, Inc. 1993. 104th Congress calculated from *Congressional Quarterly Weekly Report*, 25 March 1995 (Supplement to No. 12).

tees. From the 92nd to the 103rd Congresses, new Democratic subcommittee chairs on exclusive committees had served 11.4 years in the House while new subcommittee chairs on major and nonmajor committees had served 8.3 and 5.8 years, respectively. By contrast the thirty-nine "new" Republican subcommittee chairs in each of these categories—with Commerce counted in the exclusive category, as was their practice up to that time—had served 10.7 years, 5.9 years, and a scant 1.7 years in the House on average (see Deering 1996).

Inexperience? Yes. But majority Republicans were advantaged relative to their forebears in the 80th Congress, and clearly majority Republicans in the Senate faced no substantial obstacles in this respect. Moreover, it is fair to say that inexperience presented the greatest roadblock to chairs of exclusive and major-policy committees and a much less formidable roadblock to the chairs of more constituency-oriented committees—Floyd Spence (R-S.C.) on National Security, Don Young (R-Alaska) on Resources, and Bud Shuster (R-Pa.) on Transportation. Of these, Shuster is perhaps the best example. Aside from budget impacts, which were severe, Shuster's committee was relatively little affected by the Republican agenda. And throughout the 104th and into the 105th conference Shuster's panel patiently worked its way through a major rewrite of the nation's massive transportation program and commenced a battle to take the multibillion-dollar highway trust fund off budget.

Thinking about Term Limits

If experience is of any importance, positively or negatively, then term limits for committee chairs become the most intriguing of the Republican reforms. As noted earlier, both chambers have adopted a six-year term limit for full committee chairs and the House has a similar limit for subcommittee chairs. But both the timing and the form of each chamber's rule is consequential. In the House, term limits are not totally unusual inasmuch as the Budget, Intelligence, and Standards committees all have had rotating membership.

The House Republicans first adopted term limits for ranking members in the 103rd Congress—a restriction that applied only to Conference members. Thus, sixteen of the nineteen standing committee chairs of the 104th Congress already had two years "on the clock." But the Republicans ignored this fact in writing their new rule, partly on the grounds that the shift in party control necessitated resetting the clock. The new rule (Rule X 6[b]) reads as follows: "No member may serve as the chairman of the same standing committee, or as the chairman of the same subcommittee thereof, for more than three consecutive Congresses, beginning with the One Hundred and Fourth Congress (disregarding for this purpose any service for less than a full session in any Congress)."

In addition, Republican Conference rules limit members to a single committee or subcommittee chair (as do Democratic Caucus rules) and prohibit top party leaders from serving as chairs.[11] As written, the rule does not prevent a term-limited member from becoming chair of another committee or subcommittee, nor does it clearly proscribe such a member from regaining a chair after a two-year hiatus. The Senate limitation applies only to committee chairs and only to Republicans, but it is worded more strictly: "A Senator shall serve no more than six years as chair and six years as ranking member of any standing committee, effective in January 1997" (Rule V[B]). Thus, as stated, and unlike the House rule, a senator might serve in a committee leadership position for twelve years, but could not then become chair of another committee. And, assuming continued chamber control, a senator's service might be limited to six years.[12]

As the first round of forced turnover approaches, some critics have emerged. Representative Don Young (R-Alaska), who will vacate the Chair on Natural Resources, said the rule was "a stupid idea to begin with"(Gugliotta 1998b). Representative W. J. "Billy" Tauzin (R-La.), for example, has spearheaded a move that would alter or abolish the House rotation rule. "Imagine," Tauzin said, "the mad scramble, the controversy, the unnecessary bitter fights" (Palmer 1997). Late in 1997, Tauzin met with Speaker Gingrich to make his case, but the likelihood of a rules change appears remote. Indeed, proponents of congressional term limits link the two issues closely. Thus, most rank-and-file House Republicans appear to oppose any relaxation, much less the abolition, of the rule. In the House, where the first forced rotations are less than three years away, impacts have already been felt but they seem unlikely to reach the levels Tauzin has predicted.

At the outset of the 105th Congress, three committees were chaired by individuals below the top seniority slot—Bob Smith (R-Ore.) of Agriculture, Livingston on Appropriations, and James M. Talent (R-Mo.) on Small Business.

Smith retired at the end of the 105th Congress and the Livingston case has been discussed. On Small Business, however, the top two Republicans declined the chair in favor of subcommittee positions with greater electoral impact: Larry Combest (R-Tex.) for an Agriculture subcommittee and Joel Hefley (R-Colo.) for a National Security subcommittee. With Smith's retirement, Combest now stands in line to chair the full Agriculture Committee, a move that would leave Talent secure in his position beyond the first major shift.

The magnitude of change is further softened by the current Republican seniority structure. Thirteen of the sixteen House committees without rotation currently have chairs serving a second consecutive term. However, five current House chairs stand second on another House committee: Don Young (R-Alaska) chairs Resources and is second on Transportation; Benjamin Gilman (R-N.Y.) chairs International Relations and is second on Government Reform and Oversight; Bob Stump (R-Ariz.) chairs Veterans' Affairs and is second on National Security; Bill Goodling (R-Pa.) chairs Education and the Workforce and is second on International Relations; and James Sensenbrenner (R-Wis.) chairs Science and is second on Judiciary. Young and Shuster of Transportation have indicated their intention to seek the senior spot on another committee. Others are likely to follow that pattern. Only Henry Hyde has said he's content to simply relinquish his leadership role: "Having tasted the glory of chairmanship, I can live without it. I enjoy being a member. I ask only that I can put my two cents in" (Gugliotta 1998b). The impact of term limits would appear to be less than Tauzin and some others predict, with, at most, about half the incoming chairs being "new."

Impacts in the Senate are much less certain and probably hinge on the interpretation of the existing rule. Strictly enforced, the rule will require all standing committee chairs to step aside. And, although it is early, only one committee is certain to experience a leadership change prior to the 108th Congress. Senator Strom Thurmond (R-S.C.) relinquished his post on Armed Services at the end of the 105th Congress. This move allowed Senator John Warner (R-Va.) a long-sought opportunity to chair that committee and removes Armed Services from the cycle of change. Should senators be permitted to move to another committee chair, however, the venerable Senate tradition of musical chairs will continue. As has long been the case, the Senate's most senior members rank near the top of at least two committees.[13]

In sum, term limits for chairs will have an impact, but not as severe an impact as some might think insofar as the actual event is concerned. On the other hand, the impact on members' careers may be more complicated than has been presumed to date. For example, the House already has lost at least one member because of the rule and political circumstances back home. Representative Pat Roberts (R-Kan.) abandoned the chairmanship of House Agriculture after only two years to seek and win one of two open Kansas Senate seats. Roberts was the first sitting chair to run for a Senate seat in 60 years.

In other instances, the rule appears to have postponed career-ending decisions. Early in 1998, Representative Robert Livingston (R-La.) announced that he intended to retire at the end of the 105th Congress to pursue a more lucrative career in Washington lobbying (Pianin 1998). The move also would have ended his long-running battles with the Republican leadership over how to run the Appropriations Committee. Within forty-eight hours, however, Livingston reversed his decision and indicated his intention remain at the helm of Appropriations through the six years allowed under the rule. Further, Livingston declared that he would be a candidate for Speaker if Gingrich decided to resign in 1999 to make a run at the presidency. Poor election returns and criticisms from within the party induced Gingrich to resign earlier than expected, and Livingston translated his front-runner status into easy victory in the GOP Conference. Only a month later, however, Livingston shocked House members by announcing his own resignation as he too fell victim to disclosures about his personal life.

Livingston is not alone in prolonging his House career for reasons related to the new rule. In 1997, Tauzin, who stands second on Resources and on Commerce, announced that he would remain in the House rather than run for a Louisiana Senate seat. Although he did not say so publicly, his decision is presumed to have been based, in part, on the prospect of chairing the Commerce Committee. Representative Doug Bereuter (R-Neb.) *was* explicit in declaring that he would pass up a run for governor in hopes of succeeding Gilman as chairman of the International Relations Committee. But Bereuter ranks fifth on the Committee behind four other members, all of whom are currently full committee chairmen. Any one of them might stake a claim to the position and be in a good position to gain it. If the Tauzin and Bereuter cases are indicative, term limits will actually prolong some House careers. In other cases, however, particularly when senior members are forced to step down, it may lead to retirements.

Likewise, party leaders may have to choose at an earlier point whether to pursue leadership or committee careers in the House. For example, Representative John A. Boehner (R-Ohio), currently chair of the Republican Conference, stands third on the House Oversight Committee and will be no worse than third on Agriculture in the 106th Congress. Before long, assuming he remains on the leadership ladder, he will face a decision regarding whether to be a committee leader or a party leader.[14]

Agenda Control: The Contract and Congress's False Start

During the first one hundred days of the 104th Congress, House committees worked at a virtually unprecedented pace to achieve the promises made in the

TABLE 5.3
WORKLOAD INDICATORS FOR RECENT FIRST SESSIONS

			Year	
Indicator	1991	1993	1995	1997
Days in Session				
Senate	158	153	211	153
House	154	142	168	132
Hours in Session				
Senate	1201	1270	1839	1093
House	939	982	1525	1004
Average Daily Hours				
Senate	7.6	8.3	8.7	7.1
House	6.1	6.9	9.1	7.6
Public Laws	243	210	88	153
Recorded Votes				
Senate	280	395	613	298
House	444	615	885	640

Source: *Calendars of the United States House of Representatives and History of Legislation,* and "Daily Digest," *Congressional Record.*

Contract with America. Leaders and members of those committees tolerated the intrusions, but they were not always pleased with the pace required to shape the sometimes complex pieces of legislation that had been entrusted to them. The breakneck pace is, perhaps, unmatched in terms of the scope of the committees involved and the brevity of the time taken to produce the bills. During the first one hundred days, the House was in session for 58 days, for 528 hours, took 293 roll-call votes, and held 688 hearings and 134 markups. In each case these levels of activity far exceeded the first one hundred days of the previous Congress and normal levels of activity for the previous two decades.[15] And, although the remainder of the session proceeded at a more sedate pace, this first session stands in stark contrast to the two Congresses prior to it and to the one just completed. Ironically, as the data in Table 5.3 demonstrate, members worked harder in the first session of the 104th Congress but achieved dramatically less—using public laws as an indicator—than typical first sessions of recent years.

It was not without costs. The rapid pace of the Contract House exposed sensitive nerves and wore people out. Reelection-oriented members spent little time at home. Experienced chairs expected something different from majority status than what they got. Rank-and-file Republicans, like most revolutionaries, were impatient to succeed instantly and did not want committees getting in the way.

And the leadership's attention to the agenda was driven, from the bottom up, by first- and second-term members. The combination proved somewhat disastrous in the first session of the 104th Congress, and forced retrenchment and risked defeat in the second.

Some veteran Democrats squawked about the pace. Representative Henry Waxman (D-Calif.)—an experienced legislator, subcommittee chair, and political infighter—expressed his dismay early in 1995:

> What we're doing is demeaning the legislative process. All of this [Contract legislation] has been mushed together to make a political statement. . . . Everything is moving so quickly that the public and the press don't have a chance to absorb what's going on. Democrats have tried but we have not been successful in getting the Republicans to engage. (Cohen 1995)

Sour grapes? In part, certainly. But with the exception of the partisan end, Waxman's opinion reflected that of many new Republican chairs as well.

After the Contract and the first one hundred days of the 104th Congress had been successfully negotiated, the Speaker and his new Republican majority did not rest on their laurels. Gingrich continued to take a strong and direct interest in what his committees were producing. He circumvented the Ways and Means and Commerce Committees to form an ad hoc group on Medicare policy. He intervened in heated negotiations regarding a cost-cutting rewrite of agriculture subsidy programs, and ultimately dictated the removal of dairy provisions to preserve the deal. He ignored a bill produced by the Appropriations Committee's District of Columbia Subcommittee and, in effect, ordered a new one written by the same group. He rejected portions of a telecommunications bill crafted and passed by the Commerce Committee. And, he dictated the inclusion of policy riders on a variety of appropriations bills in spite of opposition from Appropriations Committee Chairman Livingston—a tactic that allowed President Clinton to gain public-relations points by vetoing several of the bills.

For the most part, Republican committee chairs tolerated these intrusions as the necessary costs of success. Said Bill Archer of Texas, Chairman of the Ways and Means Committee, "I accept that because that's part of making something happen. In the end, you have to be part of the process. You don't run out there like the Lone Ranger and do whatever you want to do" (Koszczuk 1995, 3049). Likewise, Representative Henry J. Hyde (R-Ill.), Chair of the Judiciary Committee, allowed the contract to dictate his committee's agenda to the exclusion of his own interests: "There has not been time to implement items of my personal agenda. But they are small potatoes. I'm fully in accord with the priorities of the leadership. . . . On the whole, it is a salutary way to proceed, because we have focus and direction, not drift" (Koszczuk 1995, 3052). They were tolerant, but they were not always entirely happy. After having his appropriations bill dumped, District of Columbia Subcommittee Chairman James T. Walsh (R-N.Y.) said: "[Speaker Gingrich] brings an awful lot to the table, so you may have resources, financial and otherwise, that you didn't know you had. The down side is, you do your best to put a bill together going through the normal process and all of a sudden it's not the normal process anymore" (Koszczuk 1995, 3052).

Committees thrive on "normal process." Like most institutional arrangements, they provide predictability and stability to organizations like Congress. In the House more than the Senate, their routines have become a defining characteristic of a relatively efficient but typically decentralized organizational structure. Put somewhat differently, committees are conservative—in a bureaucratic sense. High levels of partisanship, centralized leadership, and effective agenda setting all compromise committee autonomy, as we have seen. But these circumstances, at least in their intense form, are usually ephemeral. Thus, during the second session of the 104th Congress, some slack had appeared in the tight reins Gingrich had held on committee activity. Committee leaders used leadership meetings to complain about the use of task forces. Representative Bill Goodling (R-Pa.), who chairs the Education and the Workforce Committee, sounded a familiar complaint: "I feel very strongly that all policy decisions should be made by the authorizing committees. In order to carry out the agenda in the last Congress, you had to cut corners. It's our work to do, let us do it. The committee process works very well if you just allow it to." Representative Rick A. Lazio (R-N.Y.) echoed Goodling's comments: "There is a clear sense that the committees have the proper vetting process, they have the proper expertise . . . so that people don't get blindsided." (Koszczuk 1997, 2575–77).

Legislating by Task Force

The formation of leadership task forces, which reach across committees to draw interested legislators into the legislative process, is the most visible threat to committee autonomy of recent years. During the first two months of the 104th Congress (1995–1996) Gingrich had established five temporary and ten permanent task forces and working groups on a variety of issues facing the first Republican-controlled Congress in forty years. Five of these task forces were organized to fashion key elements of the Contract with America—on regulatory reform, crime, term limits, welfare, and legal reform. The remainder, which have no specific deadlines, were directed to consider specific issues, such as immigration or disabilities, or were directed to reach out to specific constituencies or potential constituencies of the party, such as the entertainment industry (chaired by the late Sonny Bono of California) and minorities (chaired by Representatives James C. Talent of Missouri and J. C. Watts of Oklahoma). Task forces bring together legislators from different committees and, frequently, with differing points of view. They are intended to short-circuit the turf-conscious committee system and to fashion legislation that might otherwise be bottled up by or reformulated in ways that suited committee members but not party members. As the Speaker's primary spokesman, Tony Blankley, put it: "We envision using task forces a lot . . . as a device for finessing some institutional obstacles to decision-making" (Kalb 1995).

A more recent development in the House is the creation of bipartisan task forces by the joint leadership or the inclusion of like-minded minority-party members on majority-party task forces. In the first session of the 101st Congress (1989–1990), task forces on the reform of congressional ethics and campaign finance held many hearings and, in the case of congressional ethics, eventually devised legislation (Hook 1989). Partisan differences on campaign-finance practices proved too wide for that task force to bridge. In the 104th Congress, Gingrich's task force on immigration included a handful of conservative and moderate Democrats, and Republicans announced that task-force membership would be available for selected Democrats (Kalb 1995).

Senate Majority Leader George J. Mitchell (D-Maine) created several Democratic task forces to address issues that crossed committees' jurisdictional lines—on rural development and government ethics, for example. Unlike earlier House counterparts, Mitchell's task-force strategy included bill formation, a characteristic that annoyed some committee chairs. During the first session of the 105th Congress, Majority Leader Trent Lott (R-Miss.) established six task forces to help shape the Senate's agenda, but not to draft bills, on education, the environment, campaign-finance reform, retirement security, health care, and the workplace. The advantage, as Senator Robert F. Bennett (R-Utah) put it, is that "the cement is a little more liquid in a task force. It hardens later on" (Cassata 1997, 1384).

Committee and subcommittee chairs have become nervous about and hostile toward task forces, which have begun to look more like committees—by having formal membership rosters, appointing leaders, holding hearings, and proposing legislation (Kenworthy 1991). Task forces cannot, in a formal sense, draft and report legislation to their parent chamber. For the most part, they remain opportunities to build bridges, brainstorm, and advertise positions. But critics have bemoaned their secrecy, partisanship, and, in some cases, the close but exclusive links they forge with organized interests. And they can also expose party splits and create hostilities. For example, in March of 1996 Speaker Gingrich formed another task force to formulate a Republican legislative strategy on the environment. When it came time to appoint task-force members, House Resources Committee Chairman Don Young (R-Alaska) skipped over Representative H. James Saxton (R-N.J.), who chaired a relevant subcommittee, to suggest Representative Richard W. Pombo of California, a more junior member of the full committee. That move apparently did not sit well with Saxton and underscored a split between eastern and western Republicans on a variety of environmental issues (Freedman 1996).

By the end of the 104th Congress, Gingrich and his fellow party leaders were feeling the heat from committee chairs. Gingrich recognized the problem, but did not give up hope: "I would like to simultaneously strengthen the committee chairs and the task force system, and do it in a way that [produces] a very sophisticated, integrated system. Whether or not that's possible, I'm not sure yet" (Koszczuk 1996b). It was not possible. At the outset of the 105th Congress, Gingrich narrowly won reelection as Speaker and was forced to backtrack on his efforts to deprive committee chairs of their independence. There were no new efforts to empower task forces and Republican party leaders made it clear that, on most matters, committees would be allowed to shape initial legislative proposals without leadership dictation. As Judiciary Chairman Hyde put it: "I think there is a general mood of granting more autonomy to the committee chairmen. I think there will be fewer dictates and fewer mandates" (Freedman 1996).

Gingrich's position vis-à-vis committees was further compromised in July when a group of dissident Republicans discussed the prospect of replacing the Speaker. The group, which was comprised largely of newer members, did not get an entirely cold shoulder from several senior members of the leadership. But no clear replacement emerged and the plot fell through. Many rank-and-file members believed that Gingrich's slide in national polls compromised his capacity to lead the party. But the rank-and-file could not fill the vacuum either. Thus, with the Speaker backing off, it is arguable that committees became even freer to go about the process of normal legislating.

Oversight Overlooked

For most of the 104th Congress, new Republican chairs paid scant attention to investigative oversight. The lack of effort was partly attributable to the all-consuming focus upon the Contract. According to Representative Christopher Shays (R-Conn.): "None of us had been in the majority before. We were so involved with the Contract with America that many did not pay attention to oversight" (Freedman 1997, 2651). Lack of experience on the part of committee chairs, an inclination to take direction on virtually all activity from the centralized leadership team, and the reduced authority of subcommittee chairs contributed as well. Former Government Reform and Oversight Chair Bill Clinger (R-Pa.) concluded, "We were in a learning mode from the beginning" (Freedman 1997, 2651). Reductions in full committee staff and the virtual elimination of independent subcommittee staff further hampered GOP committee efforts.

But perhaps most of all, a tendency to focus on what appeared to be purely "payback" partisan hearings—on the Whitewater affair, presidential-campaign finance, and the Dornan–Sanchez and Landrieu–Jenkins election contests—

sidetracked Republican efforts regarding big government, siphoned off press attention, and failed to garner much public interest. Of these investigations, only the Commerce Subcommittee on Oversight and Investigations' review of Energy Secretary Hazel O'Leary's globe-trotting netted much of substance. "I think that perhaps there has been too much emphasis on the scandal side of things," Clinger said. "I'm not saying that is a useless effort. But there should be some balancing and looking at some of the darker sides of bureaucracy" (Freedman 1997).

The key distinction is between oversight that focused on the Republican agenda—most notably on government's size and intrusiveness—and partisan oversight that focused more upon the Democrats and their president. The latter types of efforts failed to strike a chord with the American public, already jaded and cynical about politics and politicians. Indeed, although a majority of those polled said they watched hearings on Iran-Contra, the Persian Gulf, and the Federal Raid on Waco very closely or fairly closely, fewer than 40 percent reported a similar level of interest in the Whitewater, Ruby Ridge, or campaign-contributions hearings. The "us versus them" tone did not help. As freshman Senator Sam Brownback (R-Kan.) put it: "It's a Congress controlled by one party investigating the president of another party, and the public is highly suspicious of that" (Koszczuk and Carr 1997; see also Fritz 1998).

Republican oversight efforts fared better and committee members learned more when they stuck to Republican issues of government size and intrusiveness. The most dramatic achievement in this regard came with Senate Finance's three days of hearings into IRS abuses of taxpayers. The issue, which brings the tax code, abusive big government, and average citizens all into focus, was made to order. "This has put us back on the right track," said Billy Tauzin. "The party needs a big idea, and if you want a really big idea, one that really captivates people, what could be better" (Weisman 1997a). Legislation emerged in both chambers and, with the administration backing off, House Ways and Means reported IRS reform legislation by a lopsided bipartisan vote. By early November the House had passed the bill. But its stampede was met by the Senate's inclination to milk the issue a bit longer. Finance Chair William V. Roth (R-Del.) announced his intention to hold additional hearings during the second session before considering the legislation: "This is a very important reform. We have to do it right" (Weisman 1997b). And had House-committee Republicans learned anything from all this? "The hearings on the IRS were an object lesson to most," said House Majority Leader Richard Armey. "Basically, you could see the lights go on" (Freedman 1997).

CONCLUSION

During the early days of the 104th Congress, committee chairs felt bound to deliver on the promises of the Contract. By the end of the 104th Congress, however, fissures had appeared in the Republican coalition, leaders were somewhat less united than they had been, and committee chairs felt freer to stray from the wishes of their party generals. These developments were caused, in part, by fallout from the previous year's budget deadlock with President Clinton, internal party disagreements about how to handle pressing agenda items, the plummet of Speaker Gingrich's public support, and the approach of the 1996 elections. "All the factions are equally unhappy," said Representative Thomas Petri (R-Wis.) (Koszczuk 1996a). But these developments also say something about the staying power of institutions and the personal *and* collective value members derive from them. The haste with which the Contract legislation was produced and its fate in the Senate suggest that Congress simply does not work at that pace as a matter of routine. Revolutions can be very tiring; that is why they are so difficult to sustain. Representative Fred Upton (R-Mich.) seemed to agree: "We've had a long legislative session, between last year and this year, and you have a lot of frayed nerves out there" (Koszczuk 1997).

It is not surprising, therefore, that the first session of the 105th Congress looked more normal to many observers (Koszczuk 1996; Elving 1997). The legislative pace, as indicated earlier, was nearly identical to that of 1991 and 1993. Committees in both chambers operated more independently and, to judge from preliminary evidence, the dominance of House full committees, a feature of the 104th Congress, had faded a bit while the status quo, unchanged in the 104th, held in the Senate. To be sure, House chairs were still struggling to get their footing—in legislation and in oversight. But both chambers passed fairly important bills, and the Appropriations Committees and their subcommittees finished work on thirteen separate bills more or less on time and without the rancor of a government shutdown.

To conclude, three observations—consistent with Fenno's argument—seem warranted. First, concentration on the Contract prevented "normal" legislating from commencing at the outset of the 104th Congress, and success in getting all the Contract items to the floor emboldened the leadership in its quest to revolutionize the legislative process. For at least the first session and arguably for all of the 104th Congress, the centralized leadership agenda prevented most committees, and especially the prestige and policy committees, from commencing the sometimes arduous task of legislating. Timetables dictated the use of "unorthodox" law-making (Sinclair 1997). By the time sufficient pressure had built up to alter course, few committees or committee chairs had the opportunity to descend the learning curve. This meant that most chairs did not really begin to learn until the 105th. The stunted learning effects were more pronounced in the House than in the Senate, but inasmuch as the Senate followed the House's lead on the agenda for the most part, it too "wasted" half of, if not a whole, Congress.

Second, the party-driven agenda affected learning in both legislative and oversight activities. The legislative effect dictated that the new Republican chairs ignored their "experience" as committee members and/or ranking members in order to accommodate an externally driven agenda. It further necessitated a focus on matters that were more highly charged than the new chairs might otherwise have chosen. The example of the agriculture-reform legislation noted earlier is apposite. Likewise, a tendency to focus on partisan oversight probably stole from Republican committee chairs a year of time and experience in assembling a successful oversight program.

Third, the leadership itself fell into a trap by energizing newly-elected Republicans with revolutionary rhetoric and finding that they needed to heed threats from this group when the agenda strayed back toward a more moderate course. That is, the top–bottom link cut out the chairs, frustrating them in the process, and forestalled a period of meaningful legislative learning. On the other hand, to the extent that it weakened Gingrich's position, it might also have accelerated the countertrend toward increased committee autonomy in the 105th Congress. The second session of the 105th Congress proved to be somewhat more productive than the first—though neither will be remembered as a landmark. Chairs grew even more comfortable with their positions. But the battle was not quite over. The quickness with which Republican leaders marched the IRS bill to the floor, while the Senate put off final hearings and legislation until an election year, may demonstrate that there is a residual tendency to dictate from the top. Also, should rank-and-file Republicans succumb to the presidential rhetoric of Steve Forbes, who demanded that Republican congressional leaders "fight for substance and principle rather than trying to hold on to office for the sake of holding office," then the learning curve might again be disrupted.

Committees are conservative institutions, in a bureaucratic sense. As institutional features they thrive on normal process and are disrupted by unconventional process. To the extent that careers are invested in them, members are resistant to events that threaten their power. Term limits might well alter that dynamic to some degree. But so long as seniority remains a factor, parties do not remain galvanized for long periods of time, and the institution is judged by its "productivity," then committees are likely to prove resilient, useful, and powerful to one degree or another.

NOTES

The author wishes to thank Colton Campbell, Roger Davidson, Kevin Hill, Forrest Maltzman, Nicol Rae, Priscilla Regan, Lee Sigelman, and the participants in "The Impact of the New Majority: Republican Control of Congress," for helpful comments, suggestions, and observations.

1. The reference to Tsunamis is attributable to Larry Evans and Walt Oleszek (1997). The continuity-amidst-change argument is consistent with the evidence produced by Hall and McKissick (1997) in their analysis of institutional reforms and decision making in House committees.

2. Sarah A. Binder (1997) has a much more fully formed statement of the relationship between majority-party strength and minority-party rights in Congress and, therefore, upon institutional development. My point here is, I believe, in concert with Binder's analysis—although slightly more focused upon the "punctuated equilibria" that characterize institutional development and change. The notion of punctuated equilibria is from Baumgartner and Jones (1993).

3. Actually, point one of the Contract read: "Apply All Laws to Congress." But internal reforms were embraced under this rubric from an early point. The act embracing congressional accountability to federal laws passed on 17 January, and was signed by the president on 23 January 1995. In a change from the recent practice of altering caucus or conference rules—which applied only *within* the respective parties—most of these important changes were written into the standing rules of the House. Thus, if Republicans wish to repeal the rules they will need a public vote on the House floor. And if Democrats regain the majority they will have to do likewise. This puts either group in the potentially awkward position of repealing reforms. Proposals to relax term limits, discussed later in the paper, have been stoutly criticized by younger members.

4. In a change from the recent practice of altering caucus or conference rules—which apply only *within* the respective parties—most of these important changes were written into the standing rules of the House. Thus, if Republicans wish to repeal the rules they will need a public vote on the House floor. And if Democrats regain the majority they will have to do likewise. This puts either group in the potentially awkward position of repealing reforms. Proposals to relax term limits, discussed later in the paper, have been stoutly criticized by younger members. For more on reforms see Deering and Smith (1997).

5. The committees did not disappear altogether. The District Committee became a subcommittee on Government Reform and Oversight, Merchant Marine and Fisheries was split between the Resources and the Transportation committees, and Post Office and Civil Service became two subcommittees, also on Government Reform and Oversight.

6. The three violations of seniority—reminiscent of violations at the outset of the post–Watergate 94th Congress—turned somewhat less on ideology than upon energy and capacity. On Appropriations, Robert Livingston's (R-La.) appointment might have been made anyway, but the senior committee Republican, Joseph M. McDade (R-Pa.) was under the cloud of a federal bribery indictment and was ineligible to serve as chair under a new Republican Conference rule. In the other two cases the senior Republican

on the committee was Carlos J. Moorhead (R-Calif.). But Moorhead was passed over largely because of a relative lack of assertiveness rather than for ideological reasons. His party-support scores fell below 90 only once in his career and the liberal ADA organization rated him as high as 10 only once. By contrast, Gingrich permitted Gerald B.H. Solomon (R-N.Y.) to become chair of the Rules Committee even though Solomon had briefly opposed Gingrich for Speaker when Robert H. Michel (R-Ohio) retired. Solomon, whose party-support scores were slightly lower and ADA scores slightly higher than Moorhead's, opposed his party on several visible issues. Solomon had advanced to become ranking member of the Rules Committee in the 102nd Congress when the more senior but aging Representative Jamie Quillen (R-Tenn.) stepped down as ranking member during the Republican organizing meetings of December 1990. Although seniority was violated in each of these cases, the Republicans did not dip far into the lower ranks of committee members. Only Livingston ranked less than second on his respective panel. Republicans violated seniority again in the 105th Congress when freshman Representative Bob Smith (R-Ore.) was named chair of the Agriculture Committee after Kansas Representative Pat Roberts retired to run for one of Kansas's vacant Senate seats. Smith had been lured out of a two-year retirement with the promise of a chair when GOP leaders feared the loss of the Oregon seat due to a scandal surrounding Representative Wes Cooley. Smith had served six previous terms on the committee. Smith's brief encore concluded with the end of the 105th Congress.

7. Technically, the amendment failed by two votes because Dole switched sides at the last moment to ensure his parliamentary right to offer a motion to reconsider at a later date. That motion failed as well.

8. These figures include the abolished committees—Post Office, District of Columbia, and Merchant Marine. Excluding them does not change the average seniority of the Democratic chairs appreciably.

9. This figure includes the House Un-American Activities Committee and the other standing committees of the 80th Congress.

10. Of the three, only Capper, with 28 years in the Senate (and on the Committee), had a chance to chair a committee of substance. By the 72nd Congress he had risen to third on Agriculture and chaired the District of Columbia Committee. Vandenberg entered the Senate in April 1929 (71st Congress) and chaired the Committee on Enrolled bills in the 72nd Congress, second session. White was a freshman in the Republican 72nd Congress.

11. The first rule (Rule 15) excludes House Oversight, Standards, and joint, select, and special committees but includes a waiver. The second rule (Rule 2) includes the Speaker, floor leader, whip, conference chair, policy committee chair, and campaign committee chair. This group also is limited to membership on a single committee.

12. Senate Republican rules also prohibit full committee chairs from being chair (or ranking member) of any other committee or subcommittee—with the Rules and Administration Committee excepted.

13. Thurmond is senior Republican on three committees at present, Jesse Helms on three, Frank Murkowski on two, William Roth on two, and Ted Stevens on two. As this was being written, several calls to the Hill and one knowledgeable journalist failed to elicit a definitive interpretation on the rule.

14. Boehner currently avoids the existing requirement on committee assignments because, as indicated in note 11, House Oversight is exempt from the one-committee rule.

15. These data are from Gill and Thurber (1997). They conclude, inter alia, that the rapid pace reduced efficiency and deliberation and increased member dependence upon party cues for making legislative decisions.

PART THREE

Reforming the Legislative Process

CHAPTER SIX

Procedural Features of House Republican Rule

C. LAWRENCE EVANS AND WALTER J. OLESZEK

INTRODUCTION

The November 1994 election results, Czar Newt, the Contract, budgetary gridlock and government shutdowns, the "new Newt," Bob Livingston, and now Speaker Hastert. So far, the colorful personalities and events of the Republican Congress have passed by like a wave, providing new congressional anecdotes and raising enrollments in college courses about the legislative process. But can the Republican-controlled House teach us much about the nature of Congress as an institution? Does it have important ramifications for our theories of legislative structure and procedure?

In this chapter, we answer both questions with a qualified "yes." Section 1 summarizes the leading theoretical perspectives on congressional organization, particularly as they relate to the role of party-leadership prerogatives in the House of Representatives. In section 2 we briefly outline the diverse ways such procedural powers can affect lawmaking in the chamber, and argue that leadership prerogatives primarily matter because they can be used to focus institutional attention on issues that unite the majority party and overcome the political, procedural, and other obstacles to passing legislation. In section 3 we evaluate our arguments by exploring how House Republican leaders employed their procedural powers during the 1995–1997 time period.

HOUSE PROCEDURE AND THEORIES OF LEGISLATIVE ORGANIZATION

Throughout this chapter, we adopt a fairly broad view about what constitutes legislative procedure, structure, and organization (the terms are used inter-

117

changeably). By procedure, we are referring to the entire range of institutional features that can influence legislation. "Procedure" includes everything from party caucus rules and chamber precedents to the House rules that allocate staff and the special resolutions governing floor debate. As mentioned, we are especially interested in the formal prerogatives and informal powers that the House majority leadership uses to affect the timing and content of legislative outcomes.

Members of the House have a constitutional right to determine the internal structure of the chamber. These rules and procedures, however, are typically fashioned by the majority party. Because lawmakers view procedure and policy as closely related, the decisions they make on procedural matters are strategic and often subject to dispute. Within days of the 1994 elections, for instance, incoming Speaker Newt Gingrich and other GOP leaders announced major alterations in the House's procedural structure. Most observers argued that these changes were intended to enhance the Speaker's prerogatives and to make the committee system more accountable to the leadership and the GOP Conference.

These events on Capitol Hill coincided with renewed scholarly interest in the origins and impact of congressional organization. One perspective, entitled *Conditional Party Government* (CPG), derives from David Rohde's (1991) classic study of congressional parties, and a series of important papers Rohde has coauthored with John Aldrich (1995; see also Cox and McCubbins 1990). According to CPG theory, when policy preferences within the majority-party caucus or conference are homogeneous, majority-party lawmakers will delegate significant procedural prerogatives and informal powers to the Speaker, and party leaders will use these tools to advance the party's legislative program. The result, according to Aldrich and Rohde, is legislative outcomes that can diverge significantly from the policy preferences of the median voter in the chamber toward the preferences of the median voter within the majority party. They argue that such outcomes have regularly occurred in the Republican House, especially in 1995.

Conditional Party Government theory has been challenged by Keith Krehbiel (1998; see also Brady and Volden 1998), who argues that procedure and policy in the contemporary House are primarily *majoritarian*; that is, responsive to the interests of the chamber median. He points out that, absent perfect-preference homogeneity within the majority, certain members of the majority party will prefer the floor median to the majority-party median. Why would these lawmakers be willing to provide leaders with the procedural powers and political support sufficient to move policy from the floor median to an outcome they value less highly? And, Krehbiel observes, if preferences within the majority party are very homogeneous, then the chamber and majority-party medians become indistinguishable. Under such conditions, the preference-induced momentum behind the chamber/party median is so strong that there is little need for a procedurally empowered leadership. Rather than conditional party government, Krehbiel argues, legislative outcomes in the House are primarily determined by the preferences of the "pivotal voter" within the chamber—the lawmaker at the median of the preference distribution in the House.

Although the two views are fundamentally different, both capture important aspects of the legislative process. Consistent with CPG theory, congressional history reveals that lawmakers have been more likely to increase the procedural powers of the House Speaker when policy preferences within the majority party are relatively homogeneous. Many of the institutional changes implemented during the 1994 House Republican transition clearly were intended to give Gingrich the tools necessary to advance the remarkably ambitious GOP agenda. And, as significant divisions emerged within the Republican Conference, power tended to devolve somewhat toward the standing committee system.

The sheer quantity of partisan activity occurring on Capitol Hill is also consistent with CPG theory. The majority party organizes the House and drafts chamber rules. Members are assigned to panels by their party's Committee on Committees. Votes on procedural matters typically are more partisan than votes on substantive issues. House party leaders set the legislative agenda and play key roles in negotiating with Senate leaders and the executive branch. If party leaders and the procedural prerogatives they employ do not significantly influence policy, then why is so much congressional activity fundamentally partisan?

Still, Krehbiel's arguments, and the majoritarian perspective more generally, should not be dismissed. High levels of partisan activity in the House do not necessarily imply high levels of partisan power. And the use of procedural prerogatives and tactics is constrained by the majoritarian nature of the chamber. Consider the amendment rules devised by the House Rules Committee. CPG theorists rightly point out that the Rules Committee is an arm of the Speaker, and that decision making on amendment rules tends to be highly partisan and strongly influenced by majority-party leaders. However, no special resolution reported by the panel has force unless it can secure at least 218 votes on the floor. Members and staff of the Rules Committee routinely describe their panel as highly partisan, but they also emphasize that rules are always crafted with an eye toward House acceptance. The leadership, Rules Committee, and parliamentary staffers with whom we have spoken can describe examples of procedure being used to move outcomes away from the chamber median toward the party median, but there is little evidence that such distortions occur systematically. Legislative scholars should carefully consider the questions Krehbiel has raised about the logical consistency and explanatory power of CPG theory.

When Leadership Prerogatives Matter

The differences between the CPG and majoritarian perspectives raise some fundamental questions about the linkages between congressional structure and policy outcomes, particularly relating to the conditions under which leadership powers and congressional procedures have an independent impact on the contents of legislation. We believe that procedure and parties do matter a great deal, but we also are sympathetic to Krehbiel's arguments about the pivotal role of the chamber median.

It is useful to consider why party leadership powers are granted and utilized. In the House, party leaders typically employ procedural prerogatives to accomplish one or more of the following goals.[1]

Promote Committee Accountability

Lawmakers typically self-select the committees on which they serve, and they usually choose panels that appeal to important constituencies back home. The nature of the committee assignment process raises the potential of cross-pressure between constituency and party interests on issues that matter to the leadership. Although the relative powers of party and committee leaders vary over time, all House Speakers have had formal prerogatives that provide them with important leverage vis-à-vis committee leaders and members. These prerogatives can be used to make the standing committee system more accountable to the majority-party caucus or conference.

Advance or Delay Legislative Initiatives

In committee and on the floor, a majority of the membership can vote an item on or off the legislative agenda at any time. However, routinely managing the agenda via collective choice is unworkable, and lawmakers delegate disproportionate control over scheduling to the leadership. Particularly on the floor, the majority leadership decides if and when an item will be considered. And when it comes to scheduling legislation, "when" is often as important as "if." Simply delaying House action for a few weeks can reduce the time available for conference action and negotiations with the executive branch, significantly reducing the chances of adoption.

Structure the Choice Context

In addition to affecting whether and when an item is scheduled, the House majority leadership, through its influence over the Rules Committee, regulates how specific alternatives to a bill are considered. Floor outcomes can be determined by which amendments are made in order, the sequence in which alternatives are brought up, and the quantity of time allotted for consideration. Regardless of the substantive outcome, leaders can also structure the choice context to protect members from having to cast politically embarrassing votes.

Protect Prefloor Logrolling

On Capitol Hill, lawmaking is typically a process of logrolling, that is, bargaining and exchange. Deals that occur in committee and after are often fragile. They can be unraveled by opponents to a measure who offer strategically-crafted amendments. The effective introduction of so-called killer amendments, for instance, can divide a bill's supporting constituency and cause its defeat. Carefully drafted floor procedures are used by the leadership to lock in legislative compromises forged earlier on in the legislative process. Procedure can be the glue that holds together a wavering coalition.

Reduce Uncertainty

As Bach and Smith (1988) have demonstrated, procedure can also be used to reduce the uncertainty that characterizes the legislative process (see also Krehbiel 1991). Beginning in the 1970s, "[n]ew issues and new members disrupted old ways of doing business, while a variety of organizational and procedural reforms redistributed influence and resources in ways that were not always anticipated" (Bach and Smith 1988, 5). For instance, the number of unexpected and politically problematic floor amendments increased markedly during the decade, creating demands among Democrats for more restrictive amendment procedures. Particularly on the floor, majority-party leaders can use their formal prerogatives to make the process of lawmaking more stable and predictable.

This menu of what leaders can accomplish via procedural tactics is not inconsistent with the CPG notion of legislative outcomes diverging from chamber to party medians. For instance, party leaders with procedural leverage vis-à-vis committee chairs are better able to ensure that legislation reflecting party priorities is reported to the floor. Influence over the schedule enables party leaders to focus floor action on issue areas where it is possible to induce potential defectors not to stray from the reservation. The Speaker can instruct Rules Committee members to rule out-of-order floor amendments likely to prevail over the majority party's preferred position, or to place such amendments at a disadvantage in formulating the rules for floor debate on a bill. And the prefloor logrolls receiving procedural protection may derive from bargaining within the majority party.

However, it also should be apparent that these powers can matter a great deal *even if the final outcome of House consideration does not diverge much from the chamber median.* Too often, our theories of lawmaking underestimate the difficulties of drafting and passing legislation in the contemporary House. Legislating is "hard, pick-and-shovel work," observes Representative John Dingell (D-Mich.), "and it takes a long time to do it" (quoted in Kriz 1997, 2462). Consider the following common hurdles to legislative success:

- Although members typically have well-formed preferences about the ends they hope a bill will produce, considerable uncertainty can exist over how to best achieve those ends. Proponents of an initiative need to search out the policy and political information necessary to draft concrete legislative proposals and convince colleagues that such proposals will indeed achieve the desired policy outcome.
- The disagreements about policy that characterize even relatively unified partisan majorities usually require concessions and logrolling if legislation is to move and party cohesion is to be maintained. Bringing off these transactions requires time, effort, and other scarce political resources.
- Subcommittee and full committee chairs have significant say over whether and when bills are considered in committee, providing opportunities for obstruction. Committee leaders who prefer the status quo can use their prerogatives to water down, delay, or even derail a piece of legislation.
- Members of the House minority party can use a range of tactics to undermine the majority's attempts to move legislation. As mentioned, strategically-worded amendments can be used to divide the supporting coalition, and, at least in the short term, dilatory tactics can be employed to slow down legislation.
- In the contemporary House, party leaders are reluctant to bring major legislation to the floor unless a comprehensive public-relations campaign has been orchestrated and conducted on its behalf. Increasingly, House party leaders lead by going public (Sinclair 1995). These public-relations campaigns require time, money, and other resources.

The bottom line? Even in the majority-rule-oriented House, the natural tendency of the legislative process is toward inaction and maintenance of the status quo. In our view, the formal powers of party leaders are only rarely used successfully to shift outcomes from chamber toward party medians. Particularly in the House, the chamber median is the center of political gravity. Instead, the prerogatives of leadership are policy relevant primarily because they enable the majority leadership to pursue two important ends:

1. Focus attention on issues that unify the majority party, that is, issues where the party and floor medians are relatively similar; and
2. Advance legislation reflecting the chamber (and party) median toward House passage.

This argument does not trivialize the independent impact that party leaders can have on the legislative process. If the chamber median diverges significantly from the status quo, then facilitating the passage of such proposals (particularly when the party is united and chamber/party medians are similar) will be viewed as a significant political victory for the majority party and its leaders. Our argument is also fully consistent with Barbara Sinclair's (1983a) influential observation that the proximate goals of House majority leaders are to maintain peace in the family and build winning coalitions on the floor.

We are left, then, with three sets of hypotheses. First, in its boldest form, a purely majoritarian perspective provides that policy outcomes will seldom, if ever, diverge from the preferred position of the median voter in the chamber and that the formal powers of majority party leaders will not have significant consequences for policy outcomes. Second, the CPG perspective, also framed in its boldest form, predicts that the formal prerogatives of party leaders can matter a great deal and, under the right conditions, can be used to shift legislative outcomes from the chamber median toward the median of the majority party. Third, the perspective we are most comfortable with implies that significant departures from the policy mood of the entire chamber will occur only rarely, but that the majority-party leadership can still influence legislative outcomes via issue selection and by facilitating the coalition-building process.

We lack the data about member preferences, policy outcomes, and leadership behavior necessary to systematically evaluate these perspectives. However, as Aldrich and Rohde have argued in their insightful studies, useful evidence about these issues can be gathered by examining how the House Republican majority has employed procedural and other organizational means to advance its agenda. House Republican rule since 1994 provides a useful quasi-experiment for studying these prerogatives in action.

LEADERSHIP POWERS AND PROCEDURAL TACTICS IN THE REPUBLICAN HOUSE

In November 1994, the new GOP majority first turned its attention to issues of organizational reform. The institutional changes adopted by House Republicans are well known. Incoming Speaker Newt Gingrich assumed the authority to "hire and fire" committee chairs. The Speaker's influence over the GOP committee assignment process was substantially increased; he used it to place activist conservatives in key assignments. Committee staffs were reduced by one-third or more, independent subcommittee staffs were abolished, and committee chairs were granted the authority to appoint the subcommittee chairs on their panels. A range of other House procedures were altered, from the abolition of proxy voting in committee to granting the majority leader the right to end debate in the Committee of the Whole on appropriations riders. Three standing committees were abolished, with their jurisdictions parceled out to other panels. Minor alterations were made in the huge Commerce Committee jurisdiction. The process through which House bills are referred to committee was altered in subtle, but potentially important, ways. Six-year term limits were also imposed on committee and subcommittee chairmen. Most dramatically, Gingrich used his new prerogatives to violate the seniority norm in three cases, appointing like-minded conservatives to key committee chairmanships.

Elsewhere, we have analyzed these Republican organizational changes in depth (Evans and Oleszek 1997a, b). However, for certain of these reforms, it is useful to review what the GOP sought to accomplish, as well as the apparent effect of the changes on the lawmaking process. Here, we focus on three categories of procedure: the changes aimed at enhancing Gingrich's power vis-à-vis the committee chairs, the jurisdictional/referral reforms, and the amendment rules adopted by House Republicans in the 104th and 105th Congresses.

Harnessing the Committee System

The most significant institutional changes implemented by the House GOP relate to the tools party leaders have to influence the timing and content of committee legislation. At least in 1995, policy preferences within the Republican Conference were homogeneous relative to prior Democratic majorities. Still, there were important divisions within the party. Senior GOP members of important committees had been first elected to Congress in the 1970s, before the party's strong turn to the right. Although the Republicans were united behind the Contract, Gingrich was concerned that certain senior committee members might not be sufficiently aggressive in pursuing the overall party agenda. A case in point was Representative Carlos Moorhead, an eleven-term veteran from California. In November 1994, Moorhead was the most senior Republican on both the Commerce and Judiciary Committees. Together, the two panels would consider key elements of the Contract with America, which Republicans had promised to bring to the floor in the first one-hundred days of the 104th House. Moorhead was a conservative legislator and a loyal Republican. But Gingrich doubted that he was aggressive enough to match parliamentary wits with John Dingell and Representative John Conyers (D-Mich.), respectively, incoming ranking Democrats on the Commerce and Judiciary panels. As a result, Moorhead was passed over for both chairmanships.

Gingrich's efforts to keep the committee system focused on the Contract and other central elements of the GOP agenda continued throughout 1995. The leadership provided the committee chairs with a strict timetable; without the deadlines, Gingrich feared that the party would miss its 100-day commitment. Interestingly, as more significant policy divisions emerged among House Republicans in 1996, committee chairs would reclaim substantial control over their own agendas.

In general, the GOP leadership's efforts to harness the standing committee system focused on expediting the flow of legislation to the floor. Early on, Republican leaders acknowledged that there was insufficient time to use the authorization process to advance certain elements of their agenda. As a result, in 1995 they chose to rely heavily on appropriations riders to bring these items to the floor. Republicans also believed that it would be more difficult for the administration to block these changes if they were included in general appropriations bills. Appropriations Chair Robert L. Livingston (R-La.) and other committee members opposed the practice, but they bowed to pressure from the leadership and other Republicans.

Perhaps the most widely noted example of GOP leaders clamping down on committee members concerned the "Freedom to Farm Act," which included major revisions in the nation's farm program. As part of the 1995 reconciliation process, the House Agriculture Committee was instructed to slash agricultural expenditures by $13.4 billion. However, members of the panel, long dominated by agriculture interests, were reluctant to make the programmatic changes sought by the leadership. Gingrich and other Republican leaders sent Agriculture Chairman Pat Roberts a letter warning him that the panel would be circumvented unless they reported a measure acceptable to the leadership. In a September 1995 markup, four Republicans joined with committee Democrats to defeat the plan. GOP leaders threatened to sanction the defectors. They did not follow through, but responsibility for devising the cuts did shift to the leadership and the Budget Committee. The Freedom to Farm Act passed as part of the 1995 Reconciliation Bill, which drew a presidential veto.

Gingrich's actions on the agricultural bill illustrate how party leaders can use procedural and other means to circumvent committee-based obstacles to implementing the majority party's agenda. But is this an example of legislative outcomes diverging from the chamber median toward the party median? Is it an example of the strong form of Conditional Party Government? Clearly not. After Clinton vetoed the 1995 reconciliation package, GOP leaders brought the Freedom to Farm Act to the floor as a freestanding measure. It passed both chambers with large bipartisan majorities and was signed by Clinton in April 1996. There is little evidence that the House-passed version diverged from the preferences of the chamber median. Instead, the primary impact of GOP leaders on the measure was to facilitate consideration and bring it to the floor. Still, their actions were critical to final passage.

Jurisdictional/Referral Changes

By all accounts, the jurisdictional changes implemented by House Republicans have not significantly altered House operations. Of course, given the difficulties Democrats faced altering committee boundaries, abolishing three committees is not an insignificant change. But the three discarded panels were minor committees, mostly of interest to Democratic constituencies, and only slivers of the Commerce jurisdiction were transferred to other panels. To a large extent, the

TABLE 6.1
Single and Multiple Referral of Measures to House
Committees, 103rd–105th Congresses

	103rd Congress			104th Congress			105th Congress (1st session)		
Committee	Single	Multiple	(%)	Single	Multiple	(%)	Single	Multiple	(%)
Banking	235	136	(36.7%)	193	132	(40.6%)	113	63	(35.8%)
Commerce	448	467	(51.0%)	396	426	(51.8%)	271	283	(51.1%)
Education	295	235	(44.3%)	233	204	(46.7%)	201	131	(39.5%)
Resources	357	146	(29.0%)	382	139	(26.7%)	260	65	(20.0%)
Transportation	228	171	(42.9%)	368	162	(30.6%)	212	91	(30.0%)
Ways and Means	1034	474	(31.4%)	650	426	(39.6%)	591	293	(33.1%)

Source: Scorpio files, U.S. Library of Congress

primary purposes of the jurisdictional changes were symbolism and position taking, rather than to make the committee system more responsive to the Republican agenda (Evans and Oleszek 1997a, b).

However, one jurisdiction-related reform has provided Republican leaders with a potentially useful new tool: the abolition of open-ended joint referrals. Gingrich sought to end joint referrals because he wanted to avoid the intramural disputes over turf that so often characterized the Democratically-controlled House. Under the Republicans, bills are still routinely referred to more than one panel, but such referrals take the form of an "additional initial referral." The parliamentarians designate a primary, or lead, committee or jurisdiction; other committees only receive the portions of the bill within their jurisdiction, and subject to time restrictions determined by the leadership.

We have found little evidence that this referral reform has substantially affected jurisdictional politics—at least during the initial stages of committee consideration of a measure. For instance, Table 6.1 provides data about the incidence of multiple referrals in six House standing committees whose jurisdictions overlap substantially with other panels. With the exception of the Committee on Transportation, there have been few changes across the 103rd and 104th Congresses. And the decrease in multiple referrals to the Transportation panel largely results from the abolition of the Merchant Marine Committee, with which it often shared referrals during the years of Democratic control.

By all accounts, the quantity of time that the House parliamentarians spend dealing with turf disputes is way down under the Republicans. The main reason

TABLE 6.2
House Conference Delegation Sizes under
Democrats and Republicans

| | Average Size (Referral) | | |
Congress	Single	Multiple	Percent from Lead Panel
103rd	11.2	42.7	47.8%
104th	13.6	29.1	57.3%

Source: Final Calendars of the U.S. House of Representatives, 103rd and 104th Congresses

for this decline is the GOP's general intolerance for committee infighting, rather than the shift to additional initial referrals. Still, the referral change has helped Gingrich with a related problem—the increasingly unwieldy nature of conference delegations under the Democratic majority.

Prior to 1995, in multiple-referral situations, committee chairs often buffeted Speaker Thomas Foley (D-Wash.) and his predecessors with demands for positions on the conference delegation that would negotiate with the Senate. One result was that the size of House delegations increased markedly during the years of Democratic control. Larger conferences are more difficult to organize and manage because of the extensive array of viewpoints and interests. Gingrich was able to streamline the conference process by reducing the size of House delegations. By singling out one committee as the lead panel, the additional initial referral rule has provided him with the procedural rationale for resisting chairs' demands for conference slots.

Table 6.2 denotes the average sizes of House conference delegations in the 103rd and 104th Congresses, for both single and multiple referrals. There has been little change in delegation size for single referrals. But for multiple referrals, the average delegation size has dropped substantially, from 42.7 members to 29.1. For multiply-referred legislation, it also is instructive to examine the percentage of the House delegation drawn from the lead committee of jurisdiction. Compared to the 103rd Congress, that percentage has increased under the GOP from 19.1 to 28.2 percent. These data reinforce our portrayal of the Republican leadership as a leadership focused on streamlining and expediting the legislative process.

Rules Governing Floor Debate

Following the 1994 elections, House GOP leaders promised to reverse the Democratic trend toward more restrictive amendment procedures. They pledged that 70 percent or more of Republican rules would be open, without restrictions on which amendments lawmakers could offer on the floor. Clearly, a general pattern of open rules would have been inconsistent with the Republican's commitment to bring the Contract to the floor within one hundred days. Indeed, a reliance on truly open rules is not feasible even when the majority party's legislative agenda is far less ambitious than was the 1995 House Republican program. There is an inevitable conflict between extensive debates versus the need to make decisions. As a result, the GOP leadership turned to time-structured procedures that provide considerable flexibility about which amendments are introduced, but place a binding time constraint on overall debate. Democrats have complained that the time limits effectively restrict their opportunities to legislate. Republicans have responded that it is up to the minority to decide which amendments will be offered in the allotted time. Overall, the floor amendment process appears somewhat more open under the Republicans than it was under recent Democratic majorities.

Notice the implications of how the House GOP has chosen to regulate the floor. Typically, there is sufficient discretion for the minority party to offer one or more alternatives, and there is not much evidence that they are using amendment rules to keep the position of the chamber median from being considered. Instead, they place binding limits on debate as part of general efforts to keep the legislative train moving on time.

Martial Law. Another example of how Republicans have used their control over procedures involves wider use of so-called *martial-law* rules. These are special rules reported by the Rules Committee that set aside certain of the standing rules of the House so that the majority party can expeditiously process its agenda. For example, House Rule XI, clause 4, states that it is not in order for the House to take up a rule on the same day that it is granted unless the House adopts it by a two-thirds vote. A martial-law rule waives the two-thirds requirement and allows same-day special rules to be adopted by the usual majority vote. Martial-law rules may also waive any layover period identified in the rulebook for measures before they can be taken up on the floor.

During the 104th Congress, Republicans employed martial-law rules more frequently, for longer periods, and for different purposes than did the Democrats. For example, during the government shutdown period of late 1995 and into 1996, the House operated continuously (from 15 November 1995 through 1 April 1996) under martial-law procedures. Republicans wanted the flexibility to bring debt ceiling, budget reconciliation, and spending measures quickly to the floor to address this emergency situation without having to observe the "regular order." Further, martial-law rules, at least according to Democrats, provided political cover to Republican leaders who could say that, "they were ready to move the bills as soon as the President would agree to their [balanced-budget] demands" (U.S. Congress, Committee on Rules 1996, 167).

For example, the GOP adopted a martial-law rule on 25 January 1996—the earliest that such a rule had been adopted in several recent Congresses. "Having reviewed the Rules Committee survey of activities from the 98th through the 103rd," stated Joe Moakley (D-Mass.), the ranking member on Rules, "I can say with assurance, the House has not once considered a martial-law rule this early in the session" (*Congressional Record,* 31 January 1996, H1065). Republicans also used martial-law rules to cover classes of bills (all spending measures, for example), whereas Democrats limited the application of martial-law rules to a specific bill. Also in the 103rd Congress, of the five martial-law rules, not one lasted longer than a day. A total of nine different martial-law rules were adopted during the Republican-controlled 104th Congress.

Republicans countered that Democrats often did the same thing with their martial-law rules and noted that their actions are permissible under the procedures of the House. "I have it right here, House Resolution 61, February 3, 1993," said Rules member Scott McInnis (R-Colo.), "they did exactly the same thing. It is allowed under the rules" (*Congressional Record,* 31 January 1996, H1067). He added: "Our priority, the Republican leadership's priority, is to try to keep this government operating" (*Congressional Record,* 31 January 1996, H1071).

The Motion to Recommit. As part of the 1995 opening-day reforms, House Republicans extended to the minority leader or his designee the right to offer a motion to recommit with instructions on every bill. This motion essentially grants the minority party an opportunity to offer a policy alternative immediately before the vote on final passage. On occasion, the majority Democrats had denied Republicans the opportunity to offer recommittal instructions; guaranteeing in House Rules the right to offer the motion was a key Republican demand under Democratic control.

For the most part, Republicans have not tinkered with the minority's opportunity to offer the motion to recommit, and Democrats have been able to make significant changes in legislation via recommittal instructions on a number of occasions. For example, the so-called V-chip provision was added to a major telecommunications bill via this motion. However, there have been important exceptions, illustrating again the Republican leadership's willingness to use procedure to promote its agenda.

In January 1996, amid legislative–executive-branch wrangling over the budget and public furor over the partial government shutdowns, House GOP leaders wanted to bring to the floor a continuing resolution (CR) they knew would be substantially amended if Democrats had the opportunity to offer a policy alternative. In a classic example of parliamentary legerdemain, GOP leaders effectively circumvented the minority's access to the motion to recommit. The motion is only guaranteed upon initial consideration of a bill by the House. GOP leaders persuaded Senate Republicans to pass their own version of the CR as an amendment to an unrelated House-passed bill extending most-favored nation duty status to products from Bulgaria. Because the Bulgaria bill had already passed the chamber, House Rules did not require that Democrats be allowed to offer recommittal instructions on a Senate amendment to a House-passed measure. According to our interviews, a sufficient number of Republicans supported a "clean" CR that, if such a proposal had been incorporated in a recommittal motion with instructions, it probably would have passed the House. There are a few other examples of GOP leaders using procedural tactics to undermine the motion to recommit, but such instances have been relatively rare.

Appropriations Conference Reports. In another interesting procedural innovation, Republicans have almost completely ended the practice of having appropriators report back partial conference reports with amendments still in bicameral disagreement, which are presented separately to each chamber. With rare exceptions during the Democratic years, this has been the long-standing procedure for handling appropriations reports.

In the Republican House, appropriators—like authorizers—bundle all their compromises into the conference report and then seek a rule from the Rules Committee to waive all points of order against the report. Appropriators previously kept certain amendments in disagreement outside the conference report and took them up separately because these amendments violated House rules and their inclusion in the conference report might have jeopardized its passage. There has been little public complaint about this new practice from the minority, however, and the impact of the innovation probably is the more expeditious consideration of spending bills in the House. Again, the Republican leadership has usually employed procedure to facilitate legislative work, rather than shift outcomes from the chamber median.

The Democratic Response

How have the minority Democrats responded with the procedural tools available to them? Just as Republicans had to adjust to majority status, shifting from stalling action to governing the House, Democrats, as John Dingell put it, had to "accept that your place in the institution is not so August as it was" (*Congressional Record,* 31 January 1996, H2461). Democrats learned how to act as the minority, both by emulating the dilatory tactics employed by the Republicans when they were the minority and by devising new forms of parliamentary guerrilla warfare. "The job of the minority is to make trouble for the majority," remarked House Majority Leader Richard Armey (R-Tex.), "and they are doing a very good job of this" (quoted in Roman 1997, A3).

As indicated in Table 6.3, Democrats have expanded the repertoire of stalling tactics and emphasized some procedures more than others. The table

TABLE 6.3
HOUSE DILATORY TACTICS, 103RD, 104TH,
AND 105TH CONGRESSES

Type of Vote	103rd Congress	104th Congress	105th Congress (1st session)
Journal Approval	78	34	29
Motion to Adjourn	13	17	46
Motion to Rise	5	6	16
Motion to Table*	18	31	26
Total	114	88	117

Source: Congressional Quarterly Weekly Report, various issues.

*Motions to table are an indirect indicator of dilatory tactics because the majority typically employs such motions to shut off attempts at obstructionism.

includes data about how often certain classic House dilatory tactics were employed in the 103rd–105th Congresses. Republicans used many of the same dilatory motions, but Democrats have either changed the mix or innovated in their use of additional procedural blocking actions. The table reveals the Democratic drop-off in forcing votes on approval of the Journal, but underscores the sharp rise in calls for adjournment of the House. In addition, Democrats in 1997 used the motion to rise from the Committee of the Whole more than three times as often in a single year as Republicans did in the entire 103rd Congress. Finally, there has been a sharp uptick in "motions to table," which are employed by the majority Republicans to defeat minority actions designed to delay or to embarrass the majority party.

Interestingly, the large increase in dilatory behavior began in the 105th Congress, rather than the 104th. One reason is that it simply took a while for Democrats to get used to their new minority status, replacing their "majority mindset" with the perspective of the House minority party. Another reason is Democratic anger in 1997 over what they viewed as stalling tactics by the majority on campaign-finance reform. More generally, dilatory tactics tend to be more effective when the size of the majority party is relatively small (Binder 1996a); the Republican seat margin diminished following the 1996 and 1998 elections.

The guerrilla-warfare strategies of the Democrats can perhaps best be demonstrated by examining some concrete examples. Compared to other House motions (that is, to recess, to table, to amend), the motion to adjourn has the highest privilege. Although it is nondebatable and customarily offered by the majority leader or his designee at the end of a legislative day, any lawmaker can offer it whenever he/she can get the floor. Further, the motion is in order in many circumstances—when a question is under debate, after a vote is ordered but before the vote begins, during consideration of conference reports, and so on. It is a first-rate dilatory tactic.

During much of 1997, Democrats employed a variety of obstructionist tactics as part of efforts to induce the GOP leadership to schedule a vote on a campaign-finance reform bill. Like Republicans before them, Democrats pressed their case by objecting to unanimous consent agreements, requesting votes on approval of the *Journal,* and delivering scores of so-called one-minute speeches at the start of each day on the need for campaign-funding reform. As Democrat Lloyd Doggett of Texas said in a one-minute: "We will have vote after vote; we will engage in extraordinary tactics to assure debate on real [campaign] reform because of [GOP leaders'] extraordinary refusal to permit that reform" (*Congressional Record,* 4 September 1997, H6803).

An important part of those "extraordinary tactics" was repetitious use of the motion to adjourn. From Labor Day to early October, Democrats forced about thirty votes on the motion to adjourn, each one consuming fifteen or more minutes of time. On 24 September 1997, for instance, Democrats offered five motions to adjourn—all of which were rejected by the House. Moreover, they even forced roll-call votes on matters that normally are decided quickly by unanimous consent. For example, Minority Leader Richard Gephardt (D-Mo.) moved to adjourn the House and then demanded "the yeas and nays." Recorded votes in the House are usually ordered if supported by forty-four members, or one-fifth of a quorum of the House. Typically, this is a pro forma request, ostensibly as in Gephardt's case, because the Chair simply said, "the yeas and nays are ordered."

However, another Democrat immediately offered a motion to reconsider the ordering of the yeas and nays. Under House rules, this motion is debatable for one hour. To prevent that debate, a GOP lawmaker quickly moved successfully to table the motion to reconsider. Then the House voted to reject the motion to adjourn. The point here is that on a simple motion to adjourn, two votes were taken and about a half hour of time consumed before the House took up the regularly scheduled business. The Democrats have employed similar parliamentary hijinks via the motion to rise and other dilatory motions. Such tactics can sidetrack GOP efforts to expedite the legislative schedule. Again, one GOP response has been increased usage of the motion to table as part of efforts to curb these dilatory actions. In addition, Republicans have not been reluctant to adopt "rules" from the Rules Committee that limit or restrict minority-party opportunities to use certain dilatory tactics.

Sweeping away the Cobwebs?

The procedural features of House Republican rule have important implications for congressional operations and for our theories of legislative organization. Participants in the legislative process typically remark that the main change in the House is an intangible sense that lawmaking is less constrained by procedure, precedent, and tradition. On both sides of the aisle, but particularly among Republicans, there is a palpable sense that some of the procedural cobwebs from the Democratic years have been swept away. Especially in the 104th Congress, the GOP leadership demonstrated an enhanced willingness to use the rules to expedite legislation. Of course, previous Democratic majorities also used procedure in such a manner, but the Republican leaders have appeared more willing and able to innovate procedurally to promote their agenda.

Interestingly, Republicans have demonstrated an increased willingness to *amend* the formal rules of the House to move their partisan-substantive objectives. Understandably, after forty years in charge, Democrats viewed the House rules, which they had fine-tuned to their liking, as largely sacrosanct. Not so the Republicans. There have been several prominent examples (for instance, waiving House rules to allow the Government Reform Committee to have an extra census subcommittee or abolishing the House rule that allowed subpoenaed witnesses to ban the televising of their testimony) that highlight the Republicans' proclivity to amend the House rule book not just at the beginning of a new Congress, but at any time GOP leaders believe it is necessary to advance their agenda.

We began this chapter by asking what Republican House rule can teach us about the nature of Congress as an institution. The role of leadership prerogatives and procedures in the GOP-controlled House indicates that we should not gauge the importance of party leaders by their ability to move legislative outcomes from the chamber toward the party median. Such distortions appear to be rare. Instead, leaders and leadership prerogatives primarily make a difference via issue selection, focusing the agenda, and facilitating the passage of bills upon which the majority is united. The Republican House demonstrates that party leaders do matter on Capitol Hill, but a proper understanding of why they matter requires that we examine all areas of leadership activity.

Note

1. There is a large literature about the goals and tactics of party leaders in the House. For a comprehensive overview, consult Barbara Sinclair, *Legislators, Leaders, and Lawmaking: The U.S. House of Representatives in the Postreform Era* (Baltimore: Johns Hopkins University Press, 1995).

CHAPTER SEVEN

Republican Roles in Congressional Budget Reform: Twenty-Five Years of Deficit and Conflict

JAMES A. THURBER

INTRODUCTION

The congressional budget process has been transformed dramatically through both bipartisan cooperation and highly partisan battles in the last twenty-five years, with the Republican Party playing a key role in the drive to balance the budget through reform. The transformation evolved from a focus on budgetary priority in the 1974 Budget Act (1974–1985), to deficit control in the Gramm-Rudman-Hollings Deficit Reduction Act (1985–1990), to spending control measures in the 1990 Budget Enforcement Act, to the 1997 Balanced Budget Act (BBA), which resulted in the first budget surplus ($63 billion in Fiscal Year 1998) since 1969. A consistent theme from 1974 to 1998 was the Republican Party efforts to cut spending, cut taxes, and balance the budget.

This analysis describes and evaluates the impact of Republican-Party–initiated congressional budget reforms on the budgetary decision-making capacity of the Congress, on presidential and congressional budgetary power, and on the complexity, openness, and timeliness of the congressional budget process. The chapter concludes with a discussion about the implications of the Republican-led reforms for the capacity of Congress to make timely and difficult budgetary decisions.

To combat rising deficits and improve accountability over the budget process, the congressional budget process has undergone three major reforms in the last twenty-five years: the Congressional Budget and Impoundment Control Act of 1974, the Balanced Budget and Emergency Deficit Control Acts of 1985 and 1987 (Gramm-Rudman-Hollings or GRH I and II), and the Budget

Enforcement Act of 1990 (BEA) (Thurber 1989; Thurber 1991; Thelwell 1990; LeLoup 1987; Havens 1986; Fisher 1985). Republican and conservative Democratic-Party supporters of these acts suggested that their passage would promote more discipline in congressional budgeting, reduce deficits, control runaway spending, and make the process more timely and effective. As a consequence of the 1994 congressional election, Republicans were in power to push a new round of budget reforms and spending policies, such as unfunded mandates reform, the line-item veto, cuts in payments to individuals, and cuts in taxes and a balanced budget, culminating in passage of the Balanced Budget Act of 1997 and a budget surplus. Although never an important issue in the public's mind, each budget cycle brought increasing concern by members of Congress about spending, taxing, deficits, and debt, which brought calls for reforming the budget process itself.

1974 BUDGET PROCESS REFORMS

The most important change in the way Congress collects and spends money in the last fifty years was the 1974 Congressional Budget and Impoundment Control Act, a reform drafted equally by Democrats and Republicans.[1] The votes for this historic reform were bipartisan and close to unanimous in the House and Senate. The Congressional Budget Act created standing budget committees in the House and in the Senate that are responsible for setting overall tax and spending levels. It also required Congress to annually establish levels of expenditures and revenues with prescribed procedures for arriving at those spending and income totals. These procedures include three important elements. First, a timetable was established that set deadlines for action on budget-related legislation that was intended to ensure completion of the budget plan prior to the start of each fiscal year. Second, the Act required the annual adoption of concurrent budget resolutions, which do not require presidential approval. Finally, the act instituted a reconciliation process to conform revenue, spending, and debt legislation to the levels specified in the budget committees. This procedure directs other committees to determine and recommend revenue and spending actions deemed necessary to conform authorizations and appropriations to the decisions made in the budget resolutions. The Budget Committees have the option of mandating that House and Senate committees "report" legislation that will meet budget authority, outlays, and revenue targets (Schick 1981; Tate 1981). These reforms were strongly supported by Republican members of Congress because they made new spending and taxing transparent and more difficult. These reforms were a conservative effort to control spending and cut the deficit, thus limiting the size of the federal government, a key element of Republican-Party philosophy.

Republican Budget Reforms in the 1980s: Gramm-Rudman-Hollings

Republican control of the Senate in 1981 allowed those members of Congress who were increasingly concerned with Congress's inability to control the budget process and the large deficits under the 1974 budget act to enact a reform that was supposed to improve congressional capacity to control the process, the Balanced Budget and Emergency Deficit Control Act of 1985 and 1987 (GRH I and II). By the early 1980s, projected budget deficits were in the $200-billion range, far more than had ever been experienced before.[2] However, after the Republican drafted GRH reform legislation, the deficits as a percentage of gross national product and in absolute dollars continued to rise and created new demands, primarily from the Republican members of Congress, for new budget process reform.

The Republican GRH legislation changed the established budgetary deadlines for each of the major aspects of the congressional budget process in order to bring more discipline to congressional budgeting, to make the process more efficient, and to focus attention on reducing the deficit.[3] The central enforcement mechanism of GRH was a series of automatic spending cuts that occur if the federal budget did not meet the deficit targets. These automatic spending cuts are referred to as "sequestration" (Penner and Abramson 1988). Sequestration required federal spending to be cut automatically if Congress did not enact laws to reduce the deficit to the maximum deficit amount allowed for that year. The GRH deficit targets for each fiscal year are listed in Table 7.1. If the proposed federal budget did not meet the annual deficit targets established by GRH, then the president had to make across-the-board spending cuts evenly divided between domestic discretionary and defense programs until those targets were met. However, most entitlement programs (then approximately 43 percent of the budget) and interest payments (then approximately 14 percent of the budget) were "off-budget," making them partially or totally exempt from the potential cuts. Reformers wanted to fix the process without forcing them to make "hard choices," something that proved to be elusive.

The bipartisan GRH II legislation in 1987 altered the original GRH deficit-reduction plan by directing the Office of Management and Budget (OMB) to issue the report that would trigger sequestration if deficit reduction targets were not met and by revising the original deficit-reduction targets in accordance with more realistic economic assumptions (see Table 7.1). It was an expedient reform to avoid congressional-presidential gridlock and allowing for a more gradual and politically acceptable reduction of the deficit. Republicans agreed with Democrats that the sequestration would not work. The cuts to be made in a single year were too great.

The Gramm-Rudman-Hollings (GRH) deficit-reduction plan promised long-term progress toward lower deficits and a balanced budget, but these goals

TABLE 7.1
DEFICIT-REDUCTION TARGETS AND ACTUAL DEFICITS,
FY 1986–1996

Fiscal Year	1985 GRH Limits	1987 GRH Limits	1990 BEA Limits	CBO Deficit Projections[2]	Actual Deficits
	Deficit Reduction Targets (in billions of dollars)[1]				
1986	172	— —	— —		221
1987	144	— —	— —		150
1988	108	144	— —		155
1989	72	136	— —		152
1990	36	100	— —		195
1991	0	64	327	331	269
1992	— —	28	317	425	290
1993	— —	0	236	348	255
1994	— —	— —	102	318	203[5]
1995	— —	— —	83	162[3]	164[5]
1996	— —	— —	— —	176[3]	107[5]
1997	— —	— —	— —	103[4]	22[6]
1998	— —	— —	— —	105[4]	— —
1999	— —	— —	— —	115[4]	— —

[1] CBO estimates of the deficit taken from *An Analysis of the President's Budgetary Proposals for Fiscal Year 1991* (Washington, D.C.: Congressional Budget Office, March 1990), p. 8; and *The Economic and Budget Outlook: An Update* (Washington, D.C.: Congressional Budget Office, July 1990), p. x.

[2] Deficit projections excluding social security and postal service from CBO, *The Economic and Budget Outlook: An Update*, August 1991, p. xiii. Note: The budget figures include Social Security, which is off-budget but is counted for the purposes of the Balanced Budget Act targets. For comparability with the targets, the projections exclude the Postal Service, which is also off-budget.

[3] These deficit figures are from CBO, *The Economic and Budget Outlook: Update*, August 1994, p. 31.

[4] These figures are taken from *The Economic and Budget Outlook for Fiscal Years 1999–2008: A Preliminary Report*, January 1998, Table 2.

[5] These deficit figures are from the Office of Management and Budget as reported in *Historical Tables: Budget of the United States* (Washington, D.C.: U.S. Printing Office, 1997), p. 20.

[6] This figure is from the Financial Management Service, Department of the Treasury, *The Annual Report of the United States Government, Fiscal Year 1997*.

proved to be elusive and overly optimistic, much to the disappointment of the Republicans. During the implementation of the Gramm-Rudman-Hollings Balanced Budget legislation, the deficit was never as low as the law requires, as shown in Table 7.1.

As a measure of the budget conflict, an inordinate amount of Congress's time in the 1980s and early 1990s was spent on budgeting and appropriating. During the 1980s and 1990s, more than half of all roll-call votes in Congress were on budget-related bills, with a high of 56 percent in the House and 71 percent in the Senate in 1989 (Thurber 1991). Even though GRH II revised the original deficit targets, it did not reduce the partisan conflict and the deficit. The new targets were well out of reach as early as 1990 when Congress considered the budget of FY 1991 (see Table 7.1).

GRH sequestration was supposed to threaten the interests of all participants in the congressional budget process enough to make them want to avoid it. However, the threat of sequestration did not have the intended effect. Comparing the projected impacts of sequestration on their favored programs with the potential impact of cuts from regular legislation, Republican and Democratic members of Congress simply decided that their interests were best served by delaying the passage of bills until after sequestration occurred, a form of bipartisan avoidance behavior (U.S. Congress, Committee on the Budget 1990). In addition, sequestration could be avoided by using overly optimistic economic and technical assumptions as substitutes for actual policy changes—a common bipartisan practice. Republicans placed Democrats in a box that they, too, eventually wanted out of (Schick 1988).

In spite of their goals, the Budget and Impoundment Control Act and GRH did not achieve Republican goals for the budget process: to curb growth of federal spending; to bring an end to the growth in uncontrollable spending; to reduce the deficit; to complete budgeting on time; to reorder national spending priorities; to allow Congress to control fiscal policy; or to eliminate the need for continuing resolutions. With a projected sequestration of 24 percent for Fiscal Year 1991, clearly something needed to be done to counteract these loopholes and cut the deficit; and that was the 1990 Budget Enforcement Act, jointly crafted by Republican President George Bush, moderate congressional Republicans and Democrats.

THE 1990 BUDGET-PROCESS REFORMS

By early 1990, it was obvious to congressional "budgeteers" that the balanced-budget target set by the Republicans was not going to be reached and an impossible sequestration of 24 percent was going to hit federal agencies with a projected deficit of $195 billion. The deficit in 1993 (the year that the revised targets were to require a balanced budget) rose to be $255 billion (see Table 7.1); thus, Congress changed the rules yet again with the passage of the Budget Enforcement Act of 1990 (BEA). The budget goals shifted from deficit reduction to spending control by setting spending caps for three discretionary spending categories: defense, international, and domestic. "Fire walls" prevented shifting of funds between categories. The three categories were combined, forcing all programs to compete for federal appropriations.

The 1990 bipartisan BEA agreement was intended to bring more control over spending while easing potential partisan conflicts over the budget, allowing more efficient negotiated compromises to difficult economic and political questions, solving the problem of increasing deficits, and providing political cover over unpopular election-year decisions, but it did not work out that way (Yang and Mufson 1990). Several conservative Republican leaders, such as Representative Newt Gingrich (R-Ga.), then House Minority Whip, opposed the deal because it did not go far enough in cutting taxes and domestic spending.

A major consequence of the 1990 BEA reforms was to further centralize power within Congress and to force "zero-sum" choices: that is, trading reductions in one program for increases in another, or tax cuts for some in exchange for tax increases for others, keeping the total stable. This was done primarily through a Republican supported pay-as-you-go (PAYGO) procedure that required spending increases for new entitlements to be offset by cuts or tax cuts to be offset by revenue increases. PAYGO took one more step toward making it difficult to increase spending and taxing, a major goal of the Republicans.

Perhaps the most significant aspect of the BEA reforms was the spending ceilings it established. As latent consequence of this reform was a positive reaction by the Federal Reserve Board that dropped interest rates, thus creating more growth in the economy. The ceiling of each discretionary-spending category (defense, domestic, and international) was enforced by an end-of-session sequestration applied across the board to all of the programs within the category or categories that exceeded their spending limits (e.g., if the ceiling for discretionary spending in the international category was exceeded, the end-of-session sequester applied to all programs within the international category). This process is called "categorical sequestration." Categorical sequestration was only triggered if the spending limits of any or all of the categories were exceeded due to changes in legislation (e.g., an extension of the benefits of a program or of the number of people eligible to receive benefits or tax cuts). If the spending limits were exceeded because of changes in economic conditions (or, as is the case with many domestic programs, the number of eligible recipients increases), sequestration would not be triggered. If more was appropriated for discretionary spending than allowed under the discretionary limits, automatic sequestrations were to be imposed, but only on the accounts in the category in which the breach occurred. Categorical sequestration brought more discipline, a "zero-sum game," to the budget process, which was a major goal of the Republicans since the early 1970s.

Another Republican-proposed decision rule of the BEA was the requirement to look back at each legislative session to insure that legislation did not cause spending limits to be exceeded. In the past, because Congress only evaluated the budget once a year to ascertain whether it was meeting the GRH deficit targets, it was relatively free to add on new expenditures to the budget after that evaluation, often increasing the actual level of the deficit. The "look-back" legislation enacted in BEA was a further conservative Republican effort to control spending. It required that any amount added to the current year's deficit by policy changes made after the final budget snapshot would also be added to the following year's deficit-reduction target. This eliminated incentives for post-snapshot deficit increases and for schemes that reduce that year's budget deficit by shifting spending into the next fiscal year.

The 1990 BEA and Clinton's 1993 Omnibus Budget Reconciliation Act (OBRA) budget called for all tax and direct spending legislation to be "deficit neutral" in each year through FY 1998. This reform was yet another effort by Republicans to limit spending by creating tighter budget rules for Congress. PAYGO reforms in the BEA are based on the notion that any increase in outlays above the previous year's "base level" must be paid for by offsetting outlay reductions or tax increases. Although each bill need not be deficit-neutral, the net result of all bills must be. Budget-reform advocates argued that any kind of pay-as-you-go approach is an improvement over the 1980s, when a Republican president and a Democratic House allowed the huge explosion in defense spending, and entitlement programs (except Social Security) that were paid for with borrowed money. Pay-as-you-go reforms were not necessarily intended to reduce the deficit, but to limit growth in spending and deficits by requiring that new expenditures be linked to cuts. According to former CBO Director Robert D. Reischauer (1991), "To date, this pay-as-you-go requirement has proved to be an effective poison pill that has killed a number of legislative efforts to cut taxes and expand entitlements." The 1990 budget agreement also requires that all new revenues go to reduce the deficit, an important Republican effort to balance the budget. If the economy grows faster than anticipated, and revenues therefore exceed projections, the increased revenues would not be available to pay for increased spending. The primary impact of PAYGO has been to discourage spending, a goal of congressional Republicans. The difficulty of either raising taxes or cutting popular existing mandatory programs (like Social Security) has resulted in PAYGO effectively closing out Democratic-initiated new mandatory programs (like Clinton's 1993 health-care reforms). These reforms made the budget process a zero-sum game, the most important consequence of the budget reforms of the 1990s, thus meeting the overall Republican goals of reducing federal spending.

House and Senate points of order against "budget-busting" provisions as proposed primarily by Republicans are an important enforcement mechanism in the BEA. Under the 1990 act, legislation is subject to a point of order for breaching either the budget-year levels or the sum of the five-year levels set in a budget resolution (the five-year enforcement mechanisms apply to all budget resolutions through the 1995–1999 resolutions, after which the requirement sunsets). To prevent temporary savings and timing shifts (such as military pay delays), budget resolutions in each year through FY 1995 would be for five years, with five-year discretionary spending allocations (302[a]), revenue floors, and reconciliation.

The 1990 budget pact led the House and Senate to create different procedures for the appropriators. House appropriations were allowed to proceed on 15 May even in the absence of a budget resolution. The House Appropriations Committee must use the statutory caps as their 302(a) allocation, file 302(b) suballocation, and proceed on the basis of those suballocations. The Senate committees other than Appropriations Committee are allowed to proceed in the absence of a new budget resolution if their bills conform to the out-year allocations in the most recent budget resolution. This met the Republican-Party goal of more spending control by Appropriations Committees over members and other committees, but allows the House and Senate to move bills even if the budget resolution is late.

Consequences of Republican Budget Reforms for Congress and the President

What are the effects of the Republican budget reforms of the 1990s on the budget process, the internal workings of Congress (especially the appropriators), and congressional–presidential budgetary powers? The potential impact can be evaluated in terms of: the degree of centralization (i.e., the extent of top–down versus bottom–up budget-making and dispersal of the process); the control by the president versus Congress over the budget; the amount of openness in the decision-making process; the extent of complexity in decision-making rules, and the impact of the 1990s revisions on the timeliness of the process (Lynch 1991; Thurber 1989).

Collectively, these Republican-led changes have had a significant impact on the way Congress budgets in the 1990s. The 1990 BEA set spending caps for both budget authority and outlays in discretionary appropriations for five years (and 1993 OBRA caps out to 1998). Spending limits (or "ceilings") and informally "floors" (minimums) were imposed upon defense, international, and domestic discretionary spending in FY 1991–1993 in the BEA and to FY 1998 by the first Clinton budget in 1993. Appropriations bills that breach any of the three appropriation categories (defense, international, and domestic) trigger across-the-board automatic cuts (sequestration) in programs within the breached category. The BEA provided adjustments in the spending for several reasons: changes in inflation; revision of concepts and definitions; credit re-estimates; specified IRS, International Monetary Fund and debt forgiveness costs; appropriations for emergency needs; and an estimating cushion. The discretionary caps for FY 1991–1993 on spending and so-called fire walls between spending categories (domestic, defense, and international) established more controls and fewer degrees of freedom for members and committees, especially the appropriators, by not allowing funds from one category to be used to offset spending that breaks the caps in another. For example, shifts from defense to domestic were not allowed for the first three years of the agreement.

The 1990 and 1993 reforms have had mixed consequences for the distribution of power within Congress. The pay-as-you-go, zero-sum reforms had a centralizing impact, thus helping Republican leadership in the 104th and 105th Congresses to control spending. The reforms discouraged individual members from initiating their own "budget proposals" because cuts and revenue enhancements had to be instituted in other programs in order save their proposals. On the other hand, stricter enforcement of categorical sequestration, PAYGO provisions, and taking the Social Security Trust Fund surplus "off-budget" raised the public's understanding of spending priorities and the specter of heavy lobbying. The reforms intensified pressure on members and committees to protect their favorite programs and to make cuts in other programs. Such controls also centralized budget decision-making within the Republican-Party leadership and the budget committees, institutions with the power to negotiate trade-offs in the zero-sum game.

Although the more rigid constraints set by the 1990 BEA seem to reduce the autonomy of the Appropriations Committees, most budget participants argue that in fact the Appropriations Committees were the big winners in the 1990 pact. The 1990 budget-process reforms diminished the role of the House and Senate Budget Committees, by giving more degrees of freedom to the Appropriations panels. One budget expert summarized this shift: "Since the pot of money the Appropriations Committees will have to work with has already been decided, they needn't wait for a spending outline from the budget committees before divvying it up" (Yang and Mufson 1991). Appropriators are more able to determine the legislative details within the BEA constraints than through the old reconciliation process and sequestration under GRH. The appropriators have more control over "backdoor spending" that has been done regularly by the authorizers in reconciliation bills.

The reforms of the 1990s gave the Appropriations Committees more control over their own policy preferences, but with direction from Republican-Party leadership since 1995. The big losers were the authorizing committees that have significantly reduced degrees of freedom under the new zero-sum–game controls.

Complexity and Timeliness of the Budget Process

The budget reforms of the 1990s have made the congressional budget process more open to the public. The discretionary spending limits and PAYGO controls over entitlement spending for five years are visible and well known to all the players. The new rules reduced degrees of freedom for the actors while revealing the budget decisions to interest groups, the administration, and the public.

Closing the budget process is often considered one way to help control increased spending; opening budgetary decision making is often a way of increasing spending because of the pressure from interest groups and members of Congress. The BEA attempted to do the opposite: it opened up the process, making it more transparent and placing more controls on expenditures. The reforms opened the process and revealed the trade-offs within mandatory spending and the three discretionary-spending categories thus putting tough spending and taxing decisions in full public view.

The 1990 and 1993 budget agreements simplified the process only if members abided by the agreement. The innovations tended to work at cross-purposes when it came to timeliness. A five-year budget agreement theoretically should have made it easier to pass budget resolutions on time. If the budget resolutions were not passed on time, the appropriators could still pass money bills.

Several other reforms of the 1990s also increased the complexity and thus the delay in Capitol Hill budget making. Steps in the process multiplied, as did the decision-making rules. Typically, the more complex the process, the more time-consuming it is. Categorical sequestration and PAYGO provisions slowed the process by increasing the number of confrontations within Congress and between Congress and the president. Alternatively, multiple confrontations increase complexity and delay in the process as more cuts (or tax increases) are made to meet the caps. Already difficult budget decisions were made more difficult because of the budget-process changes of the 1990s.

In addition, the budget categories were frustratingly complicated and inconsistent. The twenty-one functional categories in the budget resolutions do not neatly fit the thirteen separate appropriations bills or the three categories of spending in the 1990 BEA. Appropriators are required to translate the functional allocations into appropriations allocations and report the result. It is then necessary to compare those results to the ceilings and guidelines set out in BEA, thus increasing the complexity and delay in the budget process.

Republican Budget Reform and the "Contract with America"

After the historic 1994 Republican takeover of the House and Senate, a flood of budget reforms became part of the new congressional agenda. Most of these budget-process reforms had been introduced in earlier Congresses and promised

TABLE 7.2
MAJOR BUDGET-REFORM PROPOSALS PRESENTED TO THE JCOC*
IN 1992–1993

- Item Veto/Enhanced Rescission
- Biennial Budget Resolution
- GDP Budgeting
- Zero-Based Budgeting
- Caps on Mandatory Spending
- Limit Waivers of Congressional Budget-Act Provisions in the House
- Special Treatment of Capital Expenditures/Capital Budget
- Sunset Budgeting
- Prohibit "baseline budgeting"
- Eliminate Appropriations as a Separate Jurisdiction
- Require Longer-Term Authorizations
- Prohibit Appropriations-Report Language that Contravenes Provisions in an Authorization
- Eliminate Unauthorized Appropriations without Concurrence of Authorizing Committees
- Establish a Single Joint-Budget Committee of the Leadership
- Apply Senate's Rule against Extraneous Matter in Reconciliation Bills to the House

*Joint Committee on the Organization of Congress

to reduce the deficit and balance the budget in a specific period of time. Over two dozen proposals to require a balanced budget, to limit the size or growth of the federal budget or of the public debt, or some combination of these ideas, were introduced in the 104th and 105th Congresses. A CBO listing of budget-process reform legislation in the 103rd Congress included 186 major budget process reform proposals (most being the balanced-budget amendment and the line-item veto/enhanced rescission).[4] The Joint Committee on the Organization of Congress reviewed dozens of budget proposals, but none were adopted in the 103rd Congress (see Table 7.2).

The 1994 congressional election changed the budget-reform agenda significantly. The 1994 election and the Republican's subsequent Contract with America in the 104th Congress impacted budget reforms by bringing forth the balanced-budget amendment, the line-item veto, the unfunded-mandate reform, tax cuts, cuts in payments to individuals, welfare reform and a major drive toward a balanced budget (see Table 7.3). These were at the top of the Republican congressional budget-reform agenda and led to the historic standoff between President Clinton and Congress in 1995 and 1996. The 104th Con-

TABLE 7.3
Major Republican Budget-Reform Proposals of the 104th and 105th Congresses

- The Balanced-Budget Amendment (passed in House only; defeated in Senate)
- The Line-Item Veto (passed)
- Unfunded-Mandate Reform (passed)
- Biennial Budgeting (defeated)
- Prohibit Authorizations of Less than Two Years (defeated)
- Abolish Baseline Budgeting (passed in House only)
- Restore "Fire walls" between Defense and Nondefense Spending (defeated)

gress was intent upon cutting spending and balancing the budget within seven years. For the first time in our history, the president vetoed the Reconciliation Bill. This occurred on 6 December 1995. The Republicans used a shut-down strategy (for six days in November and for almost a month from mid-December to early January 1996), designed to cut spending and control entitlements. The strategy failed. The FY 1997 budget was finally passed on 26 April 1996, showing the fundamental policy differences between the two parties. The strong performance of the economy in 1996–1998 generated over $225 billion in revenues that covered up (at least for the short term) sharp policy differences, and permitted a proposed balanced budget for FY 1999.

The first Republican budget-process reform promised in the Contract with America was the Balanced Budget Amendment (H.J. Res. 1), a constitutional amendment requiring the president to propose and Congress to adopt a balanced budget each fiscal year starting in FY 2002 (or for the second fiscal year beginning after its final ratification). According to this proposal, Congress may not adopt a budget resolution in which total outlays exceed total receipts unless three-fifths of the membership of each house approves. Congress may waive these provisions for any fiscal year in which a declaration of war is in effect or the country faces "an imminent and serious military threat to national security." A majority of each chamber must pass and the president must sign a joint resolution identifying the threat. This was a popular proposal with the public. A Gallup Poll conducted 28 November 1994 revealed that 77 percent of those questioned on the topic ranked the amendment either the top or a high priority for the 104th Congress (although surprisingly the deficit at that time was not an important issue in pubic opinion). Congress had rejected all balanced-budget amendments since the first one was introduced in 1936. The closest Congress ever came to passing it, until the vote in 1995, was in 1986 when the Senate defeated the proposal by a single vote. The balanced-budget amendment was defeated again in 1995 by a single vote in the Senate.

The second major budget reform in the Contract with America was the Line-Item Veto Act (PL 104-130), which gives the president a permanent legislative line-item veto. Under this procedure, the president may strike or reduce any discretionary budget authority or eliminate targeted tax provisions in any bill. The president must prepare a separate rescission package for each bill and must submit his proposal to Congress within five calendar days of its passage. The president's proposed rescissions take effect unless Congress passes a disapproval bill within thirty days after receiving them. Congress can overturn a president's line-item veto, but only after first passing a resolution mandating the spending. The resolution can itself be vetoed by the president. This confers substantial new budgetary powers to the president. Proponents of the line-item veto maintained that given large deficits, the president should have the authority to single out "unnecessary and wasteful" spending provisions in bills passed by Congress. Critics of the line-item veto have argued that the line-item veto gives too much power to the executive branch to control federal spending, a responsibility clearly given to the legislative branch in the U.S. Constitution. The line-item veto was overturned by the Supreme Court in June 1998 (*Clinton vs. New York*) (Taylor 1998).

The Unfunded-Mandate Reform Act (H.R. 5) restricts the imposition of unfunded requirements by the federal government on state and local government entities. Unfunded mandates are provisions in federal legislation that impose enforceable duties on state and local governments without appropriating funds to pay for them. According to the reform, the Commission on Unfunded Mandates must report to Congress and the president recommendations for suspending, consolidating, simplifying, or terminating mandates, as well as suggesting flexible means and common standards for complying with mandates. The bill requires federal agencies to assess the effects of federal regulations on state, local, tribal, and private-sector entities. CBO is required to prepare an impact statement assessing the cost of the proposed mandates for any legislation. The bill repeals mandates at the beginning of any fiscal year in which no funds are provided to cover their costs, and assigns responsibility to determine the appropriate mandate funding levels to the Budget Committees. Congress must consider the costs of any federal requirement they impose on state and local governments, thus limited their zeal to pass new costly legislation.

The balanced-budget amendment (or a balanced budget), line-item veto, and unfunded-mandate reform all increase the power of a more conservative agenda for federal spending. Cutbacks in federal spending and federal legislation have occurred as a result of the unfunded-mandates reform and the line-item veto, but the major cuts occurred as a result of the shift in party control and thus spending and taxing policy of the House and Senate in 1995.

CONCLUSIONS

What has been the impact of the Republican-initiated budget-process reforms of the 1990s? Specific policy outcomes did not change dramatically as a result of the budget reforms of the 1990s until the landslide Republican 1994 election and the deficit-reducing agenda in the Contract with America. A change of party and a change of will among members of Congress changed policy. It did not occur as a result of budget-process reforms, although those budget tools made it easier to implement the "deficit hawk" policy preferences of the new Republican majority in Congress. The rules did not change behavior; the elections of 1994 and 1996 did.

The increase in revenue as a result of the unexpected economic growth in the three years from 1996 through 1998 has lead to a proposed balanced budget for FY 1999, when just three years before, the federal government was shut down twice in a partisan clash over reducing the deficit. The constraints of previous budget decisions and especially the memory of past deficits and the projected mandatory-entitlement spending for the aged will, however, continue to limit congressional desires to cut taxes and increase spending.

Budgets are political documents and budgetary politics will continue to be center stage in Congress. The major impact of the 1990 pact and the 1994 Republican win was a tighter zero-sum budget game with more control, top–down, centralized budgeting by the congressional party leadership, but revealed little change in the appropriations process. The trade-offs between program reductions and increases are more visible at the aggregate level, as are tax reductions and increases, but the responsibility for them seems to be more diffuse. The budget battles will be struggles over spending priorities within zero-sum limits defined by the Republican-led reforms of the 1990s even though the 1999 budget promises more revenues. The Republican-initiated budget reforms in 1990 and 1995 led to more complexity in budget making (e.g., categorical caps on discretionary spending, PAYGO, and the line-item veto), while simplifying some aspects of the process (e.g., the five-year budget), which has resulted in a larger role for budget and party leaders. Even with a projected FY 1999 balanced budget, ultimately the conflict over further centralization of budget power is inevitable. The intent of the reforms of the 1990s was to create a more harmonious budget process. The economy has helped create harmony, but the partisan battle will continue over tax cuts, reduction of the debt, or more spending on domestic programs.

No budget process is policy neutral and this is certainly the case of the budget reforms of the 1990s. Policy outcomes and budget-process reforms cannot be separated politically, as the 1990 and 1995 budget negotiations demonstrated. The BEA controls had a conservative bias; they were intended to control spending. Like earlier reforms, they centralized budget power, reinforced top–down budget control, opened the process, and encouraged more discipline in congressional spending and taxing.

Budget-process reform does not work by itself; it must have the support of the actors. Members of Congress create the budget-process reforms and try to abide by them; but if the policy outcomes do not comply with the preferences of the members, they may change the process again. The budget process rules are important, but the preferences of the major budget and appropriations actors are much more important in determining the policy outcomes in the battle over the budget, as shown by the impact of the 1994 election.

Change in the budget (tax and spending cuts) came from the American electorate. The 1994 voters seemed to want a balanced budget, tax cuts, welfare reform, the line-item veto, and unfunded-mandates reform. Congress responded. In the past, the American electorate has failed to make this kind of commitment. The lesson of the last twenty-five years is that process reforms cannot make up for the lack of political will and a booming economy resulting in a revenue surge. The budget rules of the 1997 are designed to enforce the balance-budget agreement. The overriding objective is to preclude actions that could create or enlarge budget deficits. Those rules make it difficult for Congress or the president to spend budget surpluses. If the projections of budget surpluses hold up into FY 2000, Congress and the president will likely attempt to craft yet a new budget process, to permit some tax cuts and expenditure increases. Any time they craft a new fiscal policy framework, Republicans and Democrats tend to rewrite the budget rules to enforce the new agreement. Thus the test of the Republican reforms is if they hold during times of surplus as well as times of deficit. It is certain that budget-process reform will be an important item on the congressional agenda for years to come.

NOTES

This article is partially based upon interviews with House and Senate members, staff, and informed observers. The author is grateful for the time they gave and for their observations about the congressional budget process. He would like to thank the School of Public Affairs and the Center for Congressional and Presidential Studies at the American University for supporting the research for this analysis.

1. One of the important reforms instituted by the 1974 Budget Act was the creation of the Congressional Budget Office (CBO)—Congress's principal source of information and analysis on the budget and on spending and revenue legislation. The CBO has a specific mandate to assist the House and Senate Budget Committees and the spending and revenue committees. CBO responds to requests for information from other committees and individual members of Congress. Prior to the creation of CBO, Congress was forced

to rely on the president's budget estimates and economic forecasts and the annual analysis of the economy and fiscal policy done by the Joint Economic Committee.

2. Another measure of budget deficit problems is the imbalance of outlays and receipts as a percentage of the gross national product (GNP). For example, outlays were 24.3 percent of GNP and receipts were 18.1 percent of GNP in 1983; 23.7 percent outlays to 18.4 percent revenues in 1986; and 22.2 percent outlays to 19.2 percent revenues in 1989. See U.S. Congress, Congressional Budget Office, *The Economic and Budget Outlook: Fiscal Years 1991–1995* (1990), p. 123.

3. These deadlines significantly altered prior budget-process deadlines. Notably, the new deadlines have been delayed or modified informally each year since GRH I and GRH II were passed.

4. See memos by Phil Joyce to Bob Reischauer (and others) on the Budget Process Legislation from 22 January 1993 to 1 September 1994.

PART FOUR

The Congressional Republican Party

CHAPTER EIGHT

Moderate Success: Majority Status and the Changing Nature of Factionalism in the House Republican Party

ROBIN KOLODNY

INTRODUCTION

Recently, William F. Connelly, Jr., and John J. Pitney, Jr., commented on the House GOP's Civil War (Connelly and Pitney 1997). They explain that the first one hundred days of the 104th Congress was a unique time in the history of House Republicans (or really, of any congressional party) because of the remarkable unity and cohesion demonstrated by the House Republican Conference. However, Connelly and Pitney are quick to point out that the heady time of the Contract with America, based as it was on clear consensus issues, could not hide the fractious nature of the House Republicans for long. Their recent observations echo their earlier characterization of the Republican Party in Congress (Connelly and Pitney 1994). Along with works by Rae (1989) and Koopman (1996), Connelly and Pitney have illustrated the complexity of the Republican Party. Political scientists no longer make blanket statements about the Republican Party being homogeneous, and have come to appreciate how majority status exacerbates existing cleavages in the party.

In this research, I focus on the role of the moderate faction of the Republican Party in the 104th Congress. Moderate Republicans have always played an important role in their party's success, but the more decidedly conservative bent of the recent Republican majority initially made observers dismiss their influence. The slight majorities in the 104th and 105th Congress make the moderates' policy input more significant than their conservative counterparts, because as Connelly and Pitney say, "if Democrats are united, any Republican faction with more than ten members can deprive the party of a victory on a floor vote"

(Connelly and Pitney 1997, 701). Because moderate Republicans are more likely to ally with Democrats than conservative Republicans, the moderates' ability to prevail on ultimate policy outcomes is enhanced.

This research focuses on the work of the Tuesday Group (formerly known as the Tuesday Lunch Bunch) in both sessions of the 104th Congress. This group of relatively senior moderate to liberal Republicans exercised considerable *negative* influence on the congressional agenda championed by the majority of the Republican Conference. That is, they removed or blocked controversial proposals (normally regarding social issues) from final consideration by the House of Representatives, or voted against the party's position when such divisive issues did come up for a vote. As illustrated during the Contract period, this meant that many potentially divisive proposals were never publicly voted on, leaving mostly consensual measures among Republicans (usually economic in nature) on the public agenda. Such tabling of issues created artificially high records of party-line voting during the first session of the 104th Congress, giving the impression that Republicans were more highly unified than was in fact the case. Indeed, earlier in this volume Peters makes reference to the considerable ideological divide in the Conference. That controversial social issues could be displaced from the agenda demonstrates that Republicans are in fact quite divided on several significant aspects of the public-policy agenda.

CONVENTIONAL WISDOM ABOUT REPUBLICANS IN CONGRESS

This research builds on a growing body of literature about the Republican party in the United States, especially the Republican Party in Congress. Much of this literature emphasizes the factional nature of the Republican Party. Nicol Rae (1989) argues that the previously dominant liberal wing of the Republican Party has given way to far more conservative factions at the national level. Rae demonstrates that factions in the Republican Party have formed in three divisions: sectional, ideological, and purists versus professionals. This latter division was also recognized by Charles O. Jones (1970) when he demonstrated that a minority party in Congress can either try to achieve majority status or to participate in the policy-making process in a constructive manner. It cannot do both credibly. But this does not mean that all members of that party agree on which strategy to pursue. This problem has been well documented by Connelly and Pitney (1994) and Koopman (1996). Indeed, Connelly and Pitney spend a considerable amount of time documenting the many cleavages of the Republican Party in the House of Representatives. Despite the number of cleavages they identify, the matter of style, of "grandstanding" versus "governing," remains the fundamental distinction (see Connelly and Pitney 1994, 19–40). In the years between the Jones and Connelly/Pitney studies, few political scientists tried to capture the internal dynamics of the Republican Party in the House of Representatives. This omission is understandable because of the belief for most of the past forty years that the Republicans would not be able to attain majority status.

In 1996, Douglas Koopman documented the House Republicans' move from "a passive opposition accepting permanent minority status to an activist opposition, and ultimately to a majority" (p. 6). Koopman's focus is on seven factions he identifies in the House Republican Party: moralists, enterprisers, patricians, moderates, stalwarts, provincials, and placeholders. These factions are not based on a straightforward ideological scale, but rather a more complex combination of ideologies, views of the institution of Congress, and interpretations of the proper role of lawmakers (p. 84). Koopman's rich interpretation of the internal tensions of the House Republican Party illuminates the long-standing problems that the party had in the minority, and speculates that such tensions will not be ameliorated by majority status. In short, the party has made a turn away from moderation that may spell trouble for its future.

The sense that congressional Republicans are homogeneous and highly disciplined comes from studies of roll-call votes. But analyses based on votes cast on final passage of legislation really only tell part of the story (Koopman 1996, 17–21; see also Peters, this volume, chapter 3). The power of moderate Republicans to limit the consideration of controversial items has great significance in both understanding the heterogeneity of the Republican Party and in appreciating a powerful tool used to control public policy. Every congressional majority has factional problems, but what is noteworthy about the moderate wing of the contemporary House Republican Party is that they are committed to the ideal of party in a way that regionally factionalized Democrats were not. Peters explains this as a party culture difference. Republicans seem more intractable over ideological divisions than their Democratic predecessors, but the Democratic cleavages are more discernable (Peters, this volume, chapter 3). So, moderate Republicans tried to table action on issues where they reckoned that the divisions among the House Republicans were probably insurmountable, rather than subject the party to public division. They opposed initiatives on social policies that the conservative majority preferred (such as limits on abortion and environmental protections), but worked constructively with conservatives to promote change on policies at the core of the party, specifically issues of fiscal conservatism. Their approach was different from their moderate Democrat counterparts, the Blue Dog Coalition, which expressed its differences with the majority of their party primarily by introducing alternative legislation without regard to the long-term divisions it might cause (Kolodny 1997).

The Tuesday Group is not the first significant congressional organization of moderate Republicans. Many of its members also belong to the House Wednesday Group (which dates to the 1950s) as well as to the 92 Group, the Tuesday

Group's predecessor (see Peabody 1976; Rae 1989; Connelly and Pitney 1994; Koopman 1996). What distinguishes the Tuesday Group is its establishment under conditions of Republican-majority control and the thrust of its legislative agenda. Both the Wednesday Group and the 92 Group worked on alternative issue proposals relating to public policy, part of the strategy they pursued to be considered as junior partners in the policy process. However, in a majority environment, members of the Tuesday Group, who tend also to be relatively senior members holding positions of responsibility in committees or subcommittees, must now respond to initiatives from various factions of their own party, and are less concerned with initiatives from the opposing party (unless, of course, such proposals serve the Tuesday Group's needs).

This group, originally named for its meeting day, hour (noon), and subsidiary purpose (pizza), is unique because its minority veto power is not easily measured. They can block objectionable items from the common party agenda by pressuring the leadership (by threatening to oppose procedural motions or making speeches on the floor against the party's position), offering motions or amendments on the floor to counteract objectionable measures, and voting against the party if all else fails. The consequence of this united action by a group of senior, policy-oriented members is that they exercise internal influence on both the congressional agenda and the substance of specific proposals far beyond what their numbers warrant. Indeed, many observers of the Tuesday Group credit their success for the founding of the Conservative Action Team (CATs), a group of conservative Republicans that operates much as the Tuesday Group has. If the conservatives' position was secure, they would not feel compelled to form their own party caucus.

This research is based on the author's observations as a 1995 APSA congressional fellow in the office of one of the House's key moderate Republicans. Six elite interviews were conducted with former members and high-level staff involved with the Tuesday Group to ascertain information about the group's members, strategies, and concerns. The Tuesday Group has always been very protective of the full extent of its membership list and out of respect for their wishes, I do not reveal the full slate of names of Tuesday Group members. Their identities are not nearly as important as the role they play in the success of the House Republican leadership, especially in producing consensus victories that result in enacted laws.

WHAT IS THE TUESDAY GROUP/TUESDAY LUNCH BUNCH?[1]

The Tuesday Group is an informal caucus of moderate-to-liberal Republican members of the House of Representatives who generally represent constituencies in regions traditionally associated with moderate Republicanism such as the

Northeast and the Midwest. When asked to categorize the Tuesday Group, elite respondents chose words such as "caucus," "faction," and "coalition." Though the term "caucus" might not satisfy all those involved, I will use it to describe the Tuesday Group because it meets all the criteria specified by Susan Webb Hammond (1997). That is, the Tuesday Group operates outside the formal structures of Congress, it is voluntary, it has an organizational structure that includes three co-chairs, and it has continued from one Congress (the 104th) to the present one. Hammond lists the Tuesday Group as an intraparty (or just party) caucus. Intraparty caucuses are normally based on an ideology, which is true generally for the Tuesday Group (although some participants eschew ideological labels and call themselves "governing Republicans" to emphasize that Tuesday Group members' common link is creating workable solutions to public-policy problems even if that means compromise with other factions or parties). Finally, Hammond lists three general activities of caucuses: information gathering and exchange; influencing agendas; and other floor-oriented activities (1997, 281–82). Each of these functions will be dealt with in turn.

Information Gathering and Exchange

The initial reason for the creation of the Tuesday Group was for the sharing of information. Representative Steve Gunderson (R-Wis.), one of the co-founders of the group, described it this way:

> Our Tuesday lunches are very casual, but the attendance is strictly limited. Only members of the lunch bunch are invited, and any given member's staff people are welcome only if that member is present. Lobbyists, guests, and reporters are not allowed. We do ask various people to come in and speak to us. . . . But mainly we talk policy, hashing out our agenda for the week. (Gunderson and Morris 1996, 189)

Throughout the first session of the 104th Congress, the group met on average every week, although many additional meetings were scheduled at times when matters of particular concern to group members were imminent. As the legislative session stretched into the fall, group meetings took place less regularly, and very often on Wednesdays. The Tuesday Group's meetings were not as frequent in the second session, reflecting the less frenetic pace of legislative activity.

Each Monday, key staff members of Tuesday group co-chairs met to suggest agenda items for the upcoming meeting. Normally, topics for discussion concerned impending floor business. More frequent meetings coincided with floor consideration of issues most important to the group such as welfare reform, social spending priorities, and reconciliation. Occasionally, individuals would be invited to address the group. The most frequent guest was Speaker Newt Gingrich. Other guests included Majority Leader Richard Armey, members of the Democratic Blue Dog Coalition, and representatives of various conservative Republican groups.

Influencing Agendas

Hammond (1997, 281) states that most caucuses influence agendas by either *setting* agendas or *maintaining* agendas. The Tuesday Group, however, because of its size, its situation of being in a new majority, and the zealotry of the majority of the House Republican Party is most effective at limiting objectionable items. In one sense, the Tuesday Group is maintaining their agenda by asserting that the status quo is preferable to any change in an undesirable direction. But as many interview respondents indicated, the Tuesday Group's mission was not so much to hurt the majority party's agenda or position but to protect their party from being embroiled in controversial issues that would obscure the core set of issues that united them all. Of course, concerns about how their party's activities would play out in the electoral arena motivated Tuesday Group members to advocate workable policy positions over vague (and potentially unpopular) political principles. Representative Gunderson's insights are again telling:

> I insist on calling us "governing Republicans." It's the term I like to use rather than "moderate Republicans," because I think ideological labels are increasingly difficult to define and, I think, increasingly irrelevant . . . we want to work through government to get something accomplished. We're not driven by some narrow ideology; we're not willing, as some are, to throw political hand grenades in order to make an ideological point. . . . We . . . believe in the institution of Congress and believe in two parties working together to fulfill the obligations of a governing Congress. . . . (Gunderson and Morris 1996, 188–89)

Thus group members pursued activities in *reaction* to controversial proposals from the majority of the Republican Party (especially in the first session), rather than generating new proposals themselves. This is consistent with their general belief that they must be supportive of the party leadership as much as possible to preserve their majority position. The Tuesday Group would prefer to have family feuds be private rather than public matters.

Activities

As with any other caucus, the Tuesday Group developed legislation, offered amendments, and mobilized colleagues to achieve their ends. The group often used blocking tactics to prevent further consideration on controversial issues. If the group cannot convince the leadership to table discussion of a controversial issue, they then try several strategies such as lobbying the Rules Committee for a rule to allow them to present alternative amendments, opposing the rule if no concessions are made, supporting the Democrats' motion to recommit, or opposing final passage of a bill. The Tuesday Group lobbied, and received, a seat at leadership meetings, though the leadership stipulated that the position must rotate among various Tuesday Group members.[2] In 1996, the Tuesday Group was asked to send representatives to "Unity Dinners" held by Majority Leader Armey, in an effort to smooth tensions between the Tuesday Group and CATS (Eilperin 1997).

No Ordinary Caucus?

How is a party caucus different from a party faction? What difference does it make that the Tuesday Group operates as a party within a party? What binds Tuesday Group members and how is this cohesion manifested?

Who Is in the Group?

Group members in the 104th Congress were identified from a fax list used to appraise members of upcoming group meetings and agendas. Fifty-four members asked to be appraised of Tuesday Group meeting times and information, though fewer members were regular participants.[3] This fax list provided relatively little information about the core membership of the group (many press accounts cite Tuesday Group co-chairs as stating the real membership number as closer to forty). To ascertain the activity levels of group members, I asked six individuals with firsthand knowledge of the Tuesday Group in the 104th Congress to rank members by their level of activity.[4] An averaging of the judges' evaluations was used to help identify key members of the Tuesday Group.

Table 8.1 shows the distribution of members of the 104th Congress by region, party, and Tuesday Group membership. Virtually all of the New England Republicans (87.5 percent) are members of the Tuesday Group. Nearly half of the Mid-Atlantic Republicans and 40 percent of the Midwestern Republicans are in the group. Although one-fifth of the Tuesday Group's membership comes from the Great Lakes region, only 26.2 percent of all Great Lakes Republicans are Tuesday Group members. The southern and western regions account for only a very small part of the Tuesday Group and a very small proportion of the Republican Party's delegation from these areas.

Though region does a good job of characterizing the overall contours of group membership, it is less successful at explaining group activism. Table 8.2 categorizes Tuesday Group members by region and activism in the group as assessed by the six judges. Here we see that the Mid-Atlantic and Great Lakes regions are slightly overrepresented in the "core" and "supporting" categories, but this is probably due to their absolute numbers in the group. It appears that region is limited in explaining the activity levels of Tuesday Group members.

TABLE 8.1
MEMBERS BY PARTY (AND TUESDAY GROUP) AND REGION

Subregions	Democrat	Republican	(Tuesday Group)	Independent	Total
New England	14	8	(7)	1	23
Mid-Atlantic	33	33	(16)		66
Great Lakes	32	42	(11)		74
Midwest	14	17	(7)		31
South	52	64	(5)		116
Border States	14	18	(3)		32
West	6	18	(1)		24
Pacific States	34	35	(4)*		69
Total	199	235	54	1	435

Source: Fax list given to author.

*Due to a special election, there were five Pacific-state members in 1996, bringing the group's total to 55.

New England: Connecticut, Maine, Massachusetts, New Hampshire, Rhode Island, and Vermont.

Mid-Atlantic: Delaware, New Jersey, New York, and Pennsylvania.

Great Lakes: Illinois, Indiana, Michigan, Ohio, and Wisconsin.

Midwest: Iowa, Kansas, Minnesota, Missouri, Nebraska, North Dakota and South Dakota.

South: Virginia, Alabama, Arkansas, Florida, Georgia, Louisiana, Mississippi, North Carolina, South Carolina, and Texas.

Border States: Kentucky, Maryland, Oklahoma, Tennessee, and West Virginia.

West: Arizona, Colorado, Idaho, New Mexico, Nevada, Utah, and Wyoming.

Pacific States: California, Oregon, Washington, Alaska, and Hawaii.

Regional labels are mine; coding follows that of Poole and Rosenthal.

MEASURES OF PARTISANSHIP AND IDEOLOGY

The ideological composition of congressional parties has long been a subject of discussion. Although recent scholars of House Republicans have emphasized the multidimensionality of Republican factionalism (as cited above), other analysis have confirmed the regional division of Republican ideology. David Rohde (1991, 120–27) has commented on the liberalism of Northeastern Republicans compared to the rest of the Republican Party, demonstrated by lower party-unity scores for Northeastern Republicans. Recently, Cover, Pinney, and Serra (1997, 228–34) have found great distinction between Eastern Republicans and the remainder of the Republican Party based on their ADA (Americans for Democratic Action) scores measuring liberalism. Here, I look at both these measures of ideological dispersion in the 104th Congress.

TABLE 8.2
TUESDAY GROUP MEMBERS BY ACTIVITY LEVEL AND REGION

Subregions	Core	Supporting	Peripheral	Total
New England	2	4	1	7
Mid-Atlantic	6	9	1	16
Great Lakes	4	5	2	11
Midwest	1	4	2	7
South	—	4	1	5
Border States	2	—	1	3
West	1	—	—	1
Pacific States	1	3 (4)	—	4
Total	17	29 (30)	8	54 (55)

Source: Compiled from interviews by author.

The coding of activity levels was explained to the judges as follows:

(1) *Core Member:* this is an individual who was critical to the mission of the group, who was active in generating ideas and carrying forth the work of the group;

(2) *Supporting Member:* this is an individual who regularly attended group meetings, who voted with the group when asked or spoke up for the group, but who did not warrant the status of Core Member; and

(3) *Peripheral Member:* this is an individual who received information on group activities and occasionally attended group meetings, but whose support was not consistently expected.

At first glance, it would seem that any Republican divisions evaporated in 1995. Party-unity scores for Republicans are very tightly clustered together while Democrats are widely dispersed. Table 8.3 presents these party-unity scores. As expected, Southern Democrats and Northeastern Republicans deviate the most from the rest of their party, but the high means and low standard deviations of all Republicans' party-unity scores are truly remarkable. The same goes for ADA scores. Table 8.4 presents these scores for both parties. Again, the level of Republican conservatism is notable. The mean ADA scores are exceptionally low for all Republicans (indeed, the party's high scorer in 1995 was Connie Morella of Maryland with only a 45). Still, the Eastern Republicans are significantly more liberal than the remainder of their party, confirming Cover, Pinney, and Serra's earlier findings. But the degree of this liberalism fell dramatically in the first session of the 104th Congress. Included in the ADA's 1995 ratings is a special notice that liberal Republicans are now an "endangered species." The ADA explains that they normally consider members with a score in the 40- to 60-percent range to be a "moderate" of either party, and that Republicans who once had this distinction have since lost it (ADA 1996). The ADA commentary does not take into account the influence of the party structure on roll-call votes,

TABLE 8.3
PARTY UNITY BY REGION

Region	Democratic Party Unity by Region							
	Mean Party-Unity Score		St. Dev. of Party-Unity Score		Minimum Party-Unity Score		Maximum Party-Unity Score	
	1995	1996	1995	1996	1995	1996	1995	1996
East	86	86	10	9	52	59	97	97
Midwest	81	80	13	12	49	50	96	96
South	72	71	18	17	22	29	94	97
West	85	87	12	9	45	52	98	98

Region	Republican Party Unity by Region							
	Mean Party-Unity Score		St. Dev. of Party-Unity Score		Minimum Party-Unity Score		Maximum Party-Unity Score	
	1995	1996	1995	1996	1995	1996	1995	1996
East	85	77	8	11	63	45	98	95
Midwest	91	87	5	6	78	68	97	96
South	93	90	4	8	80	51	99	98
West	93	90	4	7	80	71	99	98

Sources: *Congressional Roll Call 1995: A Chronology and Analysis of Votes in the House and Senate, 104th Congress, First Session.* Washington, D.C.: Congressional Quarterly, Inc. 1996. *Congressional Roll Call 1996: A Chronology and Analysis of Votes in the House and Senate, 104th Congress, Second Session.* Washington, D.C.: Congressional Quarterly, Inc. 1997.

an observation made by Koopman. With the Republicans now in the majority, the range of options for the most marginal party members are necessarily proscribed. In other words, we should expect that Republican control of Congress, at least in year one, would polarize voting patterns of both parties. For 1996, Table 8.3 shows that the party-unity scores for Democrats remained relatively stable, but Republicans lost much of the cohesion they demonstrated the previous year. The overall Republican unity mean for 1995 was 91.19, but only 86.62 for 1996. Though the decline in party unity was found throughout the party's regions, clearly the Eastern Republicans' decline in party unity was the most significant. When considering the 1996 ADA scores, both parties seem less polarized. The Democratic ADA scores fell, while Republican ADA scores rose, especially for Eastern and Midwestern Republicans, though the magnitude of

TABLE 8.4
AMERICANS FOR DEMOCRATIC ACTION (ADA) SCORES
BY PARTY AND REGION

Region	Mean Democratic ADA Score		St. Dev. of Democratic ADA Score		Mean Republican ADA Score		St. Dev. of Republican ADA Score	
	1995	1996	1995	1996	1995	1996	1995	1996
East	84	82	13	14	18	21	12	16
Midwest	79	76	16	15	6	10	9	10
South	70	62	24	23	3	6	5	7
West	86	83	13	14	3	6	6	9

Sources: Americans for Democratic Action, *1995 U.S. House of Representatives Voting Record.* Washington, D.C.: Americans for Democratic Action; Americans for Democratic Action, *1996 U.S. House of Representatives Voting Record.* Washington, D.C.: Americans for Democratic Action.

the difference is not great. This should reinforce the idea that the rarified environment in 1995 significantly skewed normal voting behavior in both parties.

We know that region does not perfectly correspond with membership in the Tuesday Group. Table 8.5 shows that the mean party-unity and ADA scores are substantially different for Tuesday Group members and the remainder of the Republican conference in both sessions of the 104th Congress. Tuesday Group members are less likely to vote with their party almost 10 percent of the time and had six times the ADA score of their nongroup colleagues in 1995 (about three times as high in 1996), although the standard deviations of both these measures show how much more varied Tuesday Group members are than their nongroup colleagues. Even more interesting is the data for Tuesday Group members when divided by activity level. On both measures, core members of the Tuesday Group were much less likely to vote with their party and far more likely to have a higher ADA score. Analysis of variance tests for both sets of group comparisons (between Tuesday Group and nongroup Republicans and within categories of the Tuesday Group) were found to be statistically significant. This demonstrates that the Tuesday Group does indeed consist of ideological outliers. The propensity of the Tuesday Group to defect from their party increased in 1996. Both the means and standard deviations of party-unity scores of Tuesday Group members reflect significantly increased defections from the previous year. The ADA scores for 1996 are even more revealing. The means and standard deviations for Tuesday-Group ADA scores are higher for core and supporting members, and the maximum score for a Tuesday Group member rose from 45 in 1995 to 55 in 1996.

TABLE 8.5
PARTY-UNITY AND ADA SCORES FOR THE TUESDAY GROUP

Tuesday Group Members and Nongroup Republicans Compared

	Mean Party-Unity Score		St. Dev. of-Party-Unity Score		Mean ADA Score		St. Dev. of ADA Score	
	1995	1996	1995	1996	1995	1996	1995	1996
Tuesday Group Members (N=54)	84.37	78.36	6.76	8.89	19.11	21.0	11.28	15.35
Nongroup Republicans (N=181)	93.22	89.14	3.76	7.61	3.13	6.44	5.4	7.43

Tuesday Group Members Compared by Activity Level

Activity Level	N	Mean Party-Unity Score		St. Dev. of-Party-Unity Score		Mean ADA Score		St. Dev. of ADA Score	
		1995	1996	1995	1996	1995	1996	1995	1996
Core Member	17	81.0	76.18	7.11	8.67	24.24	21.76	10.08	14.25
Supporting Member	29	84.90	77.53	6.25	8.88	18.28	23.33	11.12	16.52
Peripheral Member	8	89.63	86.13	3.70	5.28	11.25	10.63	9.91	8.63

The coding of activity levels was explained to the judges as follows: (1) *Core Member:* this is an individual who was critical to the mission of the group, who was active in generating ideas and carrying forth the work of the group; (2) *Supporting Member:* this is an individual who regularly attended group meetings, who voted with the group when asked or spoke up for the group, but who did not warrant the status of Core Member; and (3) *Peripheral Member:* this is an individual who received information on group activities and occasionally attended group meetings, but whose support was not consistently expected.

While only four Republicans scored in the 40–60 ADA "moderate" range, ten did so in 1996. Not surprising, all Republicans scoring in the moderate range in 1995 and nine of the ten in 1996 are Tuesday Group members.

MEASURING TUESDAY-GROUP INFLUENCE

Although one of my purposes is to critique the over-reliance of political scientists on roll-call voting data, I analyze Tuesday-Group roll-call votes in the 104th Congress by looking at the unity within the group and between this subgroup and the larger majority party. One approach I have taken is to consider the way the Tuesday Group votes when the Republican Party experiences defections of ten or more. Part of the reason that moderates have any say at all is that the size of the Republican majority is so thin that virtually any defection by party members is potentially quite harmful. In the 104th Congress, the majority had a 12- to 18-vote margin (taking into account the gradual change of several southerners from Democrats to Republicans). Therefore, half of the 18-vote margin plus one would theoretically be enough to defeat any Republican proposal (conservative Democrats often compensated for Republican defections, though they did not go to the trouble of switching parties themselves—see Cooper and Young [1997] for discussions of this cross-partisanship). In short, I am investigating when the Tuesday Group accounted for significant proportions of the Republicans' defections and what effect this might have had on the conduct of majority business in the House.

Votes were analyzed for both sessions. In the first session, there were 136 votes where roughly half of all Republican dissenters (that is Republican members who voted against the majority of their party) were Tuesday Group members. There were 71 such votes for the second session. I selected votes with at least ten defectors, and then looked at each vote to determine if Tuesday Group members were about half that number. The reason for examining these votes is to find out on what issues the leadership experienced Tuesday Group defections. This will help us understand which issues define the division between the Tuesday Group and the majority of the Republican Conference.

First, there is the type of vote. The overwhelming number of Tuesday Group defections were on amendment votes. In the first session, amendments constitute 101 of the 136 votes (74 percent) analyzed; there were 46 amendments among the 71 second-session votes (65 percent).[5] The next highest category was votes on final passage of legislation, but there were only twelve of these in 1995 and six in 1996. There were six defecting votes on passage of the rule in 1995, but only three in 1996. Motions to recommit legislation comprised six defecting votes in 1995 and five in 1995. The remaining defections are reported in Table 8.6. The small number of defection votes that had extremely serious consequences for the party leadership (final passage, adoption of rule, motion to recommit) is truly noteworthy. This confirms the assertion of Tuesday Group insiders that such actions will only be used as a last resort. Additionally, relatively few Tuesday Group members engaged in those defections. The largest number of Tuesday Group defectors on a rule in 1995 was 34 (HR 1833: Partial Birth Abortions) and in 1996 was 28 (HR 125: Assault Weapons Ban Repeal). The largest number of defections on final passage in 1995 was 22 (HR 961: Clean Water Act Revisions) and was 42 in 1996 (HR 1227: Employee Commuting Act/Minimum Wage).

TABLE 8.6
VOTE DEFECTIONS BY TYPE AND SUCCESSES OF SUCH DEFECTIONS

Type of Vote	Number in 1995	Number of Successes	Number in 1996	Number of Successes
Amendment	101	25	47	11
Final Passage	12	1	6	1
Rule	6	—	3	—
Motion to Recommit	6	2	5	—
Motion to Instruct Conferees	3	1	1	—
Adoption of Conference Report	2	—	1	—
Motion to Order Previous Question	1	1	3	—
Constitutional Amendment	1	—	1	1
Miscellaneous	4	—	3	2
Veto Override	—	—	1	—
Total	136	30	71	15

Second, there is the success of these defections. That is, how often were Tuesday Group defectors on the winning side (defeating their party's majority)? On 30 of the 136 votes in the first session, Tuesday Group defectors joined with Democrats and other Republican defectors to defeat the majority of the Republican Party's position. Twenty-five of these defeats were on amendments, two on motions to recommit, and one each on a motion to instruct, motion to move the previous question, and final passage. In 1996, 15 of the 71 votes found Democrat–moderate-Republican victories. Eleven of these were on amendments, one on final passage, one on a constitutional amendment (Tax Limitation Constitutional Amendment) and two miscellaneous matters (suspension of the rules and question of consideration). Clearly, the Tuesday Group's greatest effectiveness on the floor is in the support or defeat of amendments to legislation. Amendments provide Tuesday Group members with opportunities to tone down the legislation's most controversial aspects and allow them to signal to their supporters that they can exercise some independence from the party. However, once they have tinkered with a bill's points, they find it harder to vote against final passage, for fear their leadership will not give them much consideration in the future.

Next we turn to the specific issues championed by the Tuesday Group as expressed through these vote defections. The votes were about evenly split between authorization and appropriation measures in both sessions. However, the group's successes (where their defections resulted in a defeat for the majority

Republican position) were twice as likely to occur on appropriations bills (20) than on authorization bills (10) in 1995, but just slightly more likely in 1996 with nine appropriations victories and six authorization victories. This confirms the sentiments of several of the interviewees that the Tuesday Group's efforts were particularly effective during the appropriations' process. One reason for this is that some conservative initiatives were formulated to end "status quo" programs by proposing significant cuts to their funding. This led to vocal defenses by Tuesday Group members of programs important to them (such as environmental programs and family-planning initiatives). Lastly, I examined each of the votes to determine the issue categories where Tuesday Group members defected from their party. In 1995, 32 of the 136 votes (roughly 24 percent of the total) were related to the environment; in 1996, 13 of 71 votes were (roughly 18 percent). This is where the group had the largest proportion of its successes (eight out of thirty) in 1995. Environmental issues accounted for only two of the fifteen successes in 1996. Abortion and family-planning matters comprised about 24 votes (18 percent) in 1995, but resulted in only two victories; in 1996, it accounted for 9 votes (13 percent) but only one victory. Civil-liberties/individual-freedoms issues received about 18 percent of the votes in 1995, with six of the group's victories; only 7 percent came from this category in 1996, accounting for no victories. Defense and foreign-policy-related issues were about 12 percent of the total, and resulted in four victories in 1995, mostly concerning support of the president's positions (in 1996, they comprised only 7 percent of defecting votes and two victories). Perhaps the most effective issue area for the group in 1995 was the arts. Although only 5 percent of these votes were on arts policy, the group's position prevailed 71 percent of the time, accounting for five of their thirty victories (by contrast, only two arts defecting votes and one arts victory occurred in 1996). The remaining 19 percent of votes included housing, homeless, infrastructure, science, fiscal, agricultural, welfare, and labor policy. This miscellaneous group accounted for five of the thirty victories combined in 1995. The biggest difference in vote type between the two years was the increase in labor-policy votes in 1996. Labor policy, mostly votes concerning the Tuesday Group's greatest victory—the minimum wage—comprised 10 percent of all defecting votes, all resulting in Tuesday Group victories.

Another interesting point is the relative distribution of these votes. In 1995, 91 of the 136 votes were part of a series of clustered initiatives on only thirteen bills. In 1996, 36 of the 71 votes were on only eight bills. Figure 8.1 lists these bills (each with at least 3 group votes) and the number of Tuesday Group votes associated with each. This gives some sense of where the group finds action prudent (though several bills cited cover a wide range of issues such as the Interior Appropriations bill). It also gives us a sense of what issue dimensions (social in particular) their blocking tactics are most often targeted towards.

1st Session (1995)

HR 961	Clean Water Act Revisions (11)
HR 1868	Fiscal 1996 Foreign Operations Appropriations (11)
HR 2099	Fiscal 1996 VA-HUD Appropriations (11)
HR 1977	Fiscal 1996 Interior Appropriations (10)
HR 2127	Fiscal 1996 Labor, HHS, Education Appropriations (9)
HR 925	Private Property Rights (6)
HR 2020	Fiscal 1996 Treasury-Postal Service Appropriations (6)
HR 1530	Fiscal 1996 Defense Authorization (5)
HR 2076	Fiscal 1996 Commerce, Justice, State Appropriations (5)
HR 2126	Fiscal 1996 Defense Appropriations (5)
HR 1158	Fiscal 1995 Emergency Supplemental Appropriations and Recissions (4)
HR 1561	Fiscal 1996–97 Foreign Aid and State Department Authorization (4)
HR 1976	Fiscal 1996 Agriculture Appropriations (4)

2nd Session (1996)

HR 3662	Fiscal 1997 Interior Appropriations (9)
HR 1227	Employee Commuting Act [Minimum Wage] (5)
HR 3230	Fiscal 1997 Defense Authorization (4)
HR 3610	Fiscal 1997 Defense Appropriations (4)
HR 3666	Fiscal 1997 VA-HUD Appropriations (4)
HR 1833	Abortion Procedure Ban (4)
HR 2202	Immigration Restrictions (3)
HR 2406	Housing Overhaul (3)

FIGURE 8.1 Legislation of great interest to the Tuesday Group (and number of votes where they contested the majority Republican position).

OMISSIONS FROM ROLL-CALL VOTES

There are at least two cases where Tuesday Group members actively lobbied on issues that did not surface in roll-call votes. One is on welfare-reform legislation (HR 4) and the other is affirmative-action legislation. There were virtually no roll-call votes on welfare-reform legislation where Tuesday Group members defected from the majority of their party. However, the Tuesday Group met frequently in the first week of March, when it was anticipated that welfare legislation would soon make it to the floor. The Tuesday Group worked behind the scenes to make changes to the bill prior to floor consideration. This included changes inserted into the chairman's en bloc amendment and several other amendments approved by voice vote. Before that point, several Tuesday Group members were on the Speaker's task force on welfare reform and the limits of Tuesday Group support were clearly spelled out to the leadership. None of this can be captured by roll-call analysis.

The group also met regularly in the summer of 1995. These meetings included much discussion of the impending appropriations bills, but also included discussion of a potential rider to the Defense Appropriations Bill (to be offered by Representative Gary Franks of Connecticut) to put an immediate end to affirmative action. Though the leadership had promised Franks a vote, the Tuesday group lobbied the leadership to delay such a tactic for the division it would cause in the party and the potential public-relations nightmare it would cause (ending affirmative action without any committee consideration or public hearings was considered unwise by many Tuesday Group members). When the leadership saw the level of potential party defection on this issue, they pulled the amendment and no vote was held.

In 1996, many Tuesday Group members joined forces with Democrats to enact an increase in the minimum wage from $4.25 an hour to $5.15 an hour over the wishes of their party's leadership. Press accounts at the time cite the efforts of Tuesday Group member Jack Quinn (along with many other Republican moderates) breaking ranks with the leadership over the considera-tion of the rule on the bill, and ultimately final passage, as being critical to the measure's success in the House (Clymer 1996; Stoddard 1996). The success of this rebellion prompted some conservatives to complain that moderates' rebel-lions did not result in any sanctions from party leaders, while conservative defec-tions often exacted swift and clear rebuffs (Stoddard 1996).

The critical position of moderates in the Republican Party was confirmed in the summer of 1997 when a prominent Tuesday Group member, Representative Jim Greenwood (R-Pa.) was named chair of the Leadership Action Team, a posi-tion vacated by Representative Bill Paxon (R-N.Y.). This was a permanent appointment for Greenwood in one of the leadership's elite groups and is quite different from the revolving seat at leadership meetings that the Tuesday Group currently enjoys. Though Greenwood denies his moderate position was the rea-son for his selection, his discussion of his new role on CNN echoes many of the Tuesday Group goals described here:

[**Bernard Shaw** asks if the party will run from the abortion issue.]

Greenwood: No, no. Abortion will be with us for the foreseeable future. I don't see a party planning its agenda around an issue that's a fault line for the party. We know that as long as any issue that can possibly have an abortion element attached to it, it will be. We'll debate that. That's secondary to the major issues, like tax reform, like looking at the cultural decline in our country, like planning for the retirement of the baby-boom generation. There are big mega-issues that we have to address in the next four years.

Shaw: Are you afraid Republicans could lose control of the House?

Greenwood: Oh, I think we should be afraid of that everyday. If we don't make sure that we're in touch with the agenda that the American people are looking for, with the values that the American people are looking for, we could go into the minority. But I think planning, making sure that as we tee-up major issues before the Congress and we communicate with the American voters, so they know what we're doing and why and that we want to go where they want to go, I think we'll stay in the majority. (CNN 1997)

Greenwood articulates the Tuesday Group's central goal: to keep the agenda focused on consensual issues that will stabilize the Republican Party's majority status. Though the moderates may owe their majority positions to conservatives, the shift in the agenda and public opinion from 1995 to 1996 (and beyond the 1996 elections) shows that Republicans need the policy stewardship of the moderates to produce tangible successes that allow them to claim legitimacy as a governing party. The items the Tuesday Group blocks from consideration have also saved the party from a number of political problems that might stem from taking strident positions on no-win issues (such as abortion).

CONCLUSIONS

The Republican Party in the House of Representatives is indeed heterogeneous and the moderate Northeastern and Midwestern wing of the party is often in disagreement with the majority of House Republicans. These members formed the Tuesday Group, a party caucus formed to prevent action on issues of high volatility within the Republican Party. As the preceding evidence shows, the Tuesday Group's purpose was to promote high party unity by removing items from consideration, while still acting to preserve the status quo on the issues on which they differed most from the remainder of the caucus. Unlike similar factions on the Democratic side, the Tuesday Group seeks to table dissent by preventing controversial votes rather than invite tensions by introducing their own legislation. While in the minority, Republican moderates were more likely to engage in aggressive moves against their brethren. But the lesson to be taken from the 104th Congress is that moderates did not disappear in the new majority, but found a new role for themselves as brokers of a governing position both within their party and between parties.

After the unique atmosphere of 1995 subsided, party leaders realized that they could not succeed as a governing party by championing conservative agenda items. Indeed, one staff aide I interviewed said conservatives complained that the Tuesday Group always got their way. Since moderates normally lose votes on their agenda items in the House, the staffer wondered how conservatives held that view until it was explained to him that they saw moderates getting their way in the end, once the Senate and the president had done their work. A quick look at events in the 105th Congress confirms this.

The Tuesday Group continued to be outspoken on the Fiscal Year 1999 budget plan (including a protest that the House leadership would not allow a vote on the Blue Dog Coalition's alternative budget, see *National Journal* 1998a), and particularly the Fiscal Year 1999 Labor-HHS Appropriations Bill (especially concerning LIHEAP—a program for heating and energy subsidies for low-income individuals, see *National Journal* 1998b). Moderate Republicans continued to disagree with the majority of their party over funding for the National Endowment of the Arts, the Legal Services Corporation, educational block grants, various environmental programs, and the proposed elimination of the Departments of Energy and Commerce.

In 1998 Representative Christopher Shays (R-Conn.) led moderate Republicans (with some conservatives) and a majority of Democrats to the successful passage of a comprehensive campaign-finance bill in the House of Representatives. The extent to which moderates can help define a consensus agenda, both within their party and between parties, should be a prime area of future research, given that the Republican majority in the House narrowed after the 1998 elections, and we can expect competitive House elections (resulting in small majorities) for the foreseeable future. Republican moderates have shown that consensus positions can be developed, and that bipartisanism can be humane. Perhaps that will be their lasting legacy to the new Republican congressional majority.

NOTES

1. The name Tuesday Group has been adopted in the 105th Congress. Though a name change has been discussed almost constantly, the Tuesday Lunch Bunch was used throughout the 104th Congress.

2. Similar representation is given to the Tuesday Group's effective counterpart CATS (Conservative Action Team).

3. Though the Tuesday Group had 55 members at the end of the 104th Congress, Tom Campbell (Calif.-15) was sworn in on 15 December 1995 and thus did not vote on most issues in 1995, the year under examination. Therefore, he is excluded from this part of the analysis.

4. The judges, six high-level staffers and former members of Congress, were asked to indicate group members as "Core," "Supportive," or "Peripheral" members.

5. These numbers also indicate a significant difference in the absolute number of roll-call votes held in each session. The first session had a historic 885 recorded roll-call votes compared to 455 in the second session.

CHAPTER NINE

The House Republicans: Lessons for Political Science

WILLIAM F. CONNELLY, JR., AND JOHN J. PITNEY, JR.

INTRODUCTION

Most of the key academic works on Congress came out during the unprecedented forty-year Democratic dominion over the House (1955–1995). According to Richard Fenno (1997, 2), political scientists assumed that House politics meant Democratic politics. "We wrote extensively about the House Democrats, and we became the victims of our Democratic diet." Two intellectual problems thus arose. First, the House GOP largely escaped the discipline's attention.[1] Scholars mistakenly saw the House Republicans as a homogeneous lot, enlivened only by some nihilistic troublemakers. Second, political scientists failed to anticipate what would happen to both sides—and to the institution—when the majority and minority swapped roles.

The Republican takeover of the House is thus a gift to political science. It should encourage scholars to look at the House GOP's ideas, interests, individuals, and institutional arrangements. It should also shed new light on theories of congressional behavior. Certain ideas hold up quite well, including some that date from James Madison. Others appear to have been time-bound artifacts of a specific historical period.

Although the perspective of future years will tell us more about the implications of GOP control, it is already possible to draw preliminary lessons for political science.

MAJORITY BEHAVIOR DIFFERS FROM MINORITY BEHAVIOR

Beginning in the late 1970s, Newt Gingrich and other House Republicans increasingly used confrontational tactics against the majority Democrats. Scholars sometimes noted these activities and the frustrations behind them (Rohde 1991). Seldom did deeper questions come up: was Gingrich-style "bomb-throwing" a peculiarly Republican enterprise, or would Democrats act the same way in the minority? And in the latter case, why?

The 104th and 105th Congresses have shown that minority Democrats can be as harsh and disruptive as minority Republicans. Conversely, the new majority is defending the institution. Before detailing this behavior, we should ponder how life in the majority differs from that on the other side.

Start with the obvious. "Being in the minority means you don't get your legislation heard, you don't get to chair a committee and you don't influence policies in other parts of the world," says Representative Maxine Waters (D-Calif.) (quoted in Doherty and Katz [1998]). Former Representative Susan Molinari (R-N.Y.) recalls

> How can I describe what the changeover from life in the minority to life in the majority felt like? Imagine having lived in Alaska all your life and abruptly waking up one morning in Florida (with all due respect to Alaska), or living in a cave and moving to a glass house on a hill. . . . We'd spent decades as outsiders. We'd alternately begged the Democrats to consider our legislation and adopted the time-honored, traditional minority stance of naysaying. All of a sudden we mattered. (Molinari with Burkett 1998, 169)

The majority controls procedure and the calendar. During their reign, the Democrats crafted restrictive rules that hindered minority-floor amendments. The GOP majority has been more open: closed or modified-closed rules made up only 43 percent of floor rules in the 104th Congress, compared with 56 percent in the 103rd (U.S. Congress, House Committee on Rules 1996). Republicans have also introduced innovations such as "Queen-of-the-Hill" rules and time caps, which foster consensus and deliberation (Davidson and Oleszek 1998). Democrats have argued that most major bills still come to the floor under restrictive rules (Sinclair 1997). They were especially critical when the GOP leadership tried to kill a campaign-finance bill by bringing it up under suspension of the rules, which requires a two-thirds vote. Some Republicans seconded the criticism. "I really am ashamed to see how this is coming up tonight," said Representative Matt Salmon (R-Ariz.), "that it is in the same manner as that of the leadership who ran the House for forty years under the Democrats. It is wrong. It is wrong when they did it, and it is wrong if we do it, and I don't think this is a service to the American people" (*Congressional Record* 30 March 1998, H1758).

The minority can sometimes pass its measures, and if the party balance is close, it can block items on the majority's agenda.[2] But because of their numerical disadvantage and the majority's procedural control, minority-party members have much less success than their majority colleagues.[3] Moreover, the grand prize of lawmaking—prime sponsorship of an enacted bill—is effectively outside the minority's grasp. Of the 295 House bills and joint resolutions that President Clinton signed during the 103rd Congress, Republicans sponsored only 35 (or 14 percent), mostly dealing with minor matters.[4] In the 104th Congress, the pattern flipped: Republicans sponsored 212 of 252 signed House measures, leaving Democrats with just 16 percent. While Republicans were making policy, Democrats were directing the Secretary of the Interior to convey the Carbon Hill National Fish Hatchery to the State of Alabama.

For members who want to pass important laws and get credit for them, service in the minority is often depressing.

In analyzing lawmakers' activities, political scientists have downplayed partisan differences. In his otherwise splendid account of congressional careers, John Hibbing (1991, 66) made only fleeting references to the minority and explicitly excluded Republicans from his chapter "The Formal Position Career." In *The Congressional Experience: A View from the Hill,* scholar-turned-congressman David E. Price (1992) (D-N.C.) tried to generalize from his time in the majority, but never noticed that minority members were undergoing a very different congressional experience. Now that he has served in the minority, a second edition might offer new insights.

Members of the majority spend their time deciding how to run the country. By contrast, members of the minority spend their time coping with frustration. During the 1980s, the GOP's customary response of accommodation gave way to confrontation. Republican bomb-throwing was partly an emotional reaction, but also involved deliberate strategy. When confrontation broadens the scope of conflict beyond the chamber's walls, a minority can influence floor votes or gain seats in the next election. Republicans think that such a strategy helped them win in 1994.

Put in the same position, Democrats have reacted with equal vehemence. Whereas Gingrich once said that Speaker Wright "is like Mussolini, believing he can redefine the game to suit his own needs" (quoted in Kirkwood [1988, 44]). Sam Gibbons (D-Fla.) stomped out of a Ways and Means meeting, shouting, "You're a bunch of dictators, that's all you are. I had to fight you guys fifty years ago" (*ABC World News Tonight* transcript 5188, September 1995). In 1995, Democrats stalled the foreign operations spending bill with repeated roll-call votes, forcing an all-night session at one point. Appropriations Democrats staged a brief committee boycott, denying a quorum and delaying a meeting. Republicans responded much like the Democrats of yesteryear. "I think they've been very immature," said Ways and Means Chair Bill Archer (R-Tex.) (quoted in Wines [1995]). Democrats won little on the floor but they did get publicity for their criticisms of the GOP. Said Democratic strategist Mark Mellman: "It's much less about improving legislation and much more about communicating a message" (quoted in Babson [1995]).

Democrats have accused the majority of sinister motives. Representative Pete Stark (D-Calif.) called his Republican colleague, Nancy L. Johnson of Connecticut a "whore of the insurance industry" (quoted in Appel [1995]). Complaining about GOP legislation cutting grants to recipients who engage in political advocacy, Representative George Miller (D-Calif.) said, "If you are a fascist, it is a glorious day" (*Congressional Record* 3 August 1995, H8384). Representative Jose E. Serrano (D-N.Y.) assailed "the meanspirited, reactionary, insensitive, indifferent, right wing, extremist, antipoor, antichildren, Constitution bashing, bordering on racist, contract on America" (*Congressional Record* 22 February 1995, H1972). Representative Charles B. Rangel (D-N.Y.) said of the Contract: "Hitler wasn't even talking about doing these things"; Representative Major R. Owens (D-N.Y.) added: "These are people who are practicing genocide with a smile; they're worse than Hitler" (quoted in Parente [1995, A38]).

Democrats attacked Gingrich's ethics just as strongly as he had attacked Wright. In part, vengeance drove them. "We have a long history with him, and you cannot dismiss that history," said Representative John Lewis (D-Ga.). "He's at risk of being consumed by some of the fires he helped start" (quoted in Toner [1995, A1]). As in the GOP's Wright attack, calculation was also at work. "Newt is the nerve center and energy source," explained George Miller (D-Calif.), "Going after him is like trying to take out command and control" (quoted in Drew [1996, 76]).

In both cases, the parties played tit for tat. In 1989, then-Representative Bill Alexander (D-Ariz.) filed an ethics complaint against Gingrich. In 1996, Republicans filed complaints against Minority Leader Richard Gephardt (D-Mo.) and Minority Whip Bonior (D-Miss.). All these retaliatory strikes fizzled, but only after bestowing aggravation and bad publicity on their targets.

During the 1980s, a turning point in interparty relations came with the McIntyre–McCloskey race, a near-even 1984 congressional contest in Indiana. House Democrats voted not to seat the certified winner, Republican Rick McIntyre, and instead launched an investigation into disputed ballots. After months of rancor in committee and on the floor, the House voted along party lines (with a few majority-party defections) to seat Democratic incumbent Frank McCloskey. Republicans railed at Democratic "cheating," disrupted floor proceedings, and even discussed ways of shutting down the chamber (Connelly and Pitney 1994).

Twelve years later, another contested election roiled the House. After narrowly losing his 1996 reelection race to Democratic challenger Loretta Sanchez, California Republican Bob Dornan triggered a House investigation by claiming that votes from illegal aliens had tipped the outcome. In certain ways, the case resembled McIntyre–McCloskey. Bill Thomas of California, the GOP point man in the earlier fight, now chaired the relevant House committee. As the probe dragged on, the new majority (like the old) claimed that it was doing its best with murky information. The new minority (like the old) cried foul, holding demonstrations and employing confrontational floor tactics.

The Democrats now enjoyed a stronger position than the Republicans of 1985. The Democratic majority of the previous decade had rallied behind one of its own, but many Republicans hesitated to support the eccentric Dornan. (In the fall of 1997, members of both parties voted to suspend his former-member floor privileges after he had a shouting match with a House Democrat.) And whereas the Republican minority failed to arouse the public about the McIntyre–McCloskey case, Democrats won national attention by suggesting that the Dornan–Sanchez probe had racist motives. Said Representative Elizabeth Furse (D-Ore.): "[T]his is a campaign not just against Congresswoman Sanchez, this is a campaign against new immigrants. This is a campaign against new citizens. It is a disgrace" (*Congressional Record* 5 November 1997, H10094). Representatives Sam Gejdenson (D-Conn.) and Robert Menendez (D-N.J.) both charged the GOP with "Gestapo tactics" (*Congressional Record* 5 November 1997, H10098; *Congressional Record* 6 November 1997, H10116).

In the McIntyre–McCloskey case, Democrats chided Republicans who talked about shutting down the chamber. "This threatens our ability to govern," said Gephardt (quoted in Roberts [1985, 5]). In the Dornan–Sanchez case, the parties switched sides, as Gephardt now made the threats: "If they continue in this immoral pursuit, the Democratic Party in the House of Representatives will shut the House of Representatives down until the investigation is shut down" (quoted in Bradley and Van Dongen [1997, 21]).

In 1998, the House accepted a recommendation from its contested-election task force to drop the investigation because Sanchez's margin slightly exceeded the number of illegal votes. For political scientists, that outcome was less significant than the episode's broader lessons: either party will resort to confrontation when in the minority.

Why has the House become so contentious? One explanation is that the departures of conservative Southern Democrats and moderate Frost-Belt Republicans have polarized the parties into ideological and demographic camps with little in common (Miller 1995). A second explanation is that divided government and a narrow majority combine to make the minority feel obstructed and the majority feel thwarted (U.S. Congress, House, Committee on Rules, Subcommittee on Rules and Organization of the House 1997). A third possibility is that the House's distemper reflects larger social problems, such as resource constraints that turn policy disputes into zero-sum games (Uslaner 1993).

Meanwhile, the war on the floor goes on. Scholars should pay closer attention to its causes and consequences, as well as the differences between the majority and minority.

REMEMBER THE MAJORITY-STATUS MOTIVE

Much of the literature assumes an atomistic Congress where members rationally pursue individual goals. The Republican takeover reminds us of a different kind of goal: majority status, which is a collective good. Whether or not a lawmaker contributes much to winning a majority, he or she will benefit. Like leaders everywhere, party chiefs try to overcome the "free rider" problem through rewards and punishments. Yet there is more behind party activity than selective incentives. Members really want their party to have the majority, and under the right conditions, this desire shapes their behavior.

Although this statement might sound like common sense, it represents a modestly revisionist viewpoint. In explaining congressional behavior, political scientists have pointed to reelection, influence in the House, and individual visions of good public policy.[5] While debating the relative importance of these goals, scholars have rarely mentioned party control of the chamber. (One recent and notable exception is Robin Kolodny [1998], whose *Pursuing Majorities* examines congressional campaign committees.) The failure to discuss majority status stemmed not from any intellectual shortcoming but from historical circumstances. From the late 1950s until the early 1990s, when the GOP never broke its "glass ceiling" of 192 seats, GOP control seemed out of the question. And by holding the White House for twenty of the twenty-four years between 1968 and 1992, the GOP suffered a handicap in House contests, since a president's party tends to lose seats over his tenure. Under these conditions, majority status became more a *latent* goal than an *active* one. Democrats took their majority for granted, and came to believe that incumbency was enough to hold it for them (Dwyre and Kolodny 1996). Republicans still wanted majority status, of course, but many resigned themselves to being the "permanent minority."

Not all Republicans succumbed to this mentality. Gingrich and other activists engaged in many activities aimed at winning a majority: floor confrontations, special-order speeches, party conferences, rallies and demonstrations. As we have explained elsewhere, the reelection motive fails to explain such activities (Connelly and Pitney 1994). Their opportunity cost is significant, since every hour at a party event is an hour that members cannot spend on their own campaigns. The direct costs are also steep, since high-profile partisans often put their own seats at risk (Niven and Zilber 1995). Voters may sensibly ask why their lawmakers are hogging the limelight in some party event rather than work-ing for district needs. And party activists draw fire from the other side. National Democrats labored to defeat Gingrich, and nearly succeeded twice. His persist-ence in the face of peril made him a poor role model for single-minded seekers of reelection.

The motives of power and good policy lay somewhere behind these party activities, but the connection was mainly *indirect*. In the short term, the GOP activists of the early 1980s hurt themselves by angering Democratic committee chairs, who governed the course of legislation and decided how much influence to allow ranking members. In GOP leadership contests during the late 1980s and early 1990s, members came to favor the confrontationists. This pattern clashed with the notion that lawmakers choose leaders to be brokers and favor-doers: Republicans were choosing leaders to be party champions. In varying degrees, all Republicans continued to pursue individual goals, but now many were also pursuing the collective goal of majority status.

If members of Congress cared only about reelection, all party campaign energy would focus on them, and all member-controlled party funding would go to incumbents. Over the years, however, the national party organizations have spent large sums on challengers and open-seat candidates. As the party seeking the majority, the GOP made a proportionately greater bid to win new seats, and in 1994, 72 percent of its party money went to nonincumbents in competitive contests (Herrnson 1997b; Dwyre 1996). Likewise, the Contract with America had less to do with incumbency than a party-wide campaign to take over the House.

After 1994, control of the chamber meant committee chairmanships and opportunities to influence public policy. The party leadership thus had some-thing that it had lacked before: real power to reward and punish members. So now that House Republicans have a majority in hand, can one explain their behavior solely in terms of their individual goals and the leadership's manipula-tion of selective incentives?

Not quite. The leadership's internal power has limits: push members too hard, and they push back. When Representative Mark W. Neumann (R-Wis.) crossed Appropriations Chair Robert L. Livingston (R-La.), Livingston got Gingrich's approval to remove him from the national security subcommittee. Protests from the large class of 1994 forced Gingrich to back down and put Neumann on Budget as a consolation prize. Gingrich also had a bad experience when he canceled a fundraising appearance for Mark Souder (R-Ind.) and other members who opposed legislation ending a government shutdown. Fellow freshman Steve Largent (R-Okla.) offered to take Gingrich's place—and his drawing power as a former NFL star enabled Souder to raise twice as much as expected (Gelbart 1996). This case illustrates a larger point: campaign money is overrated as a source of internal leverage. Give large sums to those who do not need them, and other members grow resentful. Deny funds to party rebels, and they will either raise it elsewhere—or they might lose their seats, which the party can ill afford.

Especially when the majority is narrow, leaders cannot rely on selective incentives alone. They have to engage other motives—including the desire to maintain majority status. Take, for instance, the 1997 budget agreement. On an ideological level, many Republicans wanted less spending and more tax cuts. And on an individual level, they probably could have found convincing justifications for voting no. But Gingrich and other party leaders argued that the agreement would deprive House Democrats of fiscal wedge issues. A Gingrich spokesman said that the budget accord marked "the end of the campaign for Congress. Republicans will keep their majority and grow it" (quoted in Rees [1997a, 10]).

The operation of the majority-status motive was even clearer on the other side. After a wobbly start, Democrats crafted a powerful negative message: that the Republicans were "extremist" and "mean-spirited." With impressive discipline, they pounded those terms until they stuck. Chief Deputy Whip Rosa DeLauro (D-Conn.) said, "There is a unifying principle here, which is to take the House back" (quoted in Drew 1996). For 1996, they needed a positive message as well as a negative one, so they issued their own version of the Contract, the "Families First" agenda (Dwyre and Kolodny 1996). Moreover, they changed campaign-finance strategy. Like the GOP two years earlier, they went on the offensive, directing 77 percent of their party contributions and coordinated expenditures to challengers and open-seat candidates, compared with 53 percent in 1994 (Herrnson 1997a, 81; Herrnson 1997b, 107).

They kept the pressure up in 1997. Their outbursts over the Dornan-Sanchez race were part of a strategy to use race and immigration as wedge issues against the GOP. Gephardt issued a release called "The GOP–Anti-Latino Congress," which accused the GOP of "advocating an agenda that is openly hostile to minorities in this country—particularly Hispanic Americans" (quoted in Gugliotta [1998, A1]).

Someday, the majority-status motive might again fade in prominence if the GOP pads its majority and appears to establish a long-term hold on power. But for the time being, with control of the chamber very much in play, this goal exerts a significant influence on both parties.

JAMES MADISON LIVES

Speaker Gingrich liked to quote *The Federalist Papers,* but was closer in spirit to the anti-Federalists. Like them, he argues for rotation in office (that is, term limits), accountability in government (for example, the Contract), decentralization, and legislative supremacy. As early as 1981, he wrote that decentralization would put "those closest to the citizen—the legislator—at an advantage," which would lead to "an increasing shift of power away from the executive branch and toward the legislature" (Gingrich and Gingrich 1981, 30, 32).

The anti-Federalists, however, lost the ratification debate. The Republicans' failure to remember that result explains much of their trouble in the 104th Congress.

In the early days of 1995, some Republicans hoped (and many Democrats feared) that Newt Gingrich would run the country from the Speaker's rostrum. Instead, everyone got a refresher course in the principles of *The Federalist Papers:* the separation of powers, bicameralism, and federalism. Clinton vetoes, Senate reluctance, and GOP governors' policy independence all hampered the House GOP. As Representative J. D. Hayworth (R-Ariz.) said, "We also should have remembered that this is not a parliamentary democracy. We don't have executive power here. We should never discount the reality of the Constitution and the separation of powers" (quoted in Rae [1998, 122]).

The ideal of "congressional government" hurt the Republicans, who wanted the country to think they were in charge. They got their wish. In an October 1995 survey, only 7 percent blamed President Clinton for the problems that most bothered them, while 35 percent cited Congress (Pew Research Center for the People and the Press 1995). Republicans not only overestimated their power, they underestimated Clinton's resolve. The government shutdowns, as well as their 1995 decision to take on Medicare, left them open to Clinton's attacks. President Clinton's bully pulpit trumped the Speaker's rostrum.

Balz and Brownstein (1996, 158) suggest that "Gingrich expanded his reach beyond anything the Founding Fathers had imagined." Unfortunately for House Republicans, their ambitions were not beyond the reach of James Madison. In *The Federalist Papers* he noted that the remedy for congressional dominance is "to divide the legislature into different branches; and to render them, by different modes of election and different principles of action, as little connected with each other as the nature of their common dependence on the society will admit" (*Federalist Papers* [1961]). Bicameralism keeps Congress from encroaching upon the other branches, and reinforces its tendency to do what legislatures do best: represent, deliberate, and exercise oversight. It also promotes conflict even when the same party runs both chambers. House Republicans fumed when the Senate failed to pass several elements of the Contract, and especially when Senator Mark Hatfield (R-Ore.) caused the balanced-budget constitutional amendment to fall just short of the necessary two-thirds vote. During the 105th Congress, House and Senate Republicans differed over issues such as Medicare and funding for the National Endowment for the Arts.

As advocates of legislative supremacy, the anti-Federalists saw the proposed Congress as too weak, not too strong. Instead, they warned of executive and judicial powers. Patrick Henry said that "you will find this very judiciary oppressively constructed" and that the Constitution "squints toward monarchy. Your president may easily become king" (Allen and Lloyd 1985, 133–34). The Federalists, on the contrary, thought the Constitution would appropriately limit each branch to its own sphere.

The Founders could have followed the British parliamentary model, arguably an incomplete separation of powers system (Nichols 1994). Instead, they made each branch powerful and independent. In the American system, wrote Martin Diamond (1992, 58), "the separation of powers receives its distinct and full formulation and embodiment." In only one sense does the Constitution provide for legislative supremacy: Congress is supreme within its own sphere, just as the executive and judiciary are supreme within theirs.

Congress is powerful when exercising legislative authority or performing legislative functions, which may explain why House Republican revolutionaries fell prey to the temptation of "congressional government." Such ambitions, again, can be checked by the other branches and the Senate. The Founders understood that institutions affect the behavior of individuals and factions: "Ambition must be made to counteract ambition. The interest of the man must be connected to the constitutional rights of the place" (*Federalist Papers* [1961], 322).

Constitutional rules are not merely the function of underlying nonconstitutional forces. Constitutional institutions affect behavior. Congress's general structure and processes shape what its members do (Dodd 1985). The Constitution provides for neither "congressional government" nor legislative supremacy, as the House Republicans have learned. On the other hand, the Constitution does provide for effective government and policy change. The separation of powers limits the abuse of power, while providing for its effective use. Madison understood that different institutions do different things. Congress is powerful within its realm. And as we shall see shortly, the competition between the political branches—and between the chambers—can inject energy into the policy process by promoting the interplay among competing ambitions.

Bill Clinton is President, Denny Hastert is Speaker, but James Madison still rules America.

JAMES MADISON IS NOT WOODROW WILSON

Congress is not Parliament, and the Constitution does not provide in any simple sense for party government. The Founders' constitutional system still checks national political parties. Under divided government, the House GOP clashed with the Reagan and Bush White Houses over the choice between government and opposition. This dilemma is acute for the forgotten minority in the majoritarian House. The "permanent minority" House Republicans increasingly played opposition, while the GOP White House wanted to govern. Reagan and Bush, like the Senate Republicans, were frequently willing to compromise with Democrats, much to the House GOP's consternation. Today's often-forgotten minority consists of the House Democrats, whose relations with President Clinton mirror GOP fissures under Reagan and Bush. With the two parties reversing roles, political scientists have witnessed a natural experiment confirming that such conflicts are products of the institutional structure.

To understand this inherent tension, compare the 1984 and 1996 elections, along with subsequent fights over the 1986 Tax Reform Act and the 1997 "fast track" authority. A single 1984 observation by Robert H. Michel sets the stage. House Republicans bemoaned their meager gains accompanying Reagan's 1984 landslide. Michel blamed the Reagan camp's obsession with raising the president's vote total:

> As good a communicator as the president is, he really never, in my opinion, enjoined that issue of what it really means to have the numbers in the House. . . . Here the son of a buck ended up with 59 percent and you bring in fifteen seats. I don't think people should expect too many victories when we are still that far behind. (Quoted in Connelly and Pitney [1994, 106])

Similarly, House Democrats seethed at President Clinton's apparent indifference. In January 1996 he said, "The American people don't think it's the president's business to tell them what ought to happen in the congressional elections" (quoted in Devroy and Harris [1996, A1]). Clinton did get more interested over time, but not enough to suit House Democrats. Shortly before the election, Gephardt's chief of staff echoed Michel's complaint: "It's not going to make an awful lot of difference if he [Clinton] wins forty-seven states or forty-eight states. History will record a lot of difference if he has a Democratic Congress or a Republican Congress . . . we need more help" (quoted in Drew [1997, 185]). The aide had reason to worry: Democrats failed to match even the Republicans' paltry fifteen-seat pickup of 1984.

Both presidents paid a price for their approach.

By rebuffing Reagan on the rule bringing the 1985/1986 tax-reform bill to the floor, House Republicans meant to slap a White House that had dealt them out of talks with the Ways and Means Committee. "It's not an act of petty revenge," said Vin Weber (R-Minn.). "But there certainly was a strong feeling that we had been ignored and rolled too many times, and this was a time to make a stand" (quoted in Shapiro [1985, A1]).

Similarly, 1997 House Democrats handed Clinton a setback on fast-track trade authority. They already blamed Clinton for their 1994 midterm loss, and the 1996 election made feelings worse. Moreover, the 1997 budget pact frustrated many Democrats, who thought that the White House had sold them out. Representative Peter A. DeFazio (D-Ore.) said: "They've become quite comfortable with the Republican majority" (quoted in Yang and Neal [1997, A11]). The *National Journal* clarified the differences between congressional and White House Democrats: "While the lawmakers took a partisan line in hopes of regaining their majority, Clinton focused more on consensus and the demands of governing" (Barnes and Cohen 1997, 2304). Precisely. Feeling no institutional responsibility for policy, House Democrats opted for "opposition" while Clinton sought to work with the congressional majority.

In 1985, Reagan reversed the tax-reform rule vote by an extraordinary personal appeal, whereas some observers concluded that Clinton's lobbying on fast track actually lost votes. Clinton's comment following the defeat of fast track—that it would have passed on a secret ballot—further split the presidential and congressional wings.

While the intraparty fissure would not have surprised James Madison, it would have heightened Woodrow Wilson's disdain for our separation of powers. The strategic "government or opposition" dilemma reflects our constitutional structure and affects political behavior. Clinton and the congressional GOP both had a motivation to accommodate each another in 1996, whereas Bob Dole and the congressional Democrats both had a stake in gridlock. The congressional GOP deliberately dumped Dole, just as Clinton made the Hill Democrats take a back seat. House Republicans made an explicitly Madisonian pitch to the voters: don't give Clinton a blank check (Drew 1997).

Analysis of party electoral behavior in the 1990s owes much to Madison. Before the 1992 elections, several House Republicans argued (off the record) for a strategy of losing the White House in order to win the House. In 1992 the GOP met this necessary (but not sufficient) condition. Had the House Republicans not won in 1994, Bill Clinton might have remained captive to liberal House Democrats and his second two years might have been as dismal as his first two years. By losing the House in 1994, he helped himself win the White House in 1996. Arguably, Republicans held Congress by abandoning Dole.

In their aptly titled book, *Losing to Win*, Ceaser and Busch explain the politics of "repulsion" between each party's presidential and congressional wings. Under the electoral conditions of the 1990s, "the success of one [wing] positively hurts the other" (Ceaser and Busch 1997, 121). In 1996, Bill Clinton offered himself as a check on congressional Republican "extremism." But when his victory seemed secure, Republicans offered themselves as a check on Clinton. Candidate Dole proved the loyal Republican to the last by aiding Hill Republicans. Madison's system precludes "party government," not party loyalty.

While strict party government is impossible, reformers from Woodrow Wilson to Newt Gingrich have often dreamed of responsible party government. Why? Gingrich once called himself "the most seriously professorial politician since Woodrow Wilson" (CNN 20 February 1995). Like Wilson, Gingrich favored politics of grand ideas, rhetoric, partisanship, and political education (Connelly 1996). In November 1994, he argued that although voters may be "fed up with petty partisanship, I don't think they mind grand partisanship. . . . To have a profound disagreement over the direction of your country or over the principles by which your economy works or over the manner in which your government should structure resources, that is legitimate, and the American people believe in that level of debate and relish it" (Gingrich 1994, 3297). The Contract, and a similar 1980 exercise called "Governing Team Day," are examples. Gingrich said in a 1980 floor speech: "[T]his is the first step toward a de facto constitutional amendment that will give us accountable party government by giving us accountable party campaigns and accountable party records" (quoted in Pitney [1996]).

Professors Wilson and Gingrich, both students of the American political system, each had difficulty because of intraparty dissension. Why were both tempted by party government if Madison's system precludes it? The answer can only be that the system consists of more than checks and balances. While neither complete "congressional government" nor simple "party government" is possible, the Constitution does allow both for strong party leadership and a powerful role for Congress when the institution concentrates on what it does best.

Congress can nurture creativity through democracy, diversity, and debate (Destler 1985, 345). Return to the 1985/86 tax reform. The old pluralist (or incrementalist) model fails to explain why rich interests lost cherished loopholes, or why the poor gained as much as they did. The party-government perspective cannot explain this significant reform at a time of divided government (Conlon, Wrightson, and Beam 1990). Another model, which Conlon, Wrightson and Beam (1990, 252) dub the "ideational/entrepreneurial" model, catches the system's dynamic potential for innovation. This model takes into account the power of ideas and individual leaders, including those who lack formal leadership positions. Our system promotes ambition counteracting ambition, as well as ambition *vying* with ambition.

The electoral cycles and routines associated with the separation of powers encourage politicians to compete with one another by searching for innovative ideas (Polsby 1984).

Martin Diamond (1992, 61) argued against the view that our system provides for separate institutions sharing power. Instead, he said, the Founders provided for a "functional parceling out of political power." When each branch brings to its function its proper performance, all three should form a coherent power of government. When any branch abuses its power or botches its work, the other branches should check it. The separation of powers thus promotes "not only free but also effective government" (Diamond 1992, 67).

Members of Congress, wrote Diamond, will normally act as "creatures of Congress . . . behaving above all with regard to the peculiar interests of their respective offices and duties" (Diamond 1992, 65). As Majority Leader Dick Armey noted, "We didn't win power, we gained responsibility" (quoted in Seelye [1994, B9]). The House Republicans' broader institutional perspective, especially that of their leaders, underscored both the limits of insurgency and the possibilities of governing. That is, Madison's constitutional structure taught them about the limitations of "revolution" in an structure inclined toward incrementalism. The same separation-of-powers system also taught them the potential for change even under divided government.

LEADERSHIP IS ABOUT LEARNING

As Fenno notes, House Republicans are "learning to govern." While political shocks have taught them about their limits, they are also learning more positive lessons. The relationship between the institution and its leaders is cybernetic, not merely robotic. Our constitutional structures constrain leaders—but also educate and empower them.

First, the limits. In his memoir, *Lessons Learned the Hard Way,* Gingrich says that Republicans got a vivid lesson in constitutional constraints. Though the House quickly passed the GOP agenda, "we were soon to learn why President George Washington once described the Senate as the cooling saucer into which the hot coffee from the cup of the House should be poured." He notes that Republicans had "much too cavalierly underrated the power of the president," especially his veto power. "Even if you pass something through both the House and the Senate, there is that presidential pen. How could we have forgotten that?" (Gingrich 1998, 6, 10).

Congress educates leaders not just about limits but also about self-interest properly understood. Leaders' competing constituencies and overlapping loyalties broaden their bases and redefine their self-interest. Justice Frankfurter's famous observation that "the robe changes the man" rested on his recognition that institutions affect behavior. In part, the office changes the person because of "that fortunate alchemy by which men are loyal to the obligation with which they are entrusted" (*Public Utilities Commission v. Pollack,* 343 U.S. 451, 1952).

Gingrich's cooperation with Clinton on fast track stemmed from a commitment to free trade, as well as the economic interests of businesses—but it also involved a genuine search for a productive relationship with the White House. The leadership's bipartisan efforts to recodify House rules also indicate interest in institutional maintenance.

Congress is about change as well as stasis. If Republicans have learned about limits, they have also learned about the potential for innovation. While the rapid passage of the Contract had the unhappy side effect of encouraging Republican hubris, it also had far more success than critics acknowledge. First, it led Congress to consider policy proposals that had never gotten a full legislative hearing (Gimpel 1996). Second, much of it did become law. The 104th Congress saw enactment of the Congressional Accountability Act, the line-item veto, and a far-reaching welfare reform bill. In the 105th Congress, the budget agreement included other Contract items: a $500 per-child tax cut, "American Dream" savings accounts, and tax reductions on capital gains.

Even more important than any specific item was the GOP's impact on political debate. Senator Bob Kerrey (D-Neb.), Chair of the Democratic Senatorial Campaign Committee, told his fellow Democrats that "Congress is relevant again because of the House Republicans who promised to do ten things, many of which I disagree with, but they did them all, and that has increased confidence in our democracy, I think that's very positive" (Lambro 1985, A1). House Republicans understood what they had achieved when the Democratic president proclaimed that "the era of big government is over." Gephardt confirmed the extent of the GOP victory when he attacked "new Democrats" (that is, Clinton and his supporters) "who set their compass only off the direction of others—who talk about the political center, but fail to understand that if it is only defined by others, it lacks core values" (Gephardt, 1997). The "others," of course, are congressional Republicans. Perhaps unintentionally, he was depicting them as the party of principle.

Much of the responsibility belongs to Gingrich. The Cheneys suggest "one must always keep in mind the power of strong individuals to reshape the forms that they find" (Cheney and Cheney 1996, xiv). They include Newt Gingrich along with important Speakers including Clay and Reed. Such leaders are both creatures and creators of the institution. The relationship between the institution and individual leaders is dynamic, as we have seen with the oscillation between "party government" in the 104th Congress and "committee government" in the 105th.

During normal periods in congressional history, individual behavior is largely a product of structural context. From time to time, certain individuals can seize a critical moment to mold the institution. Strahan argues that Newt Gingrich "helped create the critical moment in institutional time" (Strahan

1996, 22). Institutions affect behavior but do not determine it. Gingrich was not merely a creature of his caucus, nor is the House Republican Conference merely a creature of the electoral context. Gingrich changed the Conference and Congress. Leadership is not merely a dependent variable. Individuals do matter.

How did he do it? Unlike economics, which assumes preferences as given, political science must account for efforts to change them (Wilson 1980). Whereas congressional leaders have usually taken members and their beliefs as they found them, Gingrich used GOPAC to recruit and train members, influencing the way they thought even before they set foot on the Hill.

At times in the past few years, he may have wondered whether he succeeded too well. Once in power, Gingrich learned more about compromise. But younger members were still in the take-no-prisoners mindset that he had long been nurturing. He found that they were still emulating the bomb-throwing Gingrich of the 1980s, instead of the compromising Gingrich of the 1990s. He was no longer the young turk, but the Establishment. Sophomore David M. McIntosh (R-Ind.) elaborated: "There's been a generational divide between the younger members of the conference and the older members. The younger members want to keep fighting for reform. The older members are more pragmatic" (quoted in Raum [1997]). McIntosh is not the first to note such a divide. Former Representative Barber B. Conable, Jr. (R-N.Y.) once wrote:

> Old as I am, I recall being a "young turk" at one point and participating noisily in a successful effort to change House rules which the Establishment found adequate. I learned a lot about the institution from the effort, vented my frustrations, and gradually became part of the Establishment myself. Youth presses age, provides a good deal of the dynamic and the dialogue, and eventually ages. Partisans may not like the tranquility of my view of these recent histories, but I find reassurance in the cycle of renewal. (1984)

The generational divide may just be part of growing older. But as Conable suggested, a vibrant Congress needs both the Establishment and the revolutionaries. The tension in the generational divide underscores the institution's dynamism.

The attempted "coup" against Gingrich in the summer of 1997 is a case of ambition *vying* with ambition, not merely ambition mechanically checking ambition; the competition may not simply be a zero-sum game. The "youthful" exuberance of the coup-plotters (complete with an apparent lack of foresight) energizes party dialogue and maintains a potentially productive tension. Young backbenchers such as McIntosh or Lindsey Graham (R-S.C.) foster the revolutionary zeal of a principled politics. Senior "bulls" such as Jerry Lewis and Bill Archer, meanwhile, help keep the party on an even keel, attentive to competing interests. Both elements are necessary in any successful House party. A similar tension appears in the House Democratic Caucus between the liberals and the "Blue Dog" conservatives.

Successful congressional leadership requires balance. Bill Gavin, an aide to Republican Leader Michel, once compared such leadership to music. His remarks are worth quoting at length:

> It's like good jazz: In the midst of his improvisatory explorations, a jazz soloist has to be willing to take musical risks because it is in spontaneous risk-taking that great things happen in jazz. But in order to succeed, the risk-taker needs a reliable, steady accompaniment that sets the formal structure within which the creative leap takes place. The underlying chord structure and rock-solid beat provide security and order: the soaring improvisation provides freedom and spontaneity. Combine both and you have the great synergism called art. The same is true in House politics. The rock-solid political establishmentarian, setting the formal "rules of the game," and the soaring political revolutionary, guided, but not dominated, by the limits, need each other. If the establishment dominates the party, it becomes paralyzed and disintegrates; if the revolutionaries dominate, the party becomes wild and explodes. A great leader uses both elements, without letting either dominate for any length of time. (Quoted in Connelly and Pitney [1994, 163])

If congressional leadership consisted only of bargaining, perhaps Congress would need only committee chairs, not party leaders. If leadership only meant ideological warfare, Congress might need only party leaders. Over two hundred years Congress has organized itself along *both* lines of leadership, and as Gavin suggests, it *needs* both. The institution needs both the "centripetal" effect of party leadership and the "centrifugal" effect of committee leaders (Davidson and Oleszek 1998, 186).

Madison observed that our system is neither wholly federal nor wholly national. Congress is both national and local in its orientation. Congressional elections typically turn on parochial concerns, yet they surely did not cause the 1994 congressional "tsunami." As we have said before, we now have the Gingrich corollary to Tip O'Neill's famous aphorism, "all politics is local"; namely, "except when it is national."

In the 1996 elections, House Republicans held on. Conventional wisdom says they won because they moderated their excesses and compromised on welfare and the minimum wage. But perhaps both their revolutionary fervor and accommodation were necessary. The former enabled them to inspire their conservative constituencies; the latter let them prove that they can make the system work. Both parties must play both games: a politics of interests and a politics of ideas, accommodation and confrontation. Like jazz, it is an art that takes time to learn.

REPUBLICANS ARE COMPLEX

In mid-1997, a group of House Republicans—including members of the leadership—mounted a brief and abortive effort to depose Gingrich as Speaker. This conflict may have puzzled observers whose knowledge of party factionalism was confined to Democrats. Unlike the other party, the congressional GOP consists mainly of white conservatives. They look alike and vote alike. What do they have to fight about?

The answer is: quite a lot. The congressional GOP is less homogeneous and more complicated than it may seem. Although a coup against a Speaker was a new wrinkle, internal conflict was an old story. Backbiting and intrigue had long plagued the Republicans, whose leadership fights generated a great deal of bile, if little national publicity. Their image as lockstep-voting "Reagan robots" was simply inaccurate: they had lower party-unity scores than Democrats throughout the Reagan years (Rohde 1991).

After they won their majority, swift action on the Contract left a misleading impression of unity. The Contract was a consensus document: party leaders included only items that already commanded broad agreement (for example, a balanced-budget amendment) and they left items that would cause arguments (for example, antiabortion legislation). Once they voted on the Contract, they were bound to start squabbling again.

Rubik's Cube™ provides a device for explaining the conflict. The roles of ideas, interests, and institutions correspond to the puzzle's three dimensions, and the actions of individuals constitute the hands that twist the cube.

Ideas

Between the 1950s and the 1980s the GOP's liberal wing shrank in numbers and influence (Rae 1989). In the 1990s, most House Republicans called themselves conservatives. Nevertheless, the "conservative" label covers diverse schools of thought. Koopman distinguishes the "old right" from both the "new right" and the "religious right," and the "neoconservatives" from the "libertarians" (Koopman 1996). The distinctions do not end there. Some favor a flat income tax, while other prefer a national sales tax. Some want to attack racial preferences, while other fear backlash from ethnic minorities.

Former Speaker Gingrich holds an odd place in the landscape of ideas. Contrary to a common assumption, he did not come out of the conservative intellectual movement: he seldom quotes Hayek, Friedman, Kirk, or other major thinkers of the right. His eclectic philosophy—a blend of Drucker, Deming, and Toffler—has enabled him to communicate with all the party's ideological factions: the moderates of the "Tuesday Lunch Bunch" regard him as far more sympathetic than Armey or Majority Whip Tom DeLay (R-Tex.). On the other hand, it can also be a liability, since no one faction thinks of him as "our guy."

Long before he became Speaker, Gingrich often found himself in ideological crossfire, particularly with the "new right" legislative service organization (LSO), the Republican Study Committee. After the GOP took the majority, he announced plans to cut funding for LSO. At the time, many observers saw the move as an attack on Democratic groups such as the Congressional Black Caucus—but perhaps not coincidentally, it also defunded a potential source of opposition within the GOP. The successor group, which operates without benefit of official resources, is the Conservative Action Team (CAT). "The House leadership is taking the approach of reconnoitering the Clinton position, trying to determine what is agreeable to the Clinton Administration," complained CAT co-chair Ernest Istook (R-Okla.). "We don't think it's good to let the opponent define and determine the debate" (quoted in D'Agostino 1997, 8).

An ad hoc informal group, dubbed "The Gang of 11," took shape in March 1997, when the House voted on the rule for consideration of committee funding. Upset at a congressional spending increase, the eleven opposed the rule, providing the Democrats with just enough votes to beat it—an embarrassing defeat for Gingrich. The eleven held meetings for a while, and became a nucleus for opposition to the Speaker.

Interests

In *The Federalist Papers*, Madison observed that one source of factionalism is diversity of interest; and throughout congressional history, geography has given rise to such diverse interests. So it is with today's House GOP.

In the 1990s, for the first time ever, Republicans from the South and West came to outnumber those from the Northeast and Midwest. Accordingly, the leadership took on a Sun-Belt complexion, with Gingrich, Armey, and DeLay all hailing from the South. Many Frost-Belt Republicans felt alienated, and they grew nervous about embracing a leadership that looked remote and unattractive to their constituents. Long Islander Peter King complained about GOP attacks on unions. "Instead of going for solid working people . . . we're driving them away. We're going to turn ourselves into a party of barefoot hillbillies who go to revival meetings" (quoted in Greenhouse 1996, 8). He later wrote an article referring to Gingrich as "road kill."

Environmental issues have supplied a battleground for this regional conflict. Said Representative James H. Saxton (R-N.J.): "The younger members, especially from the West, are less than sensitive to the environmental issues as we know them in the East, and they comprise a sizable number, or chunk, of Republicans in the House" (quoted in Cushman [1995, A1, A17]). Westerners accused the Northeasterners of failing to understand the burdens that environmental regulators had imposed on the West. Some threatened to strike back. "Certainly some in the West are going to take serious looks at issues of importance to people in the East," said Representative Wally Herger (R-Calif.). "The pressure cooker is building in such a manner that these are considerations we have to take" (quoted in Hume [1997, 1, 23]). Westerners faulted Gingrich for failing to rein in the easterners.

Institutions

Whichever party holds the majority, the leadership's priorities often clash with those of the committee chairs. New to power, the GOP chairs yielded authority to the leadership in the early days of the 104th Congress, but later reclaimed much of it. Friction resulted. In the spring of 1997, Majority Leader Armey sought to add riders to an appropriations bill, which put him at odds with Appropriations Chair Bob Livingston. Armey got his way on the riders, which triggered a politically damaging veto fight with President Clinton. Gingrich then reached a bargain with the White House, which other GOP leaders deemed a surrender. Everyone in the GOP was dissatisfied.

At the time of the coup, however, committee chairs noticed that much of the anti-Gingrich agitation was coming from those who had opposed increases in committee funding. Wanting to preserve organizational stability, they rallied behind Gingrich. As a backbencher, Gingrich had often come into conflict with "committee guys." He now made common cause with them.

Gingrich's new attitude points to another institutional dilemma: the conflict between his roles as party leader and constitutional officer. When the President belongs to the other party, a Speaker has to balance the desire to score partisan points against the need to run the institution. Seldom can any Speaker strike a balance that pleases everyone. In 1997, many Republicans groused that Gingrich had gone too far in accommodating Clinton. "So far this session it's been a lovefest," said Representative Dana Rohrabacher (R-Calif.). "And we didn't come here to have a lovefest" (quoted in Rees [1997b]).

Individuals

As the de facto leader of a congressional minority fighting forty years of Democratic rule, Gingrich took risks and made enemies. "People like Bonior hate me," he said in 1996. "It's personal. Anything they do to me is legitimate because I'm the man who took away their power" (quoted in Brooks [1996, 24]).

Every leader makes enemies, but most enjoy a reservoir of personal affection and good will. With his intense, unusual personality, Gingrich had allies but few friends. When his ethics troubles intensified, many Republicans grew fearful of his political taint and they edged away from him. Their ambivalence encouraged ambitious GOP colleagues to make their move.

First among them was Majority Whip Tom DeLay, who had an unhappy history with Gingrich. In 1989, DeLay tried to block Gingrich's ascent to the leadership by serving as campaign manager for his opponent, Edward Madigan of Illinois. After the 1994 GOP takeover, DeLay won the whip's position by defeating Bob Walker (R-Pa.), who was among Gingrich's most faithful lieutenants. In May of 1997, DeLay joined with forty-two other Republicans to defeat a floor rule backed by the rest of the leadership. "This has absolutely nothing to do with policy," said one GOP leadership aide. "It was purely leadership politics" (quoted in Bradley [1997, 22]). Soon afterward, DeLay played a major role in the coup attempt. Even after it failed, he continued to cross swords with Gingrich. When Gingrich backed a liberal Republican in a special election for a California House seat, DeLay reportedly steered as much as $30,000 to another candidate, a strong conservative (Vande Hei 1998).

As the coup passed into memory, Republicans said that they had made peace among themselves. Beneath the surface, though, they remained as fractious and complicated as ever. This was further demonstrated by the ousting of Gingrich following the 1998 midterm election.

MORE LESSONS ARE TO COME

The coming years will furnish political scientists with more lessons about the House. Some have argued that alternation of party control would restore civility to the House, since both sides would know that they could soon stand in the other side's shoes. If the Democrats regain a majority, we will see whether this idea holds up.

Another scenario is unified Republican control of the federal government, which has not happened since the election of 1952. According to the "losing to win" argument, such a circumstance would paradoxically be a blessing for the other side. Like the GOP of 1993 and 1994, the congressional Democrats would be free of the responsibility of supporting the White House, and could concentrate on playing opposition and positioning themselves for the next round. Nevertheless, there is no guarantee of success. Only time will tell whether divided government has become a natural tendency, or whether it has resulted from conditions peculiar to the late twentieth century.

Regardless of what happens in presidential elections, House Republicans might enjoy an extended period of control. In that case, would they slip into the "permanent majority" mentality of arrogance and aversion to change? Probably so: there is no reason to think that Republicans are any more immune to this malady than Democrats. And what would become of the Democrats? Currently, bomb-throwers such as Minority Whip David Bonior seem to be riding high. Would a growing sense of "permanent minority" status intensify their fervor, or would it give rise to an "accommodationist" wing?

One thing is sure: congressional scholars will enjoy a wealth of material for many years to come.

NOTES

1. The major work on congressional Republicans was Charles O. Jones, *The Minority Party in Congress* (Boston: Little, Brown, 1970).

2. For a discussion of the GOP's occasional successes in the minority, see Paul S. Rundquist, "Winning on the Left Side of the House: Minority Parliamentary Strategies in a Majoritarian Institution" (paper resented at the annual meeting of the American Political Science Association, San Francisco, 1990).

3. See the discussion of amendments in Steven S. Smith, *Call to Order: Floor Politics in the House and Senate* (Washington, D.C.: Brookings Institution, 1989), 148–51.

4. Authors' calculation from legislative data found on the Internet: thomas.loc.gov.

5. David R. Mayhew emphasizes reelection in *Congress: The Electoral Connection* (New Haven, CT: Yale University Press, 1974). Richard F. Fenno, Jr., discusses the other motives in *Congressmen in Committees* (Boston: Little, Brown, 1973). For an excellent review of the literature, see Barbara Sinclair, "Purposive Behavior in the US Congress: A Review Essay." *Legislative Studies Quarterly* 8 (February 1983): 117–31.

BIBLIOGRAPHY

Aldrich, John, and David Rohde. "Conditional Party Government Revisited: Majority Party Leadership and the Committee System in the 104th Congress." In *Extension of Remarks: The New Republican Congress: Explanations, Assessments, and Prospects,* ed. Lawrence C. Dodd. Legislative Studies Group, American Political Science Association, December 1995.

———. "Balance of Power: Republican Party Leadership and the Committee System in the 104th House." Paper presented at the annual meeting of the Midwest Political Science Association, Chicago, Ill., 1997.

———. "The Transition to Republican Rule in the House: Implications for Theories of Congressional Politics." *Political Science Quarterly* 112, no. 4 (Winter 1997–98): 541–67.

Allen, W. B., and Gordon Lloyd, ed. *The Essential Anti-Federalist.* Lanham, MD: University Press of America, 1985.

Americans for Democratic Action. *House of Representatives Voting Record.* Washington, DC: Americans for Democratic Action, 1995.

———. *House of Representatives Voting Record.* Washington, DC: Americans for Democratic Action, 1996.

Andrews, Edmund L. "A Folksy Legislator with Power over Industries." *New York Times,* 20 December 1994, D1, D11.

Appel, Adrianne. "Stark Calls Johnson 'Whore' of Insurance Industry." *States News Service,* 10 March 1995.

Apple, R. W. "Odd Couple Cross Lines for Campaign Changes." *New York Times,* 6 September 1977, A1, A14.

Babson, Jennifer. "Democrats Refine the Tactics of Minority Party Power." *Congressional Quarterly Weekly Report* (15 July 1995): 2037.

Bach, Stanley, and Steven S. Smith. *Managing Uncertainty in the House of Representatives.* Washington, DC: Brookings Institution, 1998.

Bader, John B. *Taking the Initiative: Leadership Agendas in Congress and the "Contract with America."* Washington, DC: Georgetown University Press, 1996.

Balz, Dan, and Ronald Brownstein. *Storming the Gates: Protest Politics and the Republican Revival.* Boston: Little, Brown, 1996.

Barnes, Fred. "A Cease-Fire in Place." *Weekly Standard* (4 August 1995): 12.

Barnes, James A., and Richard E. Cohen. "Divided Democrats." *National Journal* (15 November 1997): 2304.

Barnett, Timothy J., and Burdett Loomis. "Class Community in the U.S. House: The Watergate Babies and the Republican Revolutionaries." Paper presented at the annual meeting of the American Political Science Association, Boston, Mass., 1998.

Baumgartner, Frank R., and Bryan D. Jones. *Agendas and Instability in American Politics.* Chicago: University of Chicago Press, 1993.

Beth, Richard. "What We Don't Know about Filibusters." Paper presented at the annual meeting of the Western Political Science Association, Portland, Ore., 1995.

Bimber, Bruce A. *The Politics of Expertise in Congress.* Albany: State University of New York Press, 1996.

Binder, Sarah A. *Minority Rights, Majority Rule: Partisanship and the Development of Congress.* New York: Cambridge University Press, 1997.

———. "The Partisan Basis of Procedural Choice: Allocating Parliamentary Rights in the House, 1789–1900." *American Political Science Review* 90, no. 1 (1996a): 8–20.

———. "The Disappearing Political Center." *Brookings Review* 15 (Fall 1996b): 36–39.

Binder, Sarah A., and Steven S. Smith. *Politics or Principle: Filibustering in the United States Senate.* Washington, DC: Brookings Institution, 1997.

Bradley, Jennifer. "But Republicans Find Trouble on House Floor Wednesday." *Roll Call,* 15 May 1997, 22.

Bradley, Jennifer, and Rachel Van Dongen. "Democrats Blast GOP for Probe of Sanchez." *Roll Call,* 28 July 1997, 21.

Brady, David W., and Phillip Althoff. "Party Voting in the U.S. House of Representatives, 1890–1910: Elements of a Responsible Party System." *Journal of Politics* 36, no. 2 (1974): 753–75.

Brady, David, and Charles Bullock. "Is There a Conservative Coalition in the House?" *Journal of Politics* 42, no. 2 (1980): 549–59.

Brady, David, and Joseph Cooper. "The Decline of Party Voting in the U.S. House of Representatives." *Legislative Studies Quarterly* 4 (1979): 381–407.

Brady, David W., and Craig Volden. *Revolving Gridlock.* Boulder, CO: Westview Press, 1998.

Brinkley, Alan. *The Unfinished Nation: A Concise History of the American People.* New York: McGraw-Hill, 1997.

Brooks, David. "What Happened to Newt Gingrich?" *Weekly Standard* (21 October 1996): 24.

Bruck, Connie. "The Politics of Perception." *New Yorker* (9 October 1995): 50–76.

Budget Enforcement Act of 1990, Pub. L. No. 101-508, sec. 13204, 1990 U.S.C.C.A.N. (104 Stat.) 1388-616.

Carney, Dan. "As Hostilities Rage on the Hill, Partisan-Vote Rate Soars." *Congressional Quarterly Weekly Report* (27 January 1996): 199–201.

Carr, Rebecca. "GOP's Election-Year Worries Cooled Partisan Rancor." *Congressional Quarterly Weekly Report* (21 December 1996), 3432–35.

Cassata, Donna. "Lott's Task: Balance the Demands of His Chamber and His Party." *Congressional Quarterly Weekly Report* (8 March 1997): 1384–85.

Ceaser, James W., and Andrew E. Busch, *Losing to Win: The 1996 Elections and American Politics.* Lanham, MD: Rowman & Littlefield, 1997.

Center for Responsive Politics. *Congressional Operations: Congress Speaks—Survey of the 100th Congress.* Washington, DC: Center for Responsive Politics, 1988.

Cheney, Richard B., and Lynne V. Cheney, *Kings of the Hill,* rev. ed. New York: Touchstone, 1996.

Cloud, David S. "GOP Senators Limit Chairmen to Six Years Heading Panel." *Congressional Quarterly Weekly Report* (22 July 1995): 2147.

Clymer, Adam. "House Approves Increase to $5.15 in Minimum Wage." *New York Times,* 23 May 1996, A1.

CNN. 20 February 1995, transcript 7-7.

———. "Rep. Jim Greenwood Talks about His Career, His Relationship with Newt, and His Political Views." Transcript from *CNN Inside Politics,* 20 August 1997.

Cohen, Richard E. "The Transformers." *National Journal* (4 March 1995): 531.

———. "Crumbling Committees." *National Journal* (4 August 1990): 1876–81.

Conable, Barber. "Washington Report," 10 June 1984.

Congressional Management Foundation. *Working in Congress: The Staff Perspective.* Washington, DC: Congressional Management Foundation, 1995.

Congressional Record. 105th Cong., 2nd sess., vol. 144, no. 38, 30 March 1998, H1758.

———. 105th Cong., 1st sess., vol. 143, nos. 151–60, 5 November 1997, H10094.

———. 105th Cong., 1st sess., vol. 143, nos. 151–60, 5 November 1997, H10098.

———. 105th Cong., 1st sess., vol. 143, nos. 151–60, 6 November 1997, H10116.

———. 105th Cong., 1st sess., vol. 143, nos. 113–21.

———. 104th Cong., 2nd sess., vol. 142, no. 13.

———. 104th Cong., 2nd sess., vol. 142, no. 3, 3 August 1995, H8384.

———. 104th Cong., 2nd sess., vol. 142, nos. 19–22, 22 February 1995, H1972.

Congressional Yellow Book. Washington, DC: Leadership Directories, Inc., (Summer) 1997.

Conlon, Timothy J., Margaret T. Wrightson, and David Beam. *Taxing Choices: The Politics of Tax Reform.* Washington, DC: CQ Press, 1990.

Connelly, William F., Jr., "Newt Gingrich: Speaker as Educator and Intellectual." Paper presented at the annual meeting of the American Political Science Association, San Francisco, Calif., 1996.

Connelly, William F., Jr., and John J. Pitney, Jr. "The House GOP's Civil War: A Political Science Perspective." *PS: Political Science & Politics* 30 (1997): 699–702.

———. *Congress' Permanent Minority? Republicans in the U.S. House.* Lanham, MD: Rowman & Littlefield, 1994.

Conner, George E., and Bruce I. Oppenheimer. "Deliberation: An Untimed Value in a Time Game." In *Congress Reconsidered,* 5th ed., ed. Lawrence C. Dodd and Bruce I. Oppenheimer. Washington, DC: Congressional Quarterly Press, 1993.

Connolly, Ceci. "Forbes Puts Heat on GOP Leadership." *Washington Post,* 11 January 1998, A9.

Cook, Charles E. "The Onus to Beat 'Do-Nothing' Rap Falls to Chairmen." *Roll Call,* 12 May 1997, 6.

Cooper, Joseph, and David Brady. "Institutional Context and Leadership Style: The House from Cannon to Rayburn." *American Political Science Review* 75, no. 2 (1981): 411–25.

Cooper, Joseph, and Garry Young. "Partisanship, Bipartisanship, and Crosspartisanship in Congress since the New Deal." In *Congress Reconsidered,* 6th ed., ed. Lawrence C. Dodd and Bruce I. Oppenheimer. Washington, DC: Congressional Quarterly Press, 1997.

Cover, Albert D., Neil Pinney, and George Serra. "Voting Behavior in the U.S. House and Senate: Regional Shifts and Contemporary Changes in Party Coalitions." *Party Politics* 3 (1997): 221–41.

Cox, Gary, W., and Mathew D. McCubbins. *Legislative Leviathan: Party Government in the House.* Berkeley: University of California Press, 1993.

———. *Parties and Committees in the U.S. House of Representatives.* Berkeley: University of California Press, 1990.

Cushman, John H., Jr. "Moderates Soften GOP Agenda on Environment." *New York Times,* 24 October 1995, A1, A17.

D'Agostino, Joseph A. "Doolittle Spurs Conservative Action Team Forward." *Human Events* (March 7 1997).

Davidson, Roger H. "Congressional Committees in the New Reform Era: From Combat to Contract." In *Remaking Congress: Change and Stability in the 1990s,* ed. James A. Thurber and Roger H. Davidson. Washington, DC: Congressional Quarterly Press, 1995.

———. "Two Avenues of Change: House and Senate Committee Reorganization." In *Congress Reconsidered,* 2nd ed., ed. Lawrence C. Dodd and Bruce I. Oppenheimer. Washington, DC: Congressional Quarterly Press, 1981.

Davidson, Roger H., and Colton C. Campbell. "The 105th Congress: 'The Congress of Regular Order.'" In *The United States National Election and Transition of 1996–1997: Nominating, Electing, and Organizing Congress and the Presidency,* ed. Harvey L. Schantz. Albany: State University of New York Press, forthcoming.

Davidson, Roger H., and Walter J. Oleszek. *Congress and Its Members,* 6th ed. Washington, DC: Congressional Quarterly Press, 1998.

Deering, Christopher J. "Subcommittee Government in the U.S. House: An Analysis of Bill Management." *Legislative Studies Quarterly* 7 (1982): 533–46.

———. "Career Advancement and Subcommittee Chairs in the U.S. House of Representatives: 86th to 103rd Congresses." *American Politics Quarterly* 24 (January 1996): 3–23.

Deering, Christopher J., and Steven S. Smith. *Committees in Congress.* Washington, DC: Congressional Quarterly Press, 1997.

DeGregorio, Christine. "The Silent Revolution: Republican Leadership in the U.S. House of Representatives." Paper presented at the annual meeting of the Midwest Political Science Association, Chicago, Ill., 1998.

Democratic Study Group. "A Look at the Senate Filibuster," DSG Special Report (compiled by Congressional Research Service), 13 June 1994, 103–28, Appendix B.

Destler, I. M. "Executive–Congressional Conflict in Foreign Policy: Explaining It, Coping with It." In *Congress Reconsidered,* 3rd ed., ed. Lawrence C. Dodd and Bruce I. Oppenheimer. Washington, DC: Congressional Quarterly Press, 1985.

Devroy, Ann, and John F. Harris, "Clinton Says Record Shows 'Remarkable' Consistency." *Washington Post,* 31 January 1996, A1.

Dewar, Helen. "Senate GOP Urged to Shift Power, Solidify Policy Positions in Advance." *Washington Post,* 17 May 1995: A21.

Diamond, Martin. *As Far as Republican Principles Will Admit: Essays,* ed. William A. Schambra. Washington, DC: American Enterprise Institute, 1992.

Dodd, Lawrence C. "The Cycles of Legislative Change: Building a Dynamic Theory." In *Political Science: The Science of Politics,* ed. Herbert F. Weisberg. New York: Agathon, 1985.

Doherty, Carroll. "Senate Conservatives Begin to Plot the Dividing Lines of 1998." *Congressional Quarterly Weekly Report* (8 November 1997): 2743–46.

Doherty, Carroll J., and Jeffrey L. Katz. "Bucking Up: Many Democrats Thrive after Shock of '94." *Congressional Quarterly Weekly Report* (4 July 1998): 1818.

Doherty, Carroll J., and Jackie Koszczuk. "Deal Smooths Path for Senate Exit; House Still Caught in Gridlock." *Congressional Quarterly Weekly Report* (1 November 1997): 2662–64.

Drew, Elizabeth. Showdown: *The Struggle between the Gingrich Congress and the Clinton White House.* New York: Simon & Schuster, 1996.

———. *Whatever It Takes: The Real Struggle for Political Power in America.* New York: Viking, 1997.

Dwyer, Paul, and John Pontius. *Legislative Branch Employment, 1960–1997.* CRS Report 97-112 GOV (6 June) 1997.

Dwyre, Diana. "Was 1996 a Return to Party-Centered Campaigning? Republican Partisan Efforts to Capture the House of Representatives." Paper presented at the annual meeting of the Western Political Science Association, San Francisco, Calif., 1996.

Dwyre, Diana, and Robin Kolodny. "Strategic Advancements toward Collective Party Goals: National Party Organizations and House Elections, 1993–96." Paper presented at the annual meeting of the American Political Science Association, San Francisco, Calif., 1996.

Eilperin, Juliet. "The Truth about Bipartisanship." *Roll Call,* 20 February, 1997.

———. "Highway Bill Lets Shuster Play His Trump Card." *Washington Post,* 6 August 1998, A17.

Eilperin, Juliet, and Jim Vande Hei. "Some Wounds Never Heal: Today's GOP Leadership Has Roots in 'Guerrilla' Warriors of the 1980s." *Roll Call,* 2 October 1997, 1.

Elving, Ronald D. "Fireworks of 104th Now a Faint Glow." *Congressional Quarterly Weekly Report* (8 March 1997): 606.

Evans, C. Lawrence, and Walter Oleszek. *Congress Under Fire: Reform Politics and the Republican Majority.* Boston: Houghton Mifflin, 1997a.

————. "Congressional Tsunami? The Politics of Committee Reform." In *Congress Reconsidered,* ed. Lawrence C. Dodd and Bruce I. Oppenheimer. Washington, DC: Congressional Quarterly Press, 1997b.

Federal News Service. Verbatim Transcript of GOP "Contract with America" event, West Front, U.S. Capitol (27 September), 1994.

Fenno, Richard F., Jr. *Congressmen in Committees.* Boston: Little, Brown, 1973.

————. *Learning to Govern: An Institutional View of the 104th Congress.* Washington, DC: Brookings Institution, 1997.

Fiorina, Morris P. *Congress: Keystone of the Washington Establishment.* New Haven, CT: Yale University Press, 1977.

Fisher, Louis. "Ten Years of the Budget Act: Still Searching for Controls." *Public Budgeting and Finance* (1985): 5.

Foley, Thomas S. "Testimony before the Joint Committee on the Organization of Congress, 103rd Congress, First Session." Washington, DC: U.S. Government Printing Office, 1993.

Freedman, Allan. "Returning Power to Chairmen." *Congressional Quarterly Weekly Report* (23 November 1996): 3300.

————. "Oversight: Lack of Focus Leaves GOP Stuck in Learning Curve." *Congressional Quarterly Weekly Report* (1 November 1997): 2649–55.

Freeman, Jo. "The Political Culture of the Democratic and Republican Parties." *Political Science Quarterly* 101, no. 3 (1986): 327–56.

Fritz, Sara. "Oversight at Its Best Was off Center Stage." *Congressional Quarterly Weekly Report* (14 February 1998): 406.

Gelbart, Marcia. "Spurned by the Speaker, GOP Frosh Court Armey." *The Hill,* 24 January 1996, 1.

Gephardt, Richard, A. "What Unites Us: Our Core Democratic Values." Address to Kennedy School of Government, Harvard University, 2 December 1997. (http://www.house.gov/democrats/speeches/demvalues.html) (accessed August 4, 1998).

Gill, Jeff, and James A. Thurber. "A Process Control Model of Legislative Productivity in the House of Representatives." Paper presented at the annual meeting of the American Political Science Association, Washington, DC, 1997.

Gimpel, James G. *Fulfilling the Contract: The First 100 Days.* Boston: Allyn & Bacon, 1996.

Gingrich, Newt. "Gingrich Address: New House Speaker Envisions Cooperation, Cuts, Hard Work." *Congressional Quarterly Weekly Report* (12 November 1994): 3297.

————. *Lessons Learned the Hard Way.* New York. HarperCollins, 1998.

Gingrich, Newt, and Marianne Gingrich. "Post-Industrial Politics: The Leader as Learner." *The Futurist* (December 1981): 30–32.

Ginsberg, Benjamin, Walter R. Mebane, Jr., and Martin Shefter. "The Presidency, Social Forces, and Interest Groups: Why Presidents Can No Longer Govern." In *The Presidency and the Political System,* 5th ed., ed. Michael Nelson. Washington, DC: Congressional Quarterly Press, 1998.

Gray, Jerry. "In Budget Battle, Advantage Goes to G.O.P. Chairmen." *New York Times,* 4 May 1997: 30.

Greenhouse, Steven. "Republicans Split over Criticism of Unions." *New York Times,* 11 May 1996: 8.

Gugliotta, Guy. "Democrats Hope to Translate Latino Distrust of GOP into Votes." *Washington Post,* 5 January 1998: A1 (1998a).

———. "Term Limit Prompts House Chairmen to Hunt New Perches." *Washington Post,* 23 March 1998: A17 (1998b).

Gunderson, Steve, and Rob Morris. *House and Home.* New York: Dutton/Penguin, 1996.

Hall, Richard L., and Gary J. McKissick. "Institutional Change and Behavioral Choice in House Committees." In *Congress Reconsidered,* ed. Lawrence C. Dodd and Bruce I. Oppenheimer. Washington, DC: Congressional Quarterly Press, 1997.

Hammond, Susan Webb. "Congressional Caucuses in the 104th Congress." In *Congress Reconsidered,* 6th ed., ed. Lawrence C. Dodd and Bruce I. Oppenheimer. Washington, DC: Congressional Quarterly Press, 1997.

Hardy-Vincent, Carol. *Senate Committee Staff and Funding.* CRS Report 97-222 GOV (10 February) 1997.

Harris, John F. "Gingrich Aide Urges Wide Berth for Clinton Initiatives." *Washington Post,* 16 January 1998: A7.

Havens, Henry. "Gramm-Rudman-Hollings: Origins and Implementation." *Public Budgeting and Finance* 6 (Autumn 1986): 4–26.

Healey, Jon. "Jubilant GOP Strives to Keep Legislative Feet on Ground." *Congressional Quarterly Weekly Report* (12 November 1994): 3210–15.

Henry, Ed. "Leader Picks a Panel On Senate Overhaul." *Roll Call,* 13 January 1997, 1, 16.

Henry, Patrick. "Speeches before the Virginia Ratifying Convention." In *The Essential Antifederalist,* ed. W. B. Allen and Gordon Lloyd. Lanham, MD: University Press of America, 1985.

Herrnson, Paul S. *Congressional Elections: Campaigning at Home and in Washington,* 2nd ed. Washington, DC: Congressional Quarterly Press, 1997a.

———. "Money and Motives: Spending in House Elections." In *Congress Reconsidered,* 6th ed., ed. Lawrence C. Dodd and Bruce I. Oppenheimer. Washington, DC: Congressional Quarterly Press, 1997b.

Hibbing, John. *Congressional Careers: Contours of Life in the U.S. House of Representatives.* Chapel Hill: University of North Carolina Press, 1991.

Hook, Janet. "Far-Reaching Rule Reforms Aren't Easy to Come by." *CQ Weekly Report* (23 September 1989): 2437–38.

Hook, Janet, and David S. Cloud. "A Republican-Designed House Won't Please All Occupants." *Congressional Quarterly Weekly Report* (19 November 1994): 3430–35.

Hosansky, David. "GOP Bid to Reform Committees Faces Intraparty Skepticism." *Congressional Quarterly Weekly Report* (19 November 1994): 3324–25.

———. "GOP Conference Will Consider Limits on Seniority System." *Congressional Quarterly Weekly Report* (20 May 1995): 1392.

House Republican Conference. "Highlights of the Rules of the House Republican Conference, 100th Congress," 1987.

Hume, Sandy. "Rep. Myers Calls It Quits." *The Hill,* 10 January 1996, 11.

————. "GOP Regional Feud Escalates." *The Hill,* 29 October 1997, 1, 23.

Jacoby, Mary. "Waiting in Wings, a Kinder, Gentler Lott?" *Roll Call,* 9 March 1995, 22.

Jamieson, Kathleen Hall. *Civility in the House of Representatives.* Philadelphia: Annenberg Public Policy Center, University of Pennsylvania, no. 10, 1997.

Jones, Charles O. *The Minority Party in Congress.* Boston: Little, Brown, 1970.

————. *The Presidency in a Separated System.* Washington, DC: Brookings Institution, 1994.

Jones, David R. "Institutions, Parties and Gridlock in the United States." Ph.D. diss., University of California, Los Angeles, 1998.

Joyce, Phil. Memos to Bob Reischauer (and others) on "Budget Process Legislation." 22 January 1993 to 1 September 1994.

Kahn, Gabriel. "GOP's Next Step in Reforming House." *Roll Call,* 23 January 1995, A44– A45.

Kalb, Deborah. "Government by Task Force: The Gingrich Model." *The Hill,* 22 February 1995, 3.

Kenworthy, Tom. "House 'Bulls' See Red Over Task Forces." *Washington Post,* 18 April 1991: A19.

Kirkwood, Cort. "Playing King of the Hill." *National Review* (22 January 1988): 44–46.

Klouda, Thomas J., et al. *1996 House Staff Employment: Salary, Tenure, Demographics, and Benefits.* Washington, DC: Congressional Management Foundation, 1996.

Kolodny, Robin. "Moderate Partisans in the 1990s: Withering Away or Digging In?" Paper presented at The State of the Parties: 1996 and Beyond. The Martin University Center, The University of Akron, Akron, Ohio, 1997.

————. *Pursuing Majorities: Congressional Campaign Committees in American Politics.* Norman: University of Oklahoma Press, 1998.

Koopman, Douglas L. *Hostile Takeover: The House Republican Party 1980–1995.* Lanham, MD: Rowman & Littlefield, 1996.

Kosova, Weston. "On the Hill, Slash and Burn." *New Republic* (2 January 1995): 12.

Koszczuk, Jackie. "Gingrich Puts More Power into the Speaker's Hands." *Congressional Quarterly Weekly Report* (7 October 1995): 3049.

————. "For Embattled GOP Leadership, A Season of Discontent." *Congressional Quarterly Weekly Report* (20 July 1996): 2019 (1996a).

————. "Unpopular, Yet Still Powerful, Gingrich Faces Critical Pass." *Congressional Quarterly Weekly Report* (14 September 1996): 2579 (1996b).

————. "With Tone, Tenor of First Session, It Seemed Like Old Times." *Congressional Quarterly Weekly Report* (6 December 1997): 2975–77.

Koszczuk, Jackie, and Rebecca Carr. "GOP Fails to Transform Probe into 'Clinton Watergate.'" *Congressional Quarterly Weekly Report* (1 November 1997): 2656.

Krehbiel, Keith. *Information and Legislative Organization.* Ann Arbor: University of Michigan Press, 1991.

————. *Pivotal Politics: A Theory of U.S. Lawmaking.* Chicago: University of Chicago Press, 1998.

Kriz, Margaret. "Still Charging." *National Journal* (6 December 1997): 2462.

Lambro, Donald. "Kerrey Has Advice for Democrats." *Washington Times,* 25 June 1985: A1.

LeLoup, Lance T., Barbara Luck, Graham Barwick, and Stacy Barwick. "Deficit Politics and Constitutional Government: The Impact of Gramm-Rudman-Hollings." *Public Budgeting and Finance* 7 (Spring 1987): 83–103.

Loomis, Burdett. *The New American Politician.* New York: Basic Books, 1988.

Lynch, Thomas S., ed. *Federal Budget and Financial Management Reform.* Westport, CT: Greenwood Press, 1991.

Madison, James, Alexander Hamilton, and John Jay. *The Federalist Papers,* ed. Clinton Rossiter. New York: Mentor, 1961.

Maisel, L. Sandy, Kara E. Falkenstein, and Alexander M. Quigley. "Rethinking Congressional Career Choices: Senate Retirements and Progressive Ambition among House Members in 1996." Paper presented at the annual meeting of the New England Political Science Association, New London, Conn., 1997.

Maraniss, David, and Michael Weisskopf. *Tell Newt to Shut Up!* New York: Touchstone, 1996.

Mayhew, David R. *Congress: The Electoral Connection.* New Haven, CT: Yale University Press, 1974.

Miller, Morna C. "Permanent Friends, Permanent Enemies: The Sorting Out in the House of Representatives." B.A. thesis, Claremont McKenna College, 1995.

Molinari, Susan, with Elinor Burkett. *Representative Mom: Balancing Budgets, Bill, and Baby in the U.S. Congress.* New York: Doubleday, 1998.

National Journal. "House Moderates Upset by Panel Slight of Blue Dog Plan." *National Journal's Congress Daily* (June 1998a): 4.

———. "House Moderates Angered over Labor–HHS Spending." *National Journal's Congress Daily* (24 June 1998b).

Nichols, David K. *The Myth of the Modern Presidency.* University Park: Pennsylvania State University Press, 1994.

Niven, David, and Jeremy Zilber. "The Role of National Prominence in Congressional Elections." Paper presented at the annual meeting of the American Political Science Association, Chicago, Ill., 1995.

Oleszek, Walter J. "Task Forces in the House 105th Congress." Working paper, Washington, DC, 1997.

Olson, Mancur. *The Logic of Collective Action.* Cambridge, MA: Harvard University Press, 1965.

Ornstein, Norman J., Thomas E. Mann, and Michael J. Malbin. *Vital Statistics on Congress 1997–1998.* Washington, DC: Congressional Quarterly Press, 1998.

Owens, John. "From Party Responsibility to Shared Responsibility, from Revolution to Concession: Institutional and Policy Change in the 104th Congress." In *The Republican Takeover on Capitol Hill,* ed. Dean McSweeney and John E. Owens. London: Macmillan, 1998.

Palmer, Elizabeth A. "Minute-by-Minute through the GOP's Momentous Day," *Congressional Quarterly Weekly Report* (7 January 1995): 10–11.

———. "Republicans Hope to Change Term Limits for Panel Leaders." *Milwaukee Journal Sentinel* (19 September 1997): 26.

Parente, Michele. "Rangel Ties GOP Agenda to Hitler." *Newsday,* 19 February 1995: A38.

Patterson, Samuel C. "The Semi-Sovereign Congress." In *The New American Political System,* ed. Anthony King. Washington, DC: American Enterprise Institute, 1978.

Peabody, Robert L. *Leadership in Congress: Stability, Succession and Change.* Boston: Little, Brown, 1976.

Penner, R., and Alan J. Abramson. *Broken Purse Strings: Congressional Budgeting 1974–1988.* Washington, DC: Urban Institute, 1988.

Peters, Ronald M., Jr. *The American Speakership: The Office in Historical Perspective,* 2nd ed. Baltimore: Johns Hopkins University Press, 1997.

Pew Research Center for the People and the Press. "Voter Anxiety Dividing GOP; Energized Democrats Backing Clinton," October 1995. (http://www.peoplepress.org/anxiety.html) (accessed 3 August 1998).

Pianin, Eric. "Budget-Cutter Livingston May Carve out a New Career." *Washington Post,* 13 February 1998: A23.

Pitney, John J., Jr., "Understanding Newt Gingrich." Paper presented at the annual meeting of the American Political Science Association, San Francisco, Calif., 1996.

Polsby, Nelson W.. "Two Strategies of Influence." In Robert L. Peabody, *Leadership in Congress: Stability, Succession and Change.* Boston: Little, Brown, 1976 [1963], chapter 3.

———. *Political Innovation in America.* New Haven, CT: Yale University Press, 1984.

Price, David E. *The Congressional Experience: A View from the Hill.* Boulder, CO: Westview, 1992.

Public Utilities Commission v. Pollack, 343 U.S. 451, 1952.

Rae, Nicol C. *The Decline and Fall of the Liberal Republicans From 1952 to the Present.* New York.: Oxford University Press, 1989.

———. *Conservative Reformers: The Republican Freshmen and the Lessons of the 104th Congress.* Armonk, NY: M.E. Sharpe, 1998.

Raum, Tom. "Gingrich Offers Congressional Critics a Wide Berth and Forum." Associated Press, 12 September 1997.

Rees, Matthew. "All aboard the Budget Boat." *Weekly Standard* (19 May 1997a): 10.

———. "Rebels with a Cause." *Weekly Standard* (23 June 1997b): 26–29.

———. "Rebel for a Day." *Weekly Standard* (4 August 1997c): 14–16.

Reischauer, Robert D. Speech to the National Tax Association, 84th Annual Conference on Taxation, Williamsburg, VA, 1991.

Richardson, Sula P. *Informal Congressional Groups and Member Organizations, 104th Congress: An Informational Directory.* Congressional Research Service Report 96-688 GOV (5 August) 1996.

Roberts, Steven V. "Republican Anger Ties up the House." *New York Times,* 28 April 1985: Section 4.

Rohde, David W. "Committee Reform in the House of Representatives and the Subcommittee Bill of Rights." *Annals of the American Academy of Political and Social Science* (January 1974): 39–47.

———. *Parties and Leaders in the Postreform House.* Chicago: University of Chicago Press, 1991.

Roll Call. "Vanishing Liberals?" 8 February 1996: 4.

Roman, Nancy E. "Disaster Measure Doubles in Its Cost." *Washington Times,* 5 June 1997: A3.

Rossiter, Clinton, ed. *The Federalist Papers.* New York: Mentor, 1961.

Rothenberg, Stuart. "My Bet: Gingrich Will Run in 2000 for White House." *Roll Call,* 14 August 1997.

Rundquist, Paul S. "Winning on the Left Side of the House: Minority Parliamentary Strategies in a Majoritarian Institution." Paper presented at the annual meeting of the American Political Science Association, San Francisco, Calif., 1990.

Salant, Jonathan. "Senate Altering Its Course in Favor of 'Contract.'" *Congressional Quarterly Weekly Report* (29 April 1995): 1151–54.

Schick, Allen. *Reconciliation and the Congressional Budget Process.* Washington, DC: American Enterprise Institute, 1981.

———. "Proposed Budget Reforms: A Critical Analysis." Congressional Research Service and the Library of Congress, 1988.

Seelye, Katharine Q. "Ascendance of an Improbable Leader: Richard Keith Armey." *New York Times,* 6 December 1994: B9.

Shapiro, Margaret. "House GOP Revolt Was Fed by Years of Feeling Ignored." *Washington Post,* 15 December 1985: A1.

Sinclair, Barbara. *Majority Leadership in the U.S. House.* Baltimore: Johns Hopkins University Press, 1983a.

———. "Purposive Behavior in the U.S, Congress: A Review Essay." *Legislative Studies Quarterly* 8 (February 1983b): 117–31.

———. *The Transformation of the U.S. Senate.* Baltimore: Johns Hopkins University Press, 1989.

———. *Legislators, Leaders, and Lawmaking: The U.S. House of Representatives in the Postreform Era.* Baltimore: Johns Hopkins University Press, 1995.

———. *Unorthodox Lawmaking.* Washington, DC: Congressional Quarterly Press, 1997.

———. "Leading the Revolution: Innovation and Continuity in Congressional Party Leadership." In *The Republican Takeover on Capitol Hill,* ed. Dean McSweeney and John E. Owens. London: Macmillan, 1998.

Skowronek, Stephen. *The Politics Presidents Make: Leadership from John Adams to George Bush.* Cambridge, MA: Harvard University Press, 1993.

Smith, Steven S. *Call to Order: Floor Politics in the House and Senate.* Washington, DC: Brookings Institution, 1989.

Smith, Steven S., and Eric D. Lawrence. "Party Control of Committees in the Republican Congress." In *Congress Reconsidered,* ed. Lawrence C. Dodd and Bruce I. Oppenheimer. Washington, DC: Congressional Quarterly Press, 1997.

Solomon, Gerald B. H., and Donald R. Wolfensberger. "The Decline of Deliberative Democracy in the House and Proposals for Reform." *Harvard Journal on Legislation* 31 (Summer 1994): 321–70.

Stid, Daniel. "Transformational Leadership in Congress?" Paper presented at the annual meeting of the American Political Science Association, San Francisco, Calif., 1996.

Stoddard, A.B. "Rep. Jack Quinn, Buffalo Republican Personifies Divisions in GOP over Minimum Wage Increase." *The Hill,* 1 May 1996: 26.

Strahan, Randall. "Reed and Rostenkowski: Congressional Leadership in Institutional Time." In *The Atomistic Congress,* ed. Allen D. Hertzke and Ronald M. Jr. Peters. Armond, NY: M.E. Sharpe, 1992.

———. "Congressional Leadership in Institutional Time: The Case of Henry Clay." Paper presented at the annual meeting of the American Political Science Association, New York City, 1994.

———. "Leadership in Institutional and Political Time: The Case of Newt Gingrich and the 104th Congress." Paper presented at the annual meeting of the American Political Science Association, San Francisco, Calif., 1996.

Tate, D. "Reconciliation Breeds Tumult as Committees Tackle Cuts: Revolutionary Budget Tool." *Congressional Quarterly Weekly Report* (23 May 1981): 887–91.

Taylor, Andrew. "GOP Pet Projects Give Boost to Shaky Incumbents." *Congressional Quarterly Weekly Report* (3 August 1996): 2169–73.

———. "Few in Congress Grieve as Justices Give Line-Item Veto the Ax." *Congressional Quarterly Weekly Report* (27 June 1998): 1747–49.

Thelwell, Raphael. "Gramm-Rudman-Hollings Four Years Later: A Dangerous Illusion." *Public Administration Review* 50 (1990): 190–97.

Thurber, James A. "Budget Continuity and Change: An Assessment of the Congressional Budget Process." In *Studies in U.S. Politics,* ed. D. K. Adams. Manchester, UK: Manchester University Press, 1989.

———. "Divided Democracy: Cooperation and Conflict Between the President and Congress." In *Rivals for Power: Presidential–Congressional Relations,* ed. James A. Thurber. Washington, DC: Congressional Quarterly Press, 1991.

Thurber, James A., and Roger H. Davidson, ed. *Remaking Congress: Change and Stability in the 1990s.* Washington, DC: Congressional Quarterly Press, 1995.

Thurber, James A., and Samantha Durst. "Delay, Deadlock, and Deficits: Evaluating Congressional." In *Federal Budget and Financial Management Reform,* ed. Thomas S. Lynch. Westport, CT: Greenwood Press, 1991.

Toner, Robin. "Quarrels and Sour Memories Fuel a Hostility to Gingrich." *New York Times,* 24 January 1995: A1.

U.S. Congress. House. Committee on Administrative Review. *Administrative Management and Legislative Management,* 2 vols., H. Doc. 95-232, 95th Cong., 1st sess. (28 September), 1977.

———. Congressional Budget Office. *The Economic and Budget Outlook: Fiscal Years 1991– 1995.* (January) 1990: 123.

———. House, Committee on the Budget. *The Fiscal Year 1991 Budget.* 101st Cong., 1990.

———. Joint Committee on the Organization of Congress. *Final Report: Organization of the Congress.* H. Rept. 103-413, vol. II, 103rd Cong., 1st sess. (December), 1993.

———. *Joint Committee on the Organization of Congress.* H-Rept. 103-413, vol. II. 103rd Cong., 2nd sess. (December), 1993.

———. House. Task Force on Committee Review. *Report on Reforming Committee Structure and Jurisdictions* (6 November), 1996.

———. House. Committee on Rules. *Survey of Activities of the House Committee on Rules, 104th Congress.* H. Rept. 104-868, 104th Cong., 2nd sess. (26 November), 1996.

———. Rules Committee. "Comparative Legislative Data for 103rd and 104th Congresses" (10 December), 1996 (http://www.house.gov/rules/comp_l.html) (accessed 31 July 1998).

———. House. Committee on Rules, Subcommittee on Rules and Organization of the House, *Civility in the House of Representatives,* 105th Cong., 1st sess. (17 April), 1997 (http://www.house.gov/rules_org/tran01.htm) (accessed 3 August 1998).

———. Senate. Committee on Appropriations. *Legislative Branch Appropriations, 1998.* Rept. 105-47. 105th Cong., 1st sess. (15 July), 1997.

Uslaner, Eric M. *The Decline of Comity in Congress.* Ann Arbor: University of Michigan Press, 1993.

Vande Hei, Jim. "Republicans Fill 'Big Three' With Vulnerable Members." *Roll Call,* 4 December 1997: 7.

———. "DeLay Secretly Aided Gingrich Foe in California." *Roll Call,* 19 January 1998: 1, 17.

Weisman, Jonathan. "Congress and Country Fired Up After Hearings on IRS Abuses." *Congressional Quarterly Weekly Report* (4 October 1997a): 2384.

———. "Clinton, Democrats Climb Aboard the IRS Overhaul Bandwagon." *Congressional Quarterly Weekly Report* (25 October 1997b): 2586.

Wilson, James Q. "The Politics of Regulation." In *The Politics of Regulation,* ed. James Q. Wilson. New York: Basic Books, 1980.

Wines, Michael. "Democrats Rock Around the Clock Till Daylight," *New York Times,* 30 June, 1995: A10.

Yang, John E., and Steven Mufson. "Package Termed Best Circumstances Permit." *Washington Post,* 29 October 1990: A4.

———. "Budget Battle Set to Begin on New Terrain." *Washington Post,* 13 February 1991: A12.

Yang, John E., and Terry M. Neal. "'Fast Track' Defeat Illustrates Division that Could Block Clinton Agenda." *Washington Post,* 16 November 1997: A11.

INDEX

ABOUT THE CONTRIBUTORS

COLTON C. CAMPBELL is assistant professor of political science at Florida International University. He is currently serving as an American Political Science Association congressional fellow.

WILLIAM F. CONNELLY, JR., is associate professor of politics at Washington and Lee University. He is co-author of *Congress' Permanent Minority? Republicans in the U.S. House* (Rowman & Littlefield, 1996), with John J. Pitney, Jr.

ROGER H. DAVIDSON is professor of government and politics at the University of Maryland, College Park. He is author and co-author of sixteen books, including *Congress and Its Members,* 6th ed. (1998); and co-editor of *The Encyclopedia of the United States Congress* (1995). He is a former senior specialist at the Congressional Research Service and presidential advisor.

CHRISTOPHER J. DEERING is professor of political science at George Washington University. He is co-author of *Committees in Congress,* 2nd ed. (1997); and editor of *Congressional Politics* (1989).

C. LAWRENCE EVANS is associate professor of political science at the College of William and Mary. He is author of *Leadership in Committee: A Comparative Analysis of Leadership Behavior in the U.S. Senate* (1991); and co-author of *Congress Under Fire: Reform Politics and the Republican Majority* (1997).

ROBIN KOLODNY is assistant professor of political science at Temple University. She is author of *Pursuing Majorities: Congressional Campaign Committees in American Politics* (1998).

WALTER J. OLESZEK is senior specialist in American national government at the Congressional Research Service, and adjunct professor of political science at American University. He is author of *Congressional Procedures and the Policy Process,* 4th ed. (1995); and co-author of *Congress and Its Members,* 6th ed. (1997). He has also served as policy director of the Joint Committee on the Organization of Congress.

RONALD M. PETERS, JR., is professor of political science and director of the Carl Albert Congressional Research and Studies Center at the University of Oklahoma. He authored and edited *The Atomistic Congress: An Interpretation of Congressional Change* (1992); *The Speaker* (1995); and *The American Speakership: The Office in Historical Perspective,* 2nd ed. (1997).

JOHN J. PITNEY, JR., is associate professor of government at Claremont McKenna College. He is co-author of *Congress' Permanent Minority? Republicans in the U.S. House* (1996), with William F. Connelly, Jr.

NICOL C. RAE is associate professor of political science at Florida International University. He is author of *The Decline and Fall of the Liberal Republicans From 1952 to the Present* (1989); *Southern Democrats* (1991); and *Conservative Reformers: The Republican Freshmen and the Lessons of the 104th Congress* (1998).

BARBARA SINCLAIR is Marvin Hoffenberg Professor of American politics at the University of California at Los Angeles. She is author of *Transformation of the U.S. Senate* (1989); *Legislators, Leaders, and Lawmaking* (1995); and *Unorthodox Lawmaking: New Legislative Processes in the U.S. Congress* (1997).

JAMES A. THURBER is professor of government and director of the Center for Congressional and Presidential Studies and the Campaign Management and Lobbying Institutes at American University. He is author and editor of *On Capitol Hill* (1972); *Setting Course: A Congressional Management Guide* (1994); *Campaigns and Elections: American Style* (1995); and *Rivals for Power* (1997).